UNDERSTANDING HUMAN NEED

Also available in the series

Understanding the finance of welfare (second edition)
What welfare costs and how to pay for it
Howard Glennerster

"... a total winner ... provides interest and excellence throughout." **SPA News**, review of first edition

PB £21.99 (US$34.95) **ISBN** 978 1 84742 108 1 **HB** £65.00 (US$85.00) **ISBN** 978 1 84742 109 8
264 pages February 2009
INSPECTION COPY AVAILABLE

Understanding social security (second edition)
Issues for policy and practice
Edited by **Jane Millar**

"This updated second edition brings together some of the leading writers in the field to provide a critical analysis of the recent changes to the social security system."
Dr. Liam Foster, Department of Sociological Studies, University of Sheffield

PB £21.99 (US$34.95) **ISBN** 978 1 84742 186 9 **HB** £65.00 (US$85.00) **ISBN** 978 1 84742 187 6
344 pages February 2009
INSPECTION COPY AVAILABLE

Understanding equal opportunities and diversity
The social differentiations and intersections of inequality
Barbara Bagilhole

This book challenges the official discourse that shapes the debates on Equal Opportunities and Diversity (EO&D) at national, regional and European level.

PB £21.99 (US$34.95) **ISBN** 978 1 86134 848 7 **HB** £65.00 (US$85.00) **ISBN** 978 1 86134 849 4
272 pages April 2009
INSPECTION COPY AVAILABLE

Understanding social welfare movements
Jason Annetts, Alex Law, Wallace McNeish and **Gerry Mooney**

The book provides a timely and much needed overview of the changing nature of social welfare as it has been shaped by the demands of social movements.

PB £19.99 (US$32.95) **ISBN** 978 1 84742 096 1 **HB** £65.00 (US$85.00) **ISBN** 978 1 84742 097 8
304 pages June 2009
INSPECTION COPY AVAILABLE

For a full listing of all titles in the series visit www.policypress.co.uk

www.policypress.co.uk

INSPECTION COPIES AND ORDERS AVAILABLE FROM:
Marston Book Services • PO Box 269 • Abingdon • Oxon OX14 4YN UK
INSPECTION COPIES
Tel: +44 (0) 1235 465500 • Fax: +44 (0) 1235 465556 • Email: inspections@marston.co.uk
ORDERS
Tel: +44 (0) 1235 465500 • Fax: +44 (0) 1235 465556 • Email: direct.orders@marston.co.uk

UNDERSTANDING HUMAN NEED

Social issues, policy and practice

Hartley Dean

First published in 2010 in Great Britain by
The Policy Press
University of Bristol
Fourth Floor, Beacon House
Queen's Road
Bristol BS8 1QU
UK

Tel +44 (0)117 331 4054
Fax +44 (0)117 331 4093
e-mail tpp-info@bristol.ac.uk
www.policypress.co.uk

North American office:
The Policy Press
c/o International Specialized Books Services (ISBS)
920 NE 58th Avenue, Suite 300
Portland, OR 97213-3786, USA
Tel +1 503 287 3093
Fax +1 503 280 8832
e-mail info@isbs.com

British Library Cataloguing in Publication Data
A catalogue record for this book is available from the British Library.

Library of Congress Cataloging-in-Publication Data
A catalog record for this book has been requested.

ISBN 978 1 84742 189 0 paperback
ISBN 978 1 84742 190 6 hardcover

Cover design by Qube Design Associates, Bristol.
Front cover: photograph kindly supplied by www.alamy.com
Printed and bound in Great Britain by Hobbs, Southampton.

To the memory of my parents,

Margaret and Harry Dean

Contents

Detailed contents

List of boxes, figures and tables

Acknowledgements

When writing a book one incurs debts to a great many friends and colleagues and to all those, especially close family members, who share your life. Special mention in this instance must go to Tania Burchardt, Bill Jordan, Mary Langan and an anonymous peer reviewer appointed by The Policy Press for reading and commenting on early drafts of some or all chapters; to Alison Shaw and Emily Watt at The Policy Press, for encouraging me to write the book in the first place and for so ably overseeing its production; to Ruth Lister for drawing my attention to things I should have known about; to Pam Dean for proof reading first drafts of the typescript and for much else besides. I am grateful to them all. However, insofar as this book exhibits errors and weaknesses, these are wholly my responsibility: none of these good people are in any way to blame.

Select glossary of terms

Note: This book has necessarily discussed an array of technical terms and abstract concepts. To define all of them would require a glossary almost as long as the book itself. Included here, therefore, are short explanations addressed to the different adjectives that may be used to define 'need'. Even this list is not exhaustive. Insofar as these key terms intersect and overlap, these definitions may help to clarify the connections between them. Where other terms have been mentioned in the book these will usually have been defined within the text and their definitions may be accessed via the index to the book.

absolute need
Most often used to denote the opposite of 'relative' need (see below). It may refer to whatever may be held to be absolutely necessary for physical survival or for human dignity, although as with the term 'absolute poverty', definitions of absolute necessity vary.

basic need
May be used as a synonym for 'absolute' need (see above) or to denote the opposite of 'higher need' (see below). The term generally refers to whatever may be fundamentally necessary for survival and the avoidance of harm. Confusingly, perhaps, it is sometimes also used as a synonym for 'universal' need, not so much in the sense referred to below, but as a way of referring to the elemental needs that every human being has.

circumstantial need
A term accorded a specific meaning in this book and which refers to need that is 'thinly' conceived and is 'interpreted'. For policy purposes, what people need is here judged in relation to what is minimally and morally justifiable in the specific context of an individual's personal circumstances. (Note: some philosophical texts may use the term more generally as a synonym for what is defined below as 'substantive' need and contrast it with constitutional need (a term not used in this book), namely needs that are in some way socially or institutionally constructed.)

common need   A term accorded a specific meaning in this book and which refers to need that is 'thickly' conceived but is 'interpreted'. For policy purposes, people's needs here stem from their social nature, to the requirements that attend one's belonging within a society or community and which are defined in terms of the functions and experiences one has in common with others.

comparative need   A form of need identified with reference to any relative deficit established through the comparative analysis of the living standards or the services received in different places, by different communities or by different social groups. One's comparative needs may be defined with reference to the things one lacks but which other people have.

derivative need   Can be used to denote the opposite of 'basic' need (see above), but like the term 'intermediate' need (see below), it refers to the things people need in order to satisfy more basic needs. Money, for example, is a need we derive from our need to buy food and clothing.

discursive need   Need that has been constituted through discourse, through the meanings people generate between themselves when they talk or communicate with one another and through their shared practices and conventions. Need constructed through popular discourse may sometimes be described as 'socially constituted'. Need constructed through political discourse may sometimes be described as 'ideologically constituted'.

experiential need   Refers to need as it is experienced. The term combines the meaning of 'felt' need on the one hand and 'substantive' need on the other (see below).

expressed need   A 'felt' need (see below) that has been formulated as a personal or political demand.

false need   The opposite of 'true' need (see below). The term is used with reference to things people want, demand, or think they need but which are (in the opinion of the observer) not needed. False need may sometimes correspond to 'subjective' need (see below) in the sense that it may occur when people are addicted, deluded or misguided, but critics contend that *any* need that is genuinely *experienced* as a 'felt' need cannot be dismissed as false.

felt need   Broadly synonymous with 'subjective' need (see below) and which refers to needs that are subjectively experienced by an individual or intersubjectively experienced by a group.

higher need   Often used to denote the opposite of morally inferior, base or 'basic' needs (see above). The concept refers not to luxuries, but to more refined human needs, such as intellectual, creative or spiritual pursuits.

inherent need   A term developed throughout this book to refer to needs that are inherent to the human individual not only because they are a biological organism, but by virtue of their very humanity. The notion of inherent need requires a theory or idea of personhood and of what it means to be a person. Such theories or assumptions may well be implicit, but they are usually *given*: they are established or prescribed abstractly, or from the top down.

instrumental need   Means much the same as 'derivative' need (see above) or 'intermediate' need, in that it refers to things we must have or do, not for their own sake, but as a means of surviving or avoiding harm. The meeting of instrumental need is a means to an end.

intermediate need   Has a meaning similar to that for 'derivative' need (see above) in that it refers to the things we need in order to fulfil other more immediate or 'basic' needs (see above). In order to be healthy, we need food, water, shelter and so forth. To achieve human autonomy, we need physical security, basic education and so forth. Intermediate needs may well be 'relative' (see below) in the sense that what is necessary to meet one's 'basic' needs can vary depending, for example, on the climate and the kind of society in which one is living.

interpreted need   A term developed throughout this book to refer to needs that are constructed or attributed to the human individual by interpretation. Interpreted needs may be established by observation or analysis, or through claims or demands, but they are established or articulated concretely, or from the bottom up.

normative need   Refers to needs determined by the normative judgement of policy makers, administrators or experts, including scientific experts and especially welfare professionals, such as doctors and other health professionals, teachers and social workers.

objective need   Most often used to denote the opposite of 'subjective' need (see below), referring to needs that are externally verifiable or scientifically observable.

ontological need   The things we need in order to maintain our individual identity, self-awareness and sense of being. Ontological need may be contrasted with existential need, which refers to what we need merely to exist in a material sense.

particular need   A term accorded a specific meaning in this book and which refers to need that is thinly conceived but inherent to the human subject. For policy purposes, what people are assumed to need is defined in terms of their objective individual interests and the opportunities they need in order to compete as freely choosing economic actors.

real need   Commonly but loosely used, sometimes to mean 'true' need (see below) but sometimes 'substantive' need (see below).

relative need   Most often used to denote the opposite of 'absolute' need (see above). The term refers to needs that are not fixed, but which are determined in relation to the climatic, socioeconomic and cultural conditions in which the human subject lives. The things required to satisfy 'intermediate' needs (see above) are by definition relative. When relative need is unmet we speak of relative poverty or relative deprivation.

social need   Commonly but loosely used as a way of distinguishing between the needs that pertain strictly to individuals and needs that are a matter of social concern: a distinction which in practice – as Titmuss observed – is hard to sustain.

subjective need   Most often used to denote the opposite of 'objective' need (see above). The term refers to the needs people think, believe or feel they have, whether they be 'true' (see below) or 'false' (see above). Subjective need, although it is founded on individual experience, is assumed by classical economists, for example, to be objectively observable through the preferences people exercise.

substantive need   A term that addresses the substance rather than the process of needing. It is generally used to signify actually existing or 'real' need (see above) and to capture the sense in which the needs referred to are not merely abstract or theoretical in nature.

technical need   Need that is technically created, through the invention of some new or more effective form of good. The term is most commonly used in the healthcare context to refer to forms of medical intervention that can relieve conditions not previously treatable.

thick need   This term has been accorded particular significance for the purposes of this book and is used to refer to needs that are optimally defined and that include the things that may be necessary for a person truly to flourish and to share a good life.

thin need   This term has been accorded particular significance for the purposes of this book and is used to refer to needs that are minimally defined but which include the things that are necessary for a person, with dignity, to achieve pleasure and avoid pain.

true need   Opposite of 'false' need (see above). But what is true, of course, depends on one's point of view, so the term may be used equally to apply, for example, to 'objective' or 'subjective' need.

universal need   A term accorded a very particular meaning in this book and which refers to need that is 'thickly' conceived but 'inherent' to the human subject. For policy purposes, people's needs here stem from their humanity and what is required for human fulfilment. They are defined or negotiated by and through the way people depend on and participate with one another. Confusingly, perhaps, it can sometimes *also* be used as a synonym for 'basic' need, not quite in the sense referred to above, but as a way of referring to the elemental needs that every human being has.

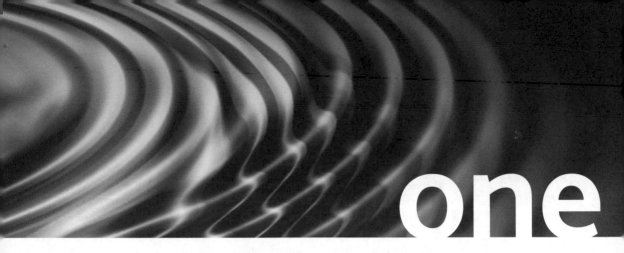

one

Introduction

- This chapter explains that 'need', although a central concept in social policy, has proved to be an elusive and contested concept.
- Four overarching kinds of response to the idea of human need will be set out, in simplified form: humanistic, economistic, paternalistic and moralistic.
- The widely used distinction between absolute and relative need is explored.
- The contents of the rest of this book are outlined.

Competing concepts of human need, whether express or implied, are present within all the social sciences. Academic social policy, as an inter- and multidisciplinary subject, draws from across the social sciences including economics, sociology and psychology. Need, it has been said, is a concept that is 'central to social policy making' (Erskine, 2002, p 158). Unfortunately, need is also a concept that is interpreted in a mind-boggling variety of ways. Des Gasper described the proceedings of an academic workshop convened in the 1990s as part of a research project on human needs and wants as follows:

> ... it became evident that the participants – psychologists, economists, philosophers, sociologists, anthropologists – held to no consistent usage of "need", as individuals, not only across disciplines. Yet most of us had read and thought about needs since the 1960s or 1970s. We jumped between different usages almost from one sentence to the next: between ... more basic needs versus satisfiers; and verbs versus nouns – and also between needs as explanatory forces and factors, needs as (pre)requisites, and needs as particular sorts of moral priority claims. (Gasper, 2007, p 54)

There is a virtually inexhaustible supply of binary distinctions between different kinds or levels of human need, many of which we shall encounter in the course of this book (see **Table 1.1** and also the Select glossary of terms). Many of these distinctions overlap or coincide with each other. Some, I shall argue, are more helpful than others. To pursue them all in any depth would be as exhausting for the reader as for the author. The literature on human need is also replete with a similarly inexhaustible supply of thought experiments and anecdotal vignettes with which to illustrate a variety of philosophical conundrums. I shall use these sparingly if at all because they can lead readers (and this author) to a sense of despair and inadequacy since nobody has been clever enough to solve every conundrum.

Table 1.1: Binary distinctions between different kinds or levels of need

absolute	...	relative
objective	...	subjective
basic	...	higher
material	...	non-material
positive	...	negative
non-instrumental	...	instrumental
non-derivative	...	derivative
physical/somatic	...	mental/spiritual
physiological	...	cultural
viscerogenic	...	sociogenic
intrinsic	...	procedural
natural	...	artificial
true	...	false
inherent	...	interpreted
constitutional	...	circumstantial
thin	...	thick
hedonic	...	eudaimonic

In this book I attempt to weave the disputed threads into a simplified and, I hope, comprehensible meta-classification of needs concepts. I do not present a wholly new theory of need, but I do develop a theoretical proposition concerning the relationship between human interdependency, needs and rights. The aim is to pick out and develop an encompassing and comprehensible concept of human need. I argue that human need represents a pivotally important concept and, arguably, the single most important organising principle in social policy. It is pivotal in the sense that it connects an understanding of our *interdependency* as human beings with arguments about the *rights* that we can assert against each other. While it remains, potentially, an elusive concept, human need is the concept from which other eminently practical and strategic approaches can flow. Or, to put it more precisely, it is through contests over human need that social policy is made. My concluding argument will be essentially normative: I will map out how I think we *ought* to think about human need, but along the way I will address a great many essential empirical questions, questions about *what is* going on in the world around us. It is acknowledged that 'the concept of a need involves both "is" and "ought"' (Thomson, 1987, p 109).

I start in this introductory chapter with a few remarks that will emphasise why the topic is important to social policy, before providing an outline of the way in which I will develop my argument in the rest of the book.

Why is need important?

I have already suggested that the way we think about human need is relevant to the ways in which social policies are organised. Functionalist accounts suggest that the analysis of human need 'provides a clear basis for the analysis of society. And though we should expect the forms of these social institutions to vary among different types of society, some institutions centring about these human needs there must always be' (Fletcher, 1965, p 21). It may be supposed that there is a distinction that could be drawn here between individual and social need. Richard Titmuss provided the classic riposte to this suggestion:

> All collectively provided services are deliberately designed to meet certain socially recognised "needs"; they are manifestations, first, of society's will to survive as an organic whole and, secondly of the expressed wish of all the people to assist the survival of some people. "Needs" may therefore be thought of as "social" and "individual" ... [but] ... no complete division between the two is conceptually possible; the shading of one into the other changes with time over the life of all societies; it changes with time over the cycle of needs of the individual and the family; it depends on prevailing notions of what constitutes a "need" and in what circumstances; and to what extent, if at all, such needs, when recognised, should be met in the interests of the individual and/or of society. (Titmuss, 2001 [1955], p 62)

It has been said that need is only one of several perspectives from which we might define what we mean by human welfare (Fitzpatrick, 2001, p 5). However, the goals of social policy, if they are not directly informed, as Titmuss asserts, by concerns about human need, will indirectly reflect assumptions about human need. Governmental and academic social policy are each preoccupied – more or less explicitly – with processes of resource distribution on the one hand, and the development of human services on the other. Social policy interventions may entail the distribution or redistribution of resources through: the administration of taxes and the provision of cash transfers; the provision of education and training and the regulation of employment; the regulation of land use and the environment and the control or provision of housing; and the organisation of health and social care and social protection for people who are vulnerable.

Significance of need

This kind of provision must be informed at some level by assumptions or principles relating to what human beings (as citizens, customers, subjects or clients) might need. However, there are other candidates for the job of prime organising principle, such as wants or preferences, desert and merits, and security and social protection. My contention would be that, at root, these all amount to different interpretations, or approaches, to need. Although philosophers may seek it (see for example Thomson, 1987), there cannot be one true meaning of a word like 'need'. It is a word with a myriad of vernacular meanings. The particular concept of human need that I advocate throughout this book might be characterised as a 'humanistic' or 'humanitarian' approach. There are clearly other ways to approach need. For the moment we can group these together in a rough and ready way and characterise them in everyday language as the 'economistic', 'moralistic/moral-authoritarian' and 'paternalistic' approaches. Although each approach represents a different attitude to need and instils a different meaning, something called 'need' is always retained.

Consider some of the things that you might say you will need in the course of your own life, or the needs that you consider yourself fortunate to have already met. This will by no means be an exhaustive list, but the important things that might immediately occur are the need for a job, for a place to live, for time to relax and for somebody to love. Our needs as human beings relate to such fundamentals as work, space, time and relationships. The responses I am about to define amount to no more than caricatures of broad, principled and sometimes complex arguments. Nonetheless, this outline (summarised in ***Table 1.2***) may help set the scene for what follows and it prefigures elements of the conclusions at which we shall eventually arrive.

The *humanistic* or *humanitarian* approach embraces all four of these expressions of need as important and interprets them broadly, in terms of what it is that defines us as human:

• People in fact need more than just jobs. They need the means to obtain a livelihood, but this should not necessarily depend on wages. In some parts of the world it is possible to obtain livelihoods without recourse to a cash economy through subsistence farming, or in others, to sustain oneself as a lone parent or informal carer through social security benefits. Nonetheless people most certainly need to be meaningfully active in 'work', regardless of whether it is paid, because this is part of what defines our humanity. 'Work' might entail labour, but it might also entail caring, studying, artistic endeavour or all kinds of purposeful activity.

• People need more than just a place to live. While they need to be appropriately sheltered from the elements, space and place are important. People need comfortable homes and a healthy, sustainable environment.

• People need more than just time to relax. They need time to properly rest, but more particularly they need time to realise their own creativity, to play as well as rest.

• People most definitely need somebody to love and somebody to love them in return. Our humanity depends on the manner of our interconnectedness and interdependency with others.

The *paternalistic* approach acknowledges all four expressions of need, but not so much in terms of what defines us as human as in terms of what secures our social belonging and what is needed to establish and preserve the social order. It regards need, literally, in a conservative sense: our safety, security and material protection depend on stability.

• People need jobs as a way of joining in with society and contributing to social production. Paid employment provides an orderly means of obtaining livelihoods and can be regulated in ways that minimise hazards and maximise compliance and cooperation between social classes.

• People need somewhere to live. The places where they live should be suited to their status.

• People need to rest and should be allowed to engage in appropriate cultural pursuits.

• People need, not necessarily love, but a strong and supportive family. The family is the place where many everyday needs can most appropriately be met.

The *economistic* or *market-oriented* approach is concerned more with economic opportunities and consumer preferences than with needs. It tends to express need in terms of the opportunities that people have to satisfy their wants and the preferences they express in the marketplace. People should be free to prioritise for themselves between jobs, homes, leisure pursuits and relationships.

• People should have the opportunity of entering the labour market. This means we may need to be educated and, importantly, we should be free to choose the jobs we seek. However, the point of a job is that it makes a productive contribution: it defines a key aspect of a person's engagement as an economic actor.

- People should have the opportunity to choose a place to live and to secure a home in the marketplace. Housing is an essential commodity.
- People should be free to choose how much leisure time they want and how they use it. Time is a commodity.
- People do not necessarily need somebody to love, but should be free to establish relationships. However, the human relationships that count primarily towards our standard of living are economic relationships.

The *moralistic* or *moral-authoritarian* approach is concerned more with people's behaviour than with their needs. It can be censorious in nature and expresses need in terms of what people have to do in order to deserve or to merit particular rewards and with ensuring that in attempting to satisfy their own needs, people should not get in each other's way.

- People need jobs to make a living. What matters is that people look after their own needs by working for a living. People determine their own living standards through their own effort or talent.
- People need to live somewhere. What matters is that in the process they do not intrude on other people's use of space and that their access to housing is fairly earned.
- People naturally prefer leisure to work, but there is no excuse for laziness and there is a risk that some people's leisure time might be used for miscreant activity rather than worthwhile pursuits.
- People naturally seek out somebody to love, which is all very well, but desire must always be tempered by responsibility, especially in personal relationships.

I must re-emphasise that this is very much a caricature or oversimplification of the range of approaches to need. You are not likely to meet anybody who subscribes consistently to just one of these approaches in the terms just portrayed. This has been an exercise in what is sometimes called 'heuristic modelling' and its purpose is to provide not necessarily an accurate description of what particular individuals, commentators or policy makers think or say, so much as a clearer understanding of the complexity of the issues. In practice these approaches are seldom if ever applied in isolation from one another; they tend to be muddled together. Approaches are combined – often unthinkingly but sometimes with subtlety – in contradictory or complicated ways. This will be illustrated in the chapters that follow.

Table 1.2: *Responses to need*

	humanistic (or humanitarian) response (a *human* needs based approach)	paternalistic response (an approach focused on social order and protection)	economistic response (an approach focused on the freedom to exercise preferences)	moralistic (or moral-authoritarian) response (an approach focused on desert and merits)
I need a job	You need decent work and to be meaningfully active	You need to be engaged in a properly ordered social production process	You need the opportunity to engage in freely chosen work	You need to work so as to make your own living
I need a place to live	You need shelter from the elements and to live in a decent environment	You need somewhere suitable to live	You need the opportunity to rent or buy a home and to choose the home you want	You need somewhere to live to keep you off the streets
I need time to relax	You need time for creativity and re-creation	You need rest and cultural amusement	You should be free to choose how much leisure time you have and how to spend it	The chance to rest must first be earned (and must not be misspent)
I need somebody to love	You need other people to care about and to care for you	You need a strong and supportive family	You should be free to love, but love is an elusive commodity and not necessarily essential	It is more important to provide for 'you and yours' than to worry about love

Absolute/relative distinction

A key debate that has driven much of this complexity concerns a distinction between 'absolute' and 'relative' conceptions of need. Is it possible to define what human beings need in absolute terms, or is human need always socially or culturally relative? And if human need is always relative, is there any point in seeking to define it? This has been a critical question for social policy (Doyal and Gough, 1991). The period of welfare state retrenchment that began from the 1970s onwards (Powell and Hewitt, 2002) has been associated by some writers with a 'politicisation of need' (Langan, 1998, pp 13-21). Towards the end of the last century arguments about the relativity of human need developed to the point that the very concept of need became increasingly discredited among the policy makers of the global North.

The absolute/relative distinction is intimately caught up with issues of poverty, deprivation and inequality. A person may be said to be *absolutely* poor if deprived of the necessities of life itself. They may be said to be *relatively* poor if deprived of whatever they might need in order to participate in the life of the society to which they belong. Villagers in a drought-stricken region of sub-Saharan Africa need food and water. But do relatively deprived families living in inner-city public sector housing developments in the global North really need colour televisions, simply because 99 per cent of their neighbours have them? As living standards rise around the world will human needs continue to expand indefinitely? These are questions to which I shall be returning later in the book. For now, however, I want to suggest that the absolute/relative distinction – whether applied to poverty or to need – fundamentally contains two underlying distinctions: one relates to the character of human need, the other to its extent.

Human beings are simultaneously both biological and social creatures. We have biological or physiological needs on the one hand, but we have social needs on the other. In practice, because we are embodied social beings (Ellis and Dean, 2000), it can be difficult to draw a line that distinguishes between these two kinds of need. But one element of the absolute/relative distinction is a distinction between physical sufficiency and social acceptability. We have bodily needs, but our needs have social meaning and significance. Psychological 'drives', for example, may be subject to cultural 'taboos'. We cannot escape from our bodies but some of the things that define us as human derive from our social context, from our interrelationship and interdependency with other human beings. Therefore, the distinction I have drawn in the past (Dean, 2002, pp 25-8) and will develop further in the pages that follow is between needs considered to be *inherent* to the human individual on the one hand, and *interpreted* needs which are constructed in the course of everyday experiences and policy processes on the other.

When defining need as either absolute or relative, the other distinction that may be implied relates not to the character of human needs, but to their extent – both in a quantitative and a qualitative sense. This raises questions of measurability on the one hand, and philosophy on the other. How *much* do we need and how *far* do our needs extend? Should human need be minimally or optimally satisfied? Is it enough that we should be able to *survive* minimally with some modicum of human dignity or is it important that we should be allowed, or even encouraged, so far as possible to *flourish* (Ignatieff, 1984, p 10)? Another way of thinking about this – and one I shall be adopting – is to distinguish between *thin* and *thick* needs (Drover and Kerans, 1993, pp 11-13; see also Walzer, 1994). The terms are, of course, metaphorical and one of the analogics that can be used to explain them relates to the difference between a thin insipid soup that, although it may be nutritious and wholesome, is not as thoroughly satisfying as a thick rich soup that appeals to our sense of taste and enjoyment. It is a distinction between what might respectively be called 'essentialist' and 'expansive' interpretations of need.

Outline of the book

The argument sketched out above informs the structure of this book and key distinctions that underlie the ideas that are developed throughout.

Chapters Two and Three draw out the key distinction mentioned above, between inherent and interpreted need. The former relates to needs that are held to vest in or belong to the human subject, the latter to needs that are inferred or attributed to the human subject by commentators on the human condition or which are claimed by people for themselves. The two are clearly related, but it is the ongoing nature of that relationship that matters.

Chapters Four and Five examine an array of concepts that are intimately related to that of human need. On the one hand, concepts of poverty, inequality and resource redistribution: concepts through which social policy has perennially responded to human need. On the other, concepts of exclusion, capabilities and recognition: new or newly rediscovered concepts through which fresh understandings of human need have been sought.

Chapter Six draws out the other key distinction, between 'thin' and 'thick' needs. Particular meaning is attributed to the distinction by articulating it with different understandings of human well-being. The discussion draws on classic philosophical and current debates about the nature of 'happiness'.

Chapters Seven, Eight and Nine bring the threads of the discussion together. Chapter Seven articulates the crude taxonomy of needs-based approaches presented above with the key conceptual distinctions explored in the previous chapters, and illustrates how each approach is manifested in different kinds of social policy intervention. Chapter Eight explores how needs-based approaches can be translated into rights-based approaches and Chapter Nine explores the politics of human need.

The contention of the book is that need, as a concept, is indeed central to social policy making. I agree with Doyal and Gough (1991) that a concept or concepts of human need are implicit even in the arguments of those who are critical of the uses and abuses of the term. While the book does not provide a new or distinctive theory of human need, it does offer a framework in which to articulate theories of need, and it situates the concept of need in relation to other related concepts.

The ultimate task of the book is to connect understandings of human need to understandings of human dependency on the one hand, and to demands for human rights on the other. Heclo (1986) distinguished two competing concepts of 'the general welfare': one was 'welfare as self-sufficiency', the other 'welfare as mutual dependence' (cited in Goodin, 1988, p 363). The central argument of this book is that the ascendancy of the former over the latter obscures a proper understanding of human need. To translate an appreciation of the essential nature of human interdependence into an effective range of human rights (that includes social or welfare rights) requires a politics of human need.

Summary

- This chapter has provided some insight into the complexity of human need as a concept that is used in a variety of different and contradictory ways among policy makers and social scientists alike.
- It has been suggested that the concept remains, nonetheless, of central importance to social policy.
- Four of the ways in which human need may be thought about have been broadly identified. These have been characterised (for now) as the humanitarian, paternalistic, economistic and moral-authoritarian approaches.
- It has been argued that the essential distinction between *absolute* and *relative* needs can be understood in two ways:

- first, in terms of a distinction between *inherent* and *interpreted* need; between the needs that individuals may be defined as having by virtue of being human and needs that are defined by or for them through the social nature of human existence;
- second, in terms of a distinction between *thin* and *thick* needs, a distinction concerned with the quantitative extent and qualitative nature of human need.

- In developing these arguments, I contend that human need is best understood in the context of human interdependency and as the basis on which social rights may be constructed.

Questions for discussion:

- 'Defining what human beings need is surely a simple matter.' Why might you disagree with this statement?
- In what sense would you say that *you* need a job, a place to live, the time to relax and somebody to love?
- How many of the binary distinctions set out in *Table 1.1* are meaningful to you, and how helpful do you find them?

Inherent need

- In this chapter the concept of inherent need will be developed and illustrated, which, although inevitably related to that of interpreted need, involves a variety of accounts that rely on different suppositions about the inherent nature of the individual human being.
- A range of classic theories of human need will be discussed, including:
  - utilitarian notions of needs as objective interests;
  - market-oriented notions of needs as market preferences;
  - psychologistic notions of needs as inner drives; and
  - Marxian notions of needs as constitutive human characteristics.
- Social policy perspectives on inherent need will be discussed, including:
  - the debate sparked by the 'crisis' of the capitalist welfare state; and
  - the influential theory advanced by Doyal and Gough.

In Chapter One a broad distinction was drawn between needs which appear to be 'inherent' to the human subject and those whose nature and existence is 'interpreted' (by experts, policy makers or through social custom or discourse). This is broadly similar to the distinction between 'intrinsic' and 'procedural' definitions of need made by Leiss (1978, cited by Hewitt, 1992, p 175) and to the distinction drawn by Gasper (2007) between drives and potentials on the one hand (which he calls 'mode A' needs) and normative priorities on the other (which he calls 'mode C' needs). (Incidentally, what Gasper refers to as 'mode B' needs encompass supposed needs that are a requisite for achieving a specific objective, an essentially tautologous or circular form of definition, of which he is rightly critical.)

The inherent needs of the human subject must – implicitly or explicitly – be theorised: they require suppositions about what exactly constitutes the living and embodied human actor. Therefore the distinction between inherent and interpreted needs can never be hard and fast. What are claimed to be inherent needs are likely at some stage to have been founded on interpretive assumptions, while interpretive accounts may very well lay claim to definitions of need that are inherent. The significance of this interdependence (or what is sometimes called a 'dialectic') between the two categories will be considered in later chapters. This chapter, however, will focus on key theories and debates that assert or assume human needs to be inherent to the human individual.

This chapter is in two parts. The first considers a range of classic theories. The second discusses specific social policy perspectives on human need.

Classic theories

Most discussions of need start from a distinction between needs and wants (Plant et al, 1980, chs 2 and 8; Goodin, 1988, ch 2). It is certainly a valid semantic distinction. In everyday parlance the words 'need' and 'want' can be carelessly substituted for each other as if they were synonyms. One of the most famous uses of the word 'want' was by Sir William Beveridge, architect of the modern British welfare state, who characterised Want as one of the five metaphorical giants on the road to postwar reconstruction (Beveridge, 1942; Timmins, 2001). Want stood alongside Disease, Squalor, Ignorance and Idleness and reflected a particular concern that in addition to health, housing, education and employment, people living in a cash economy need to be able to sustain a basic minimum income throughout the course of their lives. Whether the payment of social security benefits serves to meet needs or to satisfy wants remains a moot point (to which we shall return), but Beveridge's purpose was to prevent poverty. To characterise poverty as Want rather than as a need amounted to little other than a Bunyanesque rhetorical flourish. What is important is that we appreciate the different implicit and explicit theories of inherent need that underpin the way in which everyday discussions of wants and needs takes place.

We can all recognise that there are things in life that we might want that we do not need and things that we might need that we do not want. It is sometimes suggested that needs are absolute, while wants are relative. While this is, conceptually speaking, a fundamental distinction, it is a slippery one: it can easily miss some important considerations to do with motivation and constraint. The best worn examples are those of the unreformed smoker on the one hand who badly wants a cigarette, but needs to give up smoking, and the undiagnosed diabetic on the other who wants to indulge a taste for sugary foods, but badly needs a shot of insulin, not sugar.

The other important distinction to which discussions of need generally refer is that between instrumental or derivative needs and non-instrumental or basic needs (Thomson, 1987, ch 1). Instrumental or derivative needs are the things we need (such as money) in order to satisfy other needs (such as food or clothing). Non-instrumental needs are those that are fundamentally necessary for survival and the avoidance of harm. I shall illustrate later how theories of human need address this distinction, but for now we are discussing needs in general, and we can go along with Agnes Heller's assertion that 'All needs considered by humans to be real must be considered as real' (Heller, 1980, p 215).

In order initially to traverse the philosophical minefield left behind by past debates I shall characterise four different ways in which the human individual can be envisaged and the different ways in which needs might accordingly be construed. This is summarised in *Table 2.1*. It is a somewhat reductionist and essentially sociological analysis. It may be noted, however, that just because needs might be held to inhere in or belong to the individual, this does not mean that the individual is not a social being: it is just that in each of these accounts an individual's needs are regarded as intrinsic to her functioning, role or identity as a human actor. We are attempting, analytically, to unpack the principal elements of established debates.

Table 2.1: *Different accounts of inherent need*

The individual is primarily a:	Her needs are to be understood in terms of her:
utilitarian subject	objective interests
market actor	subjective preferences
psychological being	inner drives
species member	constitutive characteristics

Needs as objective interests

Each of the examples cited above implicitly casts a person's needs in terms of her objective interests, or at least a particular rationalist interpretation of what objective interests consist of. The smoker realises it is in her interests to give up smoking, even though her addiction to tobacco makes it difficult to do so. The undiagnosed diabetic, in contrast, does not realise it is in her interests to take insulin or to modify her diet so she persists in eating things that will be bad for her. Implicit in each instance is the self-evident supposition that it is in a person's interests to avoid harm – from the ingestion of carcinogens on the one hand or from the effects of raised blood sugar levels on the other.

In this way the human individual may be construed as a utilitarian subject. Utilitarianism is a philosophy premised on the assumption that, properly informed, the rational individual can normally be expected to maximise her utility. That is to say, she will act in her own best interests, by avoiding harmful things and seeking out pleasurable ones. In Chapter Six we shall discuss utilitarianism in greater depth, but in this and the next paragraph we shall concentrate on the claim that need may be defined strictly rationally in terms of the pursuit of objective interests. Interests are not necessarily the same as needs, but if the frustration or denial of our needs leads to harm, then it is our interests that define what harm consists of (Thomson, 1987, p 89).

This entails a view of humanity whose foundations lie in Enlightenment liberalism, and has been important to the development of social policy. But it is a view that can be inflected in various directions. It was the distinctively utilitarian liberalism of Jeremy Bentham that informed the paradoxically illiberal Poor Laws of the pre-welfare state era. The object was to create such disincentives as might deter any rational person from seeking relief and persuade them instead to provide for her own needs, if at all possible (Thane, 1982). On the other hand, what may be called social liberalism or even 'liberal collectivism' (Cutler et al, 1986) flows from the very different premise, most famously articulated by Franklin D. Roosevelt, that 'a necessitous man is not a free man' (1944). Non-utilitarian liberal theorists of social justice, of whom John Rawls (1972) is undoubtedly the best known, were concerned to theorise not necessarily the nature of need so much as the principles according to which what Rawls called 'primary goods' should be distributed.

It is social liberalism that substantially informed the development of the 'modern' welfare state in the global North during the post-Second World War period. Social liberalism sought to ensure that human needs – however defined – were at least minimally satisfied in order to underwrite the basic freedoms of the human subject. It also provided core elements of the 'basic needs' approach that informed international approaches to social development in the global South during the 1980s (Galtung, 1980; Wisner, 1988; Gasper, 2007). More recently, resurgent forms of economic liberalism have impacted on discussions of human welfare, whereby the human individual is cast as a member of a peculiarly rational and calculating species, a species that has been described with irony as *homo œconomicus* (see for example Persky, 1995; Douglas and Ney, 1998). However, rather than reverting to the crude disincentives of the 19th-century workhouse, current social policies in the global North – particularly in the English-speaking world – reflect a more sophisticated array of incentives, by which utilitarian subjects are not only persuaded to provide for their own needs, but presented with opportunities to do so and are enabled or enjoined to make informed choices.

Needs as subjective preferences

A further variation among economistic conceptions of human need is a market-oriented approach that is concerned not so much with the rational agency of *homo œconomicus* as with the effects of individual subjective preferences by free market actors. The individual actor is the atom (the simplest irreducible element) of the free market process and it is her choices that drive the market. In the context of market transactions, the preferences, wants or desires of one party are put at the services of the other's utility. The rationale of economic activity is seen to lie in the production of goods for the satisfaction of consumer needs or wants. But the distinction between the consumer's needs and wants becomes immaterial. Adam Smith famously observed that 'it is not from the benevolence of the butcher, the brewer, or the baker that we expect our dinner, but from their regard to their own interest' (1776, p 11). The suppliers of tobacco products and sugary foods may acknowledge that their products are actually harmful to some or all of their customers and therefore contrary to consumers' interests, but suppliers are willing nonetheless to satisfy the consumers' misguided preferences. And consumers themselves are unmindful of the needs and purposes of suppliers. Shakespeare's Romeo may have absolved the conscience of the impoverished apothecary who so reluctantly sold him the lethal potion he sought: 'I pay thy poverty and not thy will' (*Romeo and Juliet*, Act V, Scene I). But it mattered little to Romeo whether the 40 ducats he paid would satisfy the apothecary's needs. What mattered was that Romeo could now fulfil his own ostensibly irrational desire to kill himself.

It may be argued that our preferences, wants and desires have their roots in our interests (Thomson, 1987, ch IV). Our interests may drive or motivate our desires, although our desires may well conflict with certain of our fundamental needs. Romeo wanted to die! His desire to do so was motivated by his love for Juliet, or, more precisely, because having to part from Juliet would be harmful to his interests insofar as it would frustrate his need for somebody to love (see Chapter One, this book). As Freud pointed out, the aim and object of our desire are not necessarily the same thing (Freud, 2006; see also Stafford-Clark, 1965).

The desires of market actors are expressed through the preferences or choices they exercise. We shall see in Chapter Three that there are economists for whom utility is an abstract mathematical function. They argue that how much we are prepared to pay for something is a measure of how much we need it. But such an assumption cannot come into play unless real living people have substantive freedom of choice. And it is with precisely this in mind that neoliberal thinking is hostile to the very idea of state welfare intervention. The provision of public services and welfare benefits constrains the choices of those who receive them (Hayek, 1976), while the collection of taxes to pay for such services and benefits constrains the freedom of others to spend their money as they choose (Nozick, 1974). According to this account it is the free and unfettered market that can most efficiently and equitably allocate the resources necessary for the satisfaction of human need. Real need is represented by un-coerced choices that free individuals are able to make. If, in a free market, the needs of those who choose badly remain unmet, that may be unfortunate, but it is not unjust. Insofar as markets may fail or function inequitably (Le Grand et al, 1992, ch 1) there may be a role for social policy. But strict adherents to this account of human need would see this as a minimal role. The role of the state should be to provide safety nets for those whose essential needs remain unmet and to regulate external effects over which markets have no control. Beyond this the job of the state is to defend and promote the free choice of the human individual. Human beings are defined, it is supposed, by their choice making.

Needs as inner drives

A rather different account of human need is that espoused by philosophers and psychologists who focus on the inner-most human drives and the variety of needs that flow from these. I shall be concerned in later chapters with the implications of Cartesian dualism – the philosophical tradition that distinguishes between the 'base' needs of the human body as opposed to the 'higher' needs of the human mind. In this chapter I shall only introduce the philosophical tradition in order to situate a dominant account of the human individual as a psychological being with a spectrum of needs.

The tradition begins with Plato (427–347 BC) for whom the different parts of the human body called for different human virtues, reflecting, by implication, different levels of human need (Plato, 1974 edn). He saw the head as the seat of reason with the need of wisdom. The chest he saw as the source of will, with the need of courage. The abdomen he saw as the seat of appetite, with the need of temperance. Plato the rationalist appeared to regard the body and its abdominal elements with some disgust, as did Descartes (1596–1650), the philosopher who developed the classic dualist distinction between body and mind (Assiter, 2000, p 64). The point for Cartesian dualism is that the 'noumenal self' – the real me or the real you – is not located in our bodies at all. And yet we are beholden to the demands of our bodies. The tension between the embodied self, with its biological urges, and the noumenal self, with its higher callings, lies at the heart of the account developed by Sigmund Freud. I have already mentioned Freud's observation that the aims and objects of our desires are not necessarily the same: basic needs are sometimes disguised or 'sublimated' so as to drive behaviours that may turn out, for example, to be either highly creative or else profoundly dysfunctional, depending on the circumstances (Stafford-Clark, 1965, pp 164-6). Such insights into the complexity of the relationship between body and mind have informed more recent psychological accounts.

The best known is that by Abraham Maslow (1943, 1970), who posited the existence of a hierarchy of human needs. In his original formulation he contended that there were five basic kinds of need that motivated us, and he ordered them according to their potency. The first and strongest needs were physiological: for oxygen, water, nutrients, homeostasis, excretion, sleep, sex and so on. The second needs were safety: physical security, security of resources, livelihood, family and possessions. The third were love and belonging: relationships, family, friendship and sexual intimacy. The fourth were self-esteem: self-identity and respect, confidence and respect from others. The fifth kind of needs was 'self-actualisation': self-fulfilment through achievement. Before his death, Maslow added two more needs: cognitive (the need to acquire knowledge and understanding) and aesthetic (the need for creativity and the appreciation of beauty and structure). The hierarchy is illustrated in *Table 2.2*.

Table 2.2: *Maslow's hierarchy of needs*

higher needs	aesthetic needs	added to the hierarchy in 1970
↑	cognitive needs	
	need for self-actualisation	
	need for self-esteem	
	need for love and belonging	the classic 1943 hierarchy
	need for safety	
lower needs	**physiological needs**	

The hierarchy is sometimes visually presented in the form of a pyramid, with the higher needs towards the pinnacle. This can be taken, perhaps, to imply a degree of moral superiority for the higher needs, but Maslow's intention was to emphasise that the more potent needs at the bottom of the hierarchy took precedence over those above and must be satisfied before a person could 'progress'. We shall see that this contention does not hold up empirically, since people can and do risk their personal safety for the sake of another's love or to achieve social esteem. In affluent societies people on low incomes may literally go hungry in order to maintain forms of consumption by which to 'keep up appearances'. Nonetheless, Maslow's model provides a theory of motivation that has had an enduring influence. The assumptions it embodies are reflected in the ways that policy makers tend to prioritise needs. They are reflected, for example, in the kinds of children's health and education policies that emphasise the need for nurturing environments and the importance of monitoring children's development.

Needs as constitutive characteristics

Finally, in this section I turn to accounts of human need that focus on what is human about human need. What is it that members of the human species need that other living creatures do not? The most important thinker here is Karl Marx, although there is a problem with his account. Some commentators regard Marx's account of human needs as inconsistent or contradictory – there is an element of discontinuity between Marx's early and later writings. Between the two phases of Marx's work writers such as Althusser, for example, have detected an 'epistemological break' (1994), a breakthrough from an ideological account to a more scientific form of historical materialism. In his early writings Marx argued that although capitalism had advanced the human condition, it was inherently alienating and inimical to social humanity. In his later writings, he sought to expose the immanent logic of the commodity form and the wage relation under capitalism and demonstrated how this distorted our understanding of human need. I shall be discussing this later work in the next chapter; in this chapter I discuss Marx's early writings on human need.

Before doing so, however, we should note that several writers reject the claim that there is a tension between Marx's earlier and later writings. Certainly, his thinking was complex and it developed in the course of his lifetime. Despite this it has been variously argued by Geras (1983) that Marx consistently espoused a permanent or 'trans-historical' normative standard of human need, or else by Heller (1974) that Marx had assembled a holistic and dynamic account of 'truly' or 'radical' human needs. There are other writers who argue that Marx has provided an account of human need with complementary cognitive and normative elements (Soper, 1981), or else that Marx had been presenting two interdependent accounts, one concerning the need to 'humanise nature' (to shape or civilise the natural world in the interests of humanity), the other concerning the need to 'naturalise humanity' (to restore human beings' unity with nature) (Benton, 1988). A fuller discussion of these various commentaries is provided by Hewitt (2000, ch 6).

The foundation of Marx's argument rests, in the first instance, on a degree of scepticism towards Cartesian dualism. He argued that 'Thought and being are indeed distinct, but they also form a unity' (1844 [1975 edn], p 351). It is the dynamic relationship between thinking and being that characterises human action and therefore human history. Following from this, the argument rests on a rejection of the kind of utilitarian and psychological accounts of need outlined earlier in this chapter – which he regarded as superficial – and an insistence on what it is that is distinctive about humanity and human industry. By 'industry' he was referring not merely to the burgeoning manufacturing technologies of the times in which he was writing (the mid–19th century) but to what might be called the human project, to scientific understanding and the self-conscious harnessing of Nature for the benefit of Man (that is, humanity in general). Marx acknowledged that capitalist industry exploited both Man and Nature, but this represented a particular moment or phase in human history:

> ... if industry is conceived as an exoteric form of the realisation of the essential human faculties, one is able to grasp also the human essence of Nature or the natural essence of Man.... Nature as it develops in human history, in the genesis of human society, is the real nature of Man; thus Nature, as it develops through industry, though in an alienated form, is truly anthropological Nature. (1844 [1975 edn], p 355)

Anthropologists such as Markus (1978) have drawn on Marx's insights. Marx's theory of human need amounts to a theory of the essential characteristics of the human species and of its 'species being'. The account may be summarised in terms of four features of our species character and mode of existence: work, consciousness, sociality and historical development (Markus, 1978, pp 37–41; see also Hewitt, 2000, pp 129–31). Each of these is a constitutive species characteristic and amounts, therefore, to a human need. A highly simplified visual representation of the argument is presented in *Figure 2.1*. 'Work', of which wage labour can be a cruelly distorted manifestation, may be understood in terms of human beings' purposive interaction with the world around them. Through work we may satisfy our instrumental needs, but also develop the creative skills and the critical knowledge that defines our humanity. 'Consciousness' is what distinguishes human beings from other animals and makes human action possible in the sense that it is action that has meaning. 'Sociality' is definitive insofar as the meaningfulness of every individual human act is defined by its social context (through shared language and customs) and the social relations of the actor (through which human identity is realised). 'Historical development' is constitutive of human existence in the sense that we are creatures of history. When I referred above to the 'human project', this was an attempt to paraphrase the post-Enlightenment sense in which history is humanity's struggle to emancipate itself, to universalise its species characteristics, to realise its potential, to fulfil all human need.

Figure 2.1: *Marx's account of human need: a simplified visual representation*

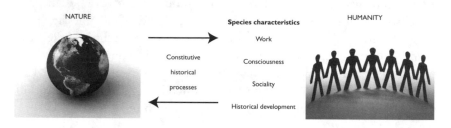

It is in this last notion of our species being that we can see what Marxism shares with liberalism as a 'modernising' project, as a 'grand narrative' whose era some would say is now past and whose substance is discredited (Fukuyama, 1992). But we can also see the difference. Marx foresaw that the culmination of human history would be a better society governed by the principle from each according to her abilities to each according to her needs. From a complex argument flows the simplest of aphorisms.

Social policy perspectives

From classic accounts I turn now to relatively recent accounts by social policy commentators. In the mid-1970s the current edition of a celebrated introductory text on social administration (as academic social policy was once described) could still claim that the 'concept of collective provision to meet individual need is the hallmark of a social service'. The task of the discipline, it was contended, is to ask 'what needs are they trying to meet; why do the needs arise; on what grounds, political, moral, economic, does society base its attempts to meet need; how effective are its policies and indeed what are our criteria for effectiveness in this context?' (Brown, 1977, p 13). Student texts of the 1970s would subsequently be criticised for reducing the discussion of need to a largely technical analysis of resource allocation and the prioritisation of competing claims (Taylor-Gooby and Dale, 1981, p 23), because by the 1980s need had become a contested issue. The politically ascendant New Right (Barry, 1987) directly questioned whether collective provision for individual need was required and those who would defend the welfare state were obliged to revisit their understanding of human need.

The welfare state or the market?

The post-Second World War welfare states that emerged throughout much of the developed world were most celebrated when – as in the case of the National Health Service in the UK – they claimed to be providing people with services on the basis of their need, rather than their ability to pay. The so-called crisis of the welfare state (Mishra, 1984) laid down a challenge. At the heart of the crisis lay a resurgent pro-market neoliberal economic orthodoxy that was opposed to social spending on welfare and believed in the efficacy of free markets as a means of satisfying human need. The ascendancy of neoliberal economic thinking was accompanied by a 'New Right' political agenda. In what was assumed to be an age of post-scarcity this agenda was hostile to the very idea of need. It was claimed by some that 'The word "need" ought to be banished from discussion of public policy' (Williams, 1974, cited in Plant et al, 1980, p 19). And so a new debate within social policy began.

An important, if guarded, defence of the welfare state was provided by Robert Goodin (1988), who started from the premise that the essential role of the welfare state was to relieve those in distress. If in the process it performed other less necessary functions or benefited people who were not in distress, this was a secondary consideration. A minimal welfare state was required in order to protect the most vulnerable members of society and to prevent those who were dependent from being exploited because of their dependency. The central task of the welfare state was indeed to meet need. But according to Goodin this did not mean that there was a compelling case for looking to the welfare state to meet needs while assuming that the market would only meet the people's less justified wants and desires. The moral justification for the welfare state has nothing to do with the primacy of needs over wants. Goodin engaged with and elaborated the tangle of arguments that I have endeavoured to present above, and emerged with the conclusion that needs did not trump wants as a principle of welfare provision and that there was no case for allowing state provision to supplant market provision. Needs claims and wants claims cannot in practice be disentangled and there is no compelling principle on which we should regard one as superior to the other.

In the course of the argument, however, two partial concessions are quietly made. Goodin contended that where needs claims related to finite resources that were not reusable (such as money), they did not necessarily take precedence over the several instrumental wants that might be satisfied by that resource. But he acknowledged nonetheless that:

> Perhaps the paradigm case of a reusable resource is health. It is a
> necessary instrument for the accomplishment of a great variety
> of goals.…Where need-statements refer to reusable resources
> of this sort, a certain measure of priority of needs over wants
> is justified. (1988, p 39)

Second, although he expressed scepticism for the argument that state
provision for basic needs promoted personal autonomy (because it would
impose a lowest common denominator on the living standards of its
citizens), Goodin acknowledged that:

> Considerations of personal autonomy might provide an
> argument for the state's providing people with needed resources
> (seen as "generalised means to any end") rather than the state's
> foisting particular goods (and through them particular ends)
> upon people. That is to say, the personal autonomy argument
> might tell in favour of a welfare state over a command economy.
> (1988, p 47)

Despite these concessions (the significance of which may shortly become
clearer), the thrust of Goodin's argument is opposed to a universal
conception of human need. While providing strong support for a limited
welfare state, Goodin attempted to kick the concept of human needs into
touch.

Doyal and Gough

The concept has been rescued from the touch line by Len Doyal and Ian
Gough (1984, 1991). Their theory of human need was prefigured in an
article in the journal *Critical Social Policy* in 1984 and then consolidated
in a book, published in 1991.

Their central concern was not to respond to Goodin, but to reclaim
some element of the Enlightenment tradition, to recapture a normative
conception of how progress in history was to be made and to articulate an
objective definition of universal human need. Their starting point, therefore,
was a critique of the subjective conception of need outlined above and of
some of the relativist theories of human need that I shall be discussing in the
next chapter. They contended that (what I characterise here as) an inherent
conception of human need remains implicit in almost every ideological
stance, even those that rail against the desirability or the possibility of
defining basic human needs. Neoliberals conceded that markets could
fail and that welfare state safety nets might be necessary in order to meet

minimal needs. Neo-Marxists conceded that need was not necessarily an ideological construct but that there were real needs, which were violated by capitalism. New social movements, while demanding recognition of the particular needs of, for example, women, gay people, disabled people, oppressed ethnic groups and others, through their opposition to human misery clearly conceded that there were universal elements to human need. Radical democrats, while insisting that needs were discursively constructed, would in practice concede that a fully democratised civil study would still require public regulation to ensure that certain needs were met. Even the most extreme cultural relativists acknowledged that there were objective contingencies – such as war and famine – that occasioned harm to human beings and from which basic needs must be inferred (Doyal and Gough, 1991, ch 2).

Doyal and Gough proceeded to advance and defend a universal theory of human need and a definition – with explicit distributional consequences – capable of application across different cultures and societies. At the heart of their theory was the claim that the universal preconditions for human action and interaction were physical health and personal autonomy. The concessions made by Goodin – the priority that may be granted to the need for health and the desirability of provision that substantively facilitates personal autonomy – find a parallel expression in Doyal and Gough's theory, save that for them health and autonomy were embraced as key tenets. The need for physical health requires the protection of all people from harm as well as the provision of the means of subsistence, shelter, healthcare and a safe environment. The need for personal autonomy requires that all people should have knowledge and understanding, capabilities and opportunities and good mental and emotional health, which would imply education or training, the prospect of productive and satisfying work, mental health and family support services. The basic needs for health and autonomy are therefore reflected in a range of intermediate needs, which may be met in a variety of different ways depending on the socioeconomic and cultural context. Doyal and Gough compiled a list of intermediate needs, the satisfaction of which was capable of empirical observation and verification. A summary is provided in *Table 2.3*.

Doyal and Gough's contention was that basic needs should be optimally met, while intermediate needs should, so far as possible, be met to the minimum optimal level. They stressed the importance of the societal conditions necessary for needs satisfaction. And here they distinguished between, on the one hand, the universal preconditions that must apply if people were to be able to avoid serious harm and minimally participate as social beings and, on the other hand, the preconditions that must apply if people were to be able to have critical autonomy and the freedom to live as they chose. The pre-conditions for the former included the existence of some means of material production and the maintenance of livelihoods (a functioning economy of some sort); social conditions conducive to the biological reproduction and renewal of society; functional arrangements for cultural transmission between generations so that a way of life could be sustained over time; and some elements of political authority for the governance of society and the making of decisions. The pre-conditions for the latter included some form of effective citizenship, including civil, political and social rights (discussed in Chapter Eight). To this extent, the normative import of Doyal and Gough's theory is a demand for 'the satisfaction of the health and autonomy needs of as many people as possible to the highest sustainable levels' (1991, p 110).

Table 2.3: Doyal and Gough's theory of human need: a summary

Basic needs	Physical health
	Personal autonomy
Intermediate needs	Adequate nutritional food and water
	Adequate protective housing
	A non-hazardous work environment
	A non-hazardous physical environment
	Appropriate health care
	Security in childhood
	Significant primary relationships
	Physical security
	Economic security
	Safe birth control and child-bearing
	Basic education

Summary

- A range of concepts of need have been discussed in this chapter, which assume that need inheres to the human subject. Implicit in each concept is a different idea or theory of the person or of personhood.
- Classic accounts of inherent need have been explored, drawing out the different ways in which the individual human actor might be regarded:
  - where the person is regarded as a self-seeking utilitarian subject her needs are constituted as objective interests. She needs whatever it is that works to her advantage or keeps her from harm;
  - where the person is regarded as an enterprising market actor her needs are constituted as subjective preferences. She needs whatever is revealed by the choices she makes;
  - where the person is regarded as a psychological being her needs are constituted as inner drives. She needs whatever serves her physical, mental and ontological well-being;
  - where the person is regarded as a member of the human species her needs are the constitutive characteristics of her humanity. She needs whatever it is that distinguishes her from other kinds of 'natural' living creature.
- Accounts from academic social policy have been explored where these have drawn on inherent conceptions of human need. It has been shown that:
  - in the first instance, the social policy debate was focused on the defence of the role of the state in the relief of human distress and, thereby, the meeting of needs which are not, or cannot be, met by markets;
  - following this, however, there has emerged what is, perhaps, the pre-eminent theory of human need in social policy: that advanced by Doyal and Gough. That theory is founded on a rejection of relativism and an assertion that all human beings have need of physical health on the one hand, and personal autonomy on the other. The satisfaction of such needs is mediated by a range of satisfiers that will be culturally specific and it is these that are the everyday concern of social policy.

Questions for discussion:

- What might it be about human need that makes it inherently human?
- Which of the four 'classic' accounts of inherent human need, if any, do you prefer, and why? And which accounts, if any, might you discount?
- To what extent would you say that Doyal and Gough's theory of human need has provided a satisfactory answer to the critics of state welfare provision?

Interpreted need

- This chapter develops and illustrates the concept of interpreted need, which, although inevitably related to that of inherent need, involves a variety of accounts that rely on inferences drawn from experience or observation of human conduct and society.
- A range of accounts are discussed that focus on social customs and patterns of consumption, including:
  - analyses that regard needs as culturally produced;
  - analyses that dismiss certain perceived needs as false or illusory; and
  - analyses that reflect on the way in which the contemporary consumer society has shaped our needs.
- Social policy perspectives on interpreted need are discussed, including:
  - pragmatic approaches to policy making that address the interpretations of needs obtained, for example, from experts, from individuals, through public opinion or by comparative analysis;
  - participatory approaches that focus specifically on finding out what people say they need; and
  - theoretical approaches that have sought to relate the social and symbolic meanings that attach to human need to the analysis of social policy.

In this chapter I turn from what I have characterised as inherent need to interpreted need. Inherent conceptions of need require a theory or construction of the individual subject or actor. Needs are the things that may be inferred as attaching to people. They are nouns (cf Gasper, 2007, p 55). Interpreted conceptions of need are concerned not with the subject or actor, but with the process of needing, with the way in which needs are generated, identified and/or responded to. Need entails observable happenings. Need becomes a verb (cf Gasper, 2007, p 55).

Although it is not a precise analogy, the distinction between inherent and interpreted need is akin to that in physics between mass and weight.[1] The mass of an object relates to the amount and density of the material it is made of, whereas its weight refers to the force that gravity exerts on it. An object's mass is an inherent property, but its weight is dependent on the context of the object, on where in the universe it happens to be. It is through the weight of an object that we interpret its mass, but there are many different ways of assessing and describing an object's weight (see **Box 3.1**). And in practical everyday life it is through the weight, not the mass, of the things around us that we generate an understanding of their properties or propensities. It is the weight not the mass of an article that influences how we would go about picking it up or throwing it. Similarly, we can differentiate between, on the one hand, the needs that attach to or characterise a human being and, on the other, the social and political context in which those needs are manifested and the ways in which, for practical everyday purposes, we understand, act on or ignore other people's needs.

We cannot feel mass, but weight. It is weight that enables us to detect the reality of mass. We may be able to feel our own needs, but we cannot feel another's. We have to judge it in some way. And judgements may be misguided. In Chapter Two, to defend the concept of inherent need, I quoted from the argument by Heller that we cannot distinguish between true and false or real and imaginary needs: if humans feel a need, Heller claimed, it must be real. Rist responded to this argument, saying 'If everything is a need, then need means nothing' (1980, p 241). Interpreted need, however, is not of itself the need that can be felt by humans (although what people say and do about needs are among the factors that can be extremely pertinent), but that which stems from observation and judgement, that which may be deduced, for example, from social customs, cultural symbols, price signals, survey data, discourse analysis or from attending to political demands. Just as mass declares itself through weight, the reality of material need declares itself through a variety of detectable evidence, signs, fashions and claims. And indeed it becomes possible to contest the difference between true and false needs. Certain needs may be interpreted in terms of the way they conceal our inherent needs. Other interpretations might, potentially, reveal them.

The interpretation of human need takes place at many different levels. In the first part of this chapter I shall discuss the ways in which need is interpreted through customs and through consumption patterns or 'lifestyle'. In the second I turn more directly to social policy perspectives, both practical and theoretical.

Box 3.1: The mass/weight analogy

An illustration of the sense in which weight is variously used to interpret mass. Just as weight is not the same as mass because it is concerned with gravity, interpreted need is not the same as inherent need because it is concerned with social effects and contextual differences.

	interpreting mass	interpreting need
When I weigh myself at home using cheap bathroom scales on the hard tiles in the bathroom, I appear to weigh 140 imperial pounds, but if I repeat the process on the soft carpet in the bedroom I appear to weigh 143 pounds (because the uneven surface distorts the scales and affects their accuracy).	weight readings may be inaccurate	need can be falsely interpreted
In outer space I would weigh nothing at all. If I could weigh myself on the moon, I would weigh 28 pounds; on Jupiter 336 pounds.	measuring weight entails observing the effects of gravity	interpreting needs entails observing the effects of social processes
If I weighed myself using metric scales, I would weigh 63.5 kilograms; using Troy measure scales, I would weigh 170 pounds. If they had had bathroom scales in ancient Rome they would have shown my weight as 195 pounds; in ancient Greece, 149 mines; and in biblical times, 112 minas.	the measurement and comparison of weights requires an arbitrary choice of units of measurement	interpreting need entails arbitrary choices concerning the criteria or conventions that may be used
From my weight and height measurements health professionals tell me that my Body Mass Indicator (BMI) is OK. But if I were 6 inches shorter than I am my BMI would be too high: I would be 'overweight'. If I were 6 inches taller my BMI would be too low: I would be 'underweight'.	to make judgements about mass, weight must be compared with other kinds of measurement	to make judgements about interpreted need several intersecting social criteria may be entailed
I am an average sized (male) human being. Average sized elephants weigh a lot more than 140 pounds; mice a lot less. But if the only information you had about me was a reading from my bathroom scales, I could for all you know be a very small elephant or a very large mouse.	interpretation based on one item of data can be meaningless	the interpretation of needs through signs devoid of human context can descend into meaninglessness

Customs and consumption

In the last chapter I briefly summarised some of the critiques advanced by Doyal and Gough in respect of certain 'relativist' notions of human need. In this section I shall address certain key relativist positions, emphasising cultural explanations of need, some critical accounts of the needs created by capitalism and concepts of need in a 'consumer society'.

Cultural meanings

The process of human civilisation (Elias, 1978) and the creation of customs and culture have, on the one hand, given meaning to human need. The observation that 'Man is a child of the customs and the things he has become used to ... not a product of his natural dispositions and temperament' had been made by the mediaeval Muslim philosopher Ibn Khaldûn (1332–1406) (cited in Callinicos, 2007, p 11). Needs depend on customs, and yet the way in which they are represented through customs may vary. Indeed they may not be represented through customs or language at all. Lederer (1980, p 8) recounts a conversation with a distinguished Japanese academic who explained to her that in Japanese there is no word for 'needs'. The Japanese language has words that translate into 'wants' or 'desires' in English, but there is no single term for the concept of need in an 'objective' sense. A similar finding from research in Hong Kong is reported by Tao (2004).

Not only are understandings of need culturally dependent, but the process of civilisation creates new needs. Four centuries after Khaldûn the realisation across Western Europe that human beings are not descended from gods, but, supposedly, risen from savages, led the philosopher Rousseau (1712–78) to regret that civilisation of the savage had, in his estimation, substituted artificial and selfish needs in place of natural and selfless ones (Springborg, 1981, ch 3). Rousseau yearned for a return to nature and the supposed innocence of the 'noble savage'. Adam Smith (1723–90), the liberal economist, was similarly mindful of the difference, for example, between 'necessities' and superficial 'luxuries', and yet he acknowledged that culture and custom could give rise to necessities. While contemporary economic liberals – as the inheritors of Smith's intellectual legacy – tend to adopt a minimalist definition of human need, it is striking that the man himself insisted that non–life sustaining commodities, if people could not forego them without some sense of *shame*, were indeed necessities. These necessities were customary: they varied in the course of history and between different parts of the world. And such variations are observable. An extended quotation from Smith's most celebrated work is set out in ***Box 3.2***. We shall see in Chapter Four that this insight has been particularly significant for certain contemporary methods for the measurement of poverty.

> ### Box 3.2: Adam Smith on the meaning of 'necessaries'
>
> 'By necessaries I understand not only the commodities which are indispensably necessary for the support of life, but whatever the custom of the country renders it indecent for creditable people, even of the lowest order, to be without. A linen shirt for example is strictly speaking not a necessity of life. The Greeks and Romans lived, I suppose, very comfortably though they had no linen. But in the present times, through the greater part of Europe, a creditable day-labourer would be ashamed to appear in public without a linen shirt.... Custom, in the same manner, has rendered leather shoes a necessary of life in England. The poorest creditable person of either sex would be ashamed to appear in public without them. In Scotland, custom has rendered them a necessary of life to the lowest order of men; but not to the same order of women, who may, without any discredit, walk about barefooted. In France, they are necessaries neither to men nor to women; the lowest rank of both sexes appearing there publicly, without any discredit, sometimes in wooden shoes and sometimes barefooted. Under necessaries therefore, I comprehend, not only those things which nature, but those things which the established rules of decency, have rendered necessary to the lowest rank of people. All other things I call luxuries....' (1776, p 691)

Illusion, falsity and wastefulness

If the process of civilisation and the evolution of customary norms may be said to have shaped human need, the coming of capitalism, according to a variety of commentators, distorted that process.

In Chapter Two I discussed the theory of human need to be found in the earlier works of Karl Marx. In his later work in particular, a different strand of his critique of capitalism also emerges in which he is not concerned with the constitutive needs of individuals as human beings but with social needs or the manner in which needs are socially produced (Heller, 1974; Soper, 1981). Through an analysis of the way in which value attaches to commodities under capitalism, he provided the basis on which to claim that capitalism generates false needs. Marx himself, it should be said, did not necessarily express it in exactly these terms, although he held that certain needs, though demonstrably and consciously experienced, are nonetheless imaginary rather than real. The essence of his argument (Marx, 1887) may be paraphrased as follows:

- There is a distinction to be made between the *use* value of a good or a service and its *exchange* value. The usefulness of something is a direct reflection of the *need* that it satisfies. But when we exchange goods or services as *commodities* under capitalism the value we attach to them relates to a notion of equivalence that has nothing to do with their usefulness to us as satisfiers of human need. Useless luxuries may be accorded greater value than necessities.
- The exchange value that we attach to a commodity is a reflection not of its usefulness, but of the amount of human labour that went into producing it. A diamond ring appears more valuable than a loaf of bread because the time, effort, risks and skills of the miners and the jeweller that produced the diamond ring are proportionately greater than that of the farmer and the baker that produced the loaf of bread.
- Under capitalism, however, labour power itself becomes a commodity that is sold in return for wages. Remember that in Chapter Two I explained that Marx regarded work as a species characteristic: we need to work because that is what defines us as human. But when we work for wages the wage does not reflect the use value of our work, but rather the exchange value of our labour power. And we are 'alienated' from the goods and services we produce in the sense that we do not use them ourselves to satisfy our own needs.
- Capitalism is based on the exploitation of labour power. And the exchange value of the goods and services sold under capitalist relations of production includes an element of 'surplus value' that derives from that exploitation. That surplus value accrues to the capitalist at the expense of the workers.
- Marx therefore argues that we end up with material relations between people and social relations between things. When we buy and sell our labour power we are not satisfying our human needs but behaving as commodities. It is a dehumanising process. At the same time we evaluate the goods and services that we need and equate them with each other in terms of socially constituted characteristics; in terms of what other people have had to do to produce them.
- It is on this basis that Marx coined the term 'commodity fetishism'. The world of commodities, he claimed, is an upside down world in which the nature of the exploitation that is suffered is obscured. The way in which the prices consumers have to pay and the profits that entrepreneurs can make may fluctuate according to the state of the market conceals an underlying perversity to the way in which we attribute value to things and the extent to which the everyday perception of human needs is distorted. Interpreted through the machinations of capitalist social relations of production, our needs become estranged from us.

This analysis – although it is easily misinterpreted and misapplied – has been influential in several ways. In particular it informed the Frankfurt School of critical theorists, among whom it was Marcuse who explicitly declared that, through indoctrination and manipulation, capitalist society implants 'false needs in people' (1964; see also Springborg, 1981, ch 9).

This kind of observation is made by progressive liberals as well as Marxist thinkers. In his excoriating critique of late 19th-century US-style capitalism, Veblen (1899) coined the term 'conspicuous consumption'. Veblen, a cofounder of the institutional economic movement, was interested in the effects of social and cultural change, in particular the process by which the ostentatious and wasteful consumption of the rich set fashions and standards that the poor aspired to but could never achieve. It is a process that Townsend would later characterise as 'the proselytisation of lifestyles' (1979, p 366). The same insight informed Kenneth Galbraith's iconoclastic account of *The affluent society* (1958). Galbraith was a Keynesian economist and an adviser to Democratic US Presidents F.D. Roosevelt, Johnson and Kennedy. His argument was that despite increasing wealth under capitalism and the absence of scarcity, human needs were never wholly satisfied. This, he claimed, was partly because of the power wielded by oligopolies, but also because of the new needs generated by a burgeoning advertising industry, needs not everybody could satisfy. Affluence fuelled chronic dissatisfaction.

Hirsch (1977) similarly contended that needs and wants proliferated with economic growth, but that there were inevitably social limits. It was not material scarcity that was the problem, but *social* scarcity. It was not simply that the spectacular consumption of the super-rich could never be emulated by everybody, but that the value of newly created needs to which people of modest means might realistically aspire may depend on their scarcity. Certain goods were necessarily 'positional goods' since they conferred an advantage on those who first acquired them, an advantage that diminished or might be lost as more people acquired them. The advantage obtained by those at the very back of a crowd by standing on tip-toe is instantly negated as soon as those immediately in front of them do the same. In the same way, the freedom and privileges enjoyed by the first motorists in a country are rapidly negated when everybody feels they need (and eventually can afford) a motor car and the roads become congested. It is not merely that extravagant needs become ordinary; they become unsustainable (Taylor-Gooby and Dale, 1981, pp 230-1).

Consumer society

This leads us beyond the point at which human needs may be understood by observing culture and custom to consider whether in consumer-oriented societies it is consumption itself that signals what needs are.

In the last chapter on inherent need I identified subjective preference as a way of conceptualising the needs that inhere or reside in a human individual when the individual is conceived of as a market actor. I mentioned that there are economists for whom utility is an abstract mathematical function. There is a form of 'welfare economics' in which the human actor becomes invisible and it is not the preferences people experience but the prices that are paid for goods that become an indicator or measure of human need (Pigou, 1928, 1965). It is what people will pay for things that provides the only meaningful way to interpret needs. This is an extreme economistic approach which, when fully developed, exemplifies what disaffected economics students at the Sorbonne once mischievously (and potentially offensively) dubbed 'autistic economics' (Monaghan, 2003) (and see www. autisme-economie.org/article142.html). This kind of welfare economics is quite literally disengaged from the dynamics of social reality. It is insensitive to social context and responds only to the signal provided by the mechanism of price. Marx had contended that price was a 'surface category' that concealed the nature of exchange value and the way in which this elided human need. And yet the powerful internal logic of this kind of welfare economics and the way in which it privileges the meaning of price signals has been influential.

An equally autistic (in the literal rather than a pejorative sense) but quite different form of logic is demonstrated through the work of the sociologist Baudrillard. Baudrillard's work is highly abstract and, to many readers, baffling. His earlier writing, however (1970; and see also 1988), provided a significant alternative approach to that of other thinkers. He argued, against Marx, that it was consumption not production that drove capitalism. The need of the consumer became institutionalised as the productive force in developed capitalist societies (Giradin, 2000). Baudrillard offered an alternative theory to account for the value of objects. In place of the distinction between use value and exchange value made by Marx, he asserted a distinction between symbolic value (which has its roots in pre-capitalist forms of gift exchange) and sign value (the significance of objects within a socially constructed system of needs). A diamond ring has symbolic value when given as a token of love or of betrothal. A loaf of bread, depending on the context, can signify lifestyle. Readers from the UK will recognise that, through the images we receive from advertising and entertainment media, a traditional English brown loaf signifies homely working-class cottage living, while a trendy Italian ciabatta signifies stylish middle-class bistro living. According to Baudrillard, it is *these* signs (not prices) that tell us about needs.

In later work Baudrillard contended that the infinite plasticity of capitalist values was realised in the age of mass ideological communication and information technology to the extent that the system of signs (or 'simulacra') imploded into a form of what he called 'hyperreality', a meaningless spiral in which there is nothing but symbols and signs. We need not go there! The essential insight that must be drawn from Baudrillard, I suggest, is the idea that exchange between human beings is not necessarily or primarily a function of need. His anthropological account of symbolic exchange proceeds from the basis that in pre-modern society it was acts, not goods, which were exchanged: for example, eating and drinking, not food and drink. Even basic survival was not necessarily recognised as a 'need' in the sense we may now understand it until a system of object values could be established. Need is, he claimed, entirely a cultural invention. Needs are no more and no less than what we may interpret through a socially constructed system of culturally generated signs (for a critique, see Hefner, 2000).

Zygmunt Bauman's (1998) account of 'consumerism' has features in common with Baudrillard's work. Bauman's argument is that in the post-modern age the work ethic has been displaced by an 'aesthetic of consumption' (1998, ch 2). Like Baudrillard, therefore, he is arguing that it is consumption not production that characterises human need. With the shift from an industrial to a service economy, consumer confidence is more important to the health of the economy than full employment. And like Baudrillard, he is mindful of the ephemeral nature of consumption: that which we consume, we destroy. But Bauman's concern is not with signs, but with the 'spirit' of consumption. As Townsend was concerned with the proselytisation of lifestyles (see above), Bauman is concerned with the proliferation of aesthetic tastes. The consumer's restless quest is for ever more satisfying sensations and experiences and 'the promise and hope of satisfaction will precede the need' (1998, p 28). One incidental implication is that there can be no satisfaction in work that is boring, so crude coercion may be required to make people work. The poor, however, are not failed workers, but failed consumers who cannot satisfy the tastes they have come to share with the rich and must therefore endure a chronic sense of insufficiency.

The point is that within these highly theoretical and sometimes extreme accounts need does not inhere in the individual but is an artefact of the consumer society.

Social policy perspectives

I turn now to interpreted need conceptions to be found in the social policy literature. The focus is on how responses to need have been, or are to be, shaped. Langan characterises this approach with her assertion that needs 'are socially constructed, historically specific and contested', and to understand them 'we need to examine the wider social and historical context and the influences of ideological and political conflicts as well as questions of resources and policy' (1998, p 7). There is a spectrum of approaches here and I shall outline first, pragmatic approaches to deciding on what needs should be met; second, approaches based on service user participation as a means to determine need; and third, the way in which some social policy academics have engaged with more theoretical accounts of how needs are socially or symbolically constructed.

Pragmatic interpretations

Public policy makers, social administrators and service providers might look at the discussion I have outlined above and ask, what's all the fuss about? The old social administration tradition within academic social policy tended to think that needs present no problem: 'they are simply what the state has chosen to recognise' (Taylor-Gooby and Dale, 1981, p 214). From within this tradition, in a celebrated article in *New Society*, Jonathan Bradshaw asserted: 'The history of the social services is the story of the recognition of social needs and the organisation of society to meet them' (1972, p 640). On the face of it this is a tautological or circular sort of argument: human need becomes whatever we decide it is. In practice, however, Bradshaw was making an important point about the different ways in which policy makers, social administrators and service providers decide to interpret human need.

Table 3.1: Bradshaw's taxonomy of need

	basis of needs interpretation	how it is determined
normative need	expert judgement	by professionals
felt need	what people feel	by opinion surveys/ qualitative research
expressed need	what people demand	by elections/petitions/ participatory assessment
comparative need	what everybody else has	by social condition surveys and/or service evaluations

Bradshaw presented a simple taxonomy of social needs (see ***Table 3.1***). By social needs he was referring to needs that were in various ways socially interpreted. He distinguished between four kinds of need. First, he identified *normative* needs and here he was referring not to need defined by cultural or customary norms, but to the judgements made by experts and welfare professionals as to what people might 'normally' and legitimately need and what services should be provided. When we discuss poverty in Chapter Four, we shall encounter the different ways in which experts have sought to define what basic needs are and where, for example, to draw a poverty line, threshold or standard below which people may be said to be in need. Second, he identified *felt* need, by which he was referring to what people might subjectively believe they need. Bradshaw is not concerned with philosophical arguments as to whether people's feelings can disclose real needs as opposed to mere 'wants'. He was pointing out the relevance of how people felt about the services they should have. In Chapter Four we shall encounter the ways in which poverty or deprivation thresholds have also been formulated using survey techniques to determine the popular consensus as to what people feel to be necessities. Third, Bradshaw identified *expressed* needs: the things that people not only feel they need, but which they demand. Once again, Bradshaw was not making judgements about the distinction between needs and demands. He was merely pointing to the relevance of what people individually ask for, or what through voting, campaigning or other forms of participation they might collectively demand in terms of benefits and services. I shall return to discuss service user participation below, and in Chapters Eight and Nine I shall return to the question of just how needs are translated into claims and claims into rights.

Finally, Bradshaw identified *comparative* needs: needs which may be said to arise when there is a shortfall or deficiency in the services received by one person or group and those received by another similarly placed person or group. At issue here are comparisons between people and what they are getting and an assumption that if a resource or service is unfairly distributed, this may leave some people in relative need. In practical terms, policy makers can draw on a variety of data relating to social and economic inequalities and studies or procedures that evaluate existing public service provision in order to identify inequities or gaps that might be said to constitute unmet needs, requiring a response. Elements of this approach have been resurrected in a recent study of 'unmet needs' in the UK (Vale et al, 2009).[2] Unless resources are available for the meeting of such needs, the idea of comparative or relative need when applied as a basis for service planning opens up a spectrum of potential objections. The concern in some quarters might be that an approach focused on comparative or relative needs could spiral out of control. On the one hand, it could result in an endless and counterproductive inflation of expectations, such that the welfare state could never satisfy need. On the other hand, if resources are finite, such an approach will not be sustainable.

The first of these points has been raised by Robert Goodin, whose discussion of needs and wants we discussed in Chapter Two. Goodin (1990) voiced a more particular concern in relation to the idea that societies should necessarily aim to maximise the provision of resources for the satisfaction of unmet relative need. In the nature of things, more means less. Goodin, like Bauman, contended that growing social inequality fuelled dissatisfaction and dissatisfaction in turn drove up demand as people discovered new unmet needs. If, assuming that basic or absolute needs could be met, policy makers were concerned to limit social and economic inequality, they should not seek to satisfy relative need by bringing everybody's living standards up to the median. This would perversely serve to accelerate the growth in expectations and ratchet up the extent of inequality. Goodin argued, controversially, that to minimise the distribution of resources while distributing them on a uniform basis would be more equitable and was more conducive in the longer term to achieving an egalitarian society.

Policy makers and social administrators themselves will usually have less principled objections and are usually more concerned to find ways to ration people's access to limited resources. Rationing is a particular issue in developed countries when it comes to access to healthcare provision. Forder (1974, cited by Liddiard, 2007, p 122) added to Bradshaw's four categories of need what he called 'technical need', which related to needs for new and often expensive forms of provision that did not previously exist. Scientific and technological advances now mean that computers in schools, central heating (or air conditioning) in houses and the latest forms of medical treatment might all come to be regarded as necessaries. Much of the literature on rationing has been developed in relation to access to medical care, where significant ethical issues can arise. Procedures once undreamt of such as heart transplants, hip replacements, advanced cancer treatments, IVF fertility treatment and gender reassignment are all now possible, but cannot necessarily be made available on demand within the budgetary constraints of publicly funded health provision. Not everyone's comparative needs can be met. Radical critics of modern healthcare, such as Ivan Illich (1977), argued that technologically created needs of this nature were not human needs at all. Access even to routine forms of service may in any event be rationed – whether by formal or informal means – if the time of welfare professionals or the money to pay for services was short (Foster, 1983; Klein et al, 1996).

Participatory approaches

The third of Bradshaw's categories was expressed need, and I have already alluded to the possibility that users of human services might give expression to their needs through various forms of participation. The ability to voice one's needs and to participate in deliberative processes concerning the satisfaction of one's needs may be regarded as a need in itself or, indeed, as a right of citizenship, and this will be a recurring theme in later chapters. For now, however, I want to touch on issues relating to the application of participatory approaches to the assessment of need.

Participation might be regarded as axiomatically desirable. However, the techniques for facilitating and managing consultation can work in a variety of different ways. Arnstein (1969) proposed a 'ladder' of participation with eight 'rungs' or levels of participation. The first rungs did not actually entail participation at all, since they were concerned with the ways in which service providers might seek to manipulate or change people's opinions or behaviour, or did no more than offer them information. The next rungs promoted purely tokenistic forms of participation, involving consultation exercises or placatory public meetings. The higher rungs of the ladder afforded people varying degrees of power: through partnership arrangements or delegation, whereby people might be co-opted into decision-making processes, or else, possibly, more direct and meaningful forms of citizenship control. The important insight here is that participation can potentially emancipate people and enable them to express their needs in ways that make a difference, or it can work to disempower them and re-shape or silence their expressions of need.

It is sometimes contended (see for example Croft and Beresford, 1992; Bochel and Bochel, 2004, ch 7) that there are two broad approaches to participation: the democratic and the consumerist. While this distinction provides important insights, it can also lead to confusion, because each heading includes approaches with very different origins and because the techniques developed by one approach are often borrowed or colonised by the other. Democratic approaches can be traditional or 'associative'; consumerist approaches can be community-focused or market-focused. And any of them may operate at different levels or on different 'rungs' of Arnstein's ladder.

Democracy has many variants (Held, 1987). The form of 'classical' democratic rule established in ancient Athens was in one sense radical, since it required every citizen to participate in his or her own governance. In practice, however, such participation was restricted to a patrician male elite and ignored the needs of women and slaves. Were it otherwise, as Aristotle (382–322 BC) recognised, 'in democracies the poor [would] have more power than the rich; for they are more numerous' (cited in Held, 1987, p 19). Such a possibility has been frustrated by mediating the power of the masses through various kinds of electoral process. The spread of universal suffrage throughout the industrialised Western world has clearly played an important part in empowering the working classes and enabling them to give expression to their needs (Bottomore, 1992), but representative democracy mediates power. Constitutional checks and balances, the power of the modern state and the arcane machinery of party politics can stifle, dilute or divert everyday expressions of need. Democracies have in some instances sought to legitimise decision making without recourse to electoral processes, through public consultation mechanisms. In large and complex societies, however, the issuing of consultation documents or the holding of public meetings are not necessarily effective means of consultation and can as easily disempower as empower the inarticulate or those who are not already effectively represented. Innovative mechanisms

---

Box 3.3:   Famous referenda: majority self-interest vs. minority needs

California Proposition 13 – 1978

The state of California in the US makes provision in its constitution for the holding of referenda. The constitution governs issues such as property taxes. Proposition 13 (the 'People's Initiative to Limit Property Taxation') was successfully promoted in the 1970s by an association of property owners who objected, amongst other things, that property taxes levied in affluent districts subsided public services in poor districts. The proposition limited property taxes to 1% of property values and restricted increases to 2% per annum. Additionally, it limited the scope of state lawmakers to enact new taxes. The overall effect was to cut property taxes by 57%. Local government services and public schools bore the brunt of the resulting cuts in public expenditure. Minority and poor communities were seen to be worst affected. Since Proposition 13, expenditure per pupil in Californian state schools has lagged behind that in the rest of the US. Private school enrolment increased for higher-income families and public schools in affluent districts have been able to top up funds through parental donations. The initiative presaged a wider tax revolt across the US and is widely thought to have contributed to Ronald Reagan's election to the Presidency in 1980 (see Smith, D. [1998] *Tax Crusaders and the Politics of Direct Democracy*, New York: Routledge). The US Supreme Court upheld the legality of the measure and successive attempts to overturn or substantially modify it have been resisted. Supporters of Proposition 13 claim it made services more efficient and California more economically competitive. Opponents argue that this supposedly democratic initiative allowed the demands of higher and middle-income property owners to trump the needs of less advantaged members of the community.

Swiss Asylum Law Referendum – 2006

Switzerland is a country that allows citizens to petition for initiatives to instigate parliamentary legislation or for referenda to challenge it. Since the 1960s there have been six initiatives instigated by right wing political parties or groupings to limit the number of foreigners entering the country. These had always been defeated, not least because the Swiss economy was seen to depend on foreign workers. There have, nonetheless, been a succession of legislative changes to tighten immigration and asylum law in Switzerland, culminating in laws that have been criticised for their severity by the UNHCR (www.unhcr.org) and by Human Rights Watch (http://hrw.org). In 2006 a coalition of centre-left parties, trade unions, churches and aid organisations petitioned for a referendum to oppose the asylum reforms. In the event, the referendum was lost and Swiss voters who had until then by a majority supported humanitarian principles and opposed the most draconian restrictions on refugees supported the reforms by a margin of almost 70%. This outcome reflected the influence of the far-right Swiss People's Party which in 2007 went on to become the largest single party in Parliament (69 out of 246 members) and which has since campaigned to reinforce the deportation of foreign offenders, using an explicitly xenophobic, if not racist, poster depicting a herd of white sheep kicking a black sheep out from an enclosure bearing the Swiss emblem. The climate of opinion has clearly been changing in Switzerland. Direct democracy can result in decisions that, some would argue, violate the human rights of potentially highly vulnerable refugees.

of democratic consultation and deliberation, such as popular referenda on specific policy issues or the organisation of citizens' juries, can also allow for the expression of need. But referenda may have consequences that are inimical to the needs of vulnerable minorities (see ***Box 3.3***) and devices such as citizens' juries have enjoyed mixed results (Beresford and Croft, 2001; Goodin and Dryzek, 2006).

The rise since the 1970s of civil society activism and new social movements (Scott, 1990) entailed challenges to traditional democratic methods and a discussion about a variety of more or less abstract radical alternatives (Walzer, 1983; Keane, 1988). Perhaps the most persuasive alternative was that characterised by Hirst (1994) as 'associative democracy', in which voluntary and self-help groups would substitute for the kind of bureaucratic and unresponsive institutions spawned by traditional representative democracy. What emerged was an emphasis within new and emerging service user movements, voluntary organisations and self-help organisations on direct participation at a community or 'grass roots' level (Hadley and Hatch, 1981), and a shift to greater pluralism in social policy approaches (Johnson, 1987). However, a proliferation and expansion of non-governmental and civil society organisations does not of itself overcome the democratic deficit unless there are ways to ensure that the social entrepreneurs who lead such organisations are accountable and that their members are actively involved.

These trends intersected with evolving practices in the sphere of social and community development. Traditional neocolonial approaches to social development in the global South and community development in deprived urban neighbourhoods of the global North had been premised on particular kinds of interpretive account of human need. The basic needs approach adopted by social development agencies in the post-colonial era (Wisner, 1988) could be seen as a counterpart to the kind of urban community development work founded by the 19th-century university settlements, such as Toynbee Hall and Cambridge House. The former involved Western aid workers seeking to identify and fulfil the basic needs and deficiencies suffered by culturally diverse populations. The latter involved (at first) well-to-do students and (later) middle-class social workers interpreting the needs and social pathologies of deprived working-class neighbourhoods (Cockburn, 1977, ch 4). The basic needs approach gradually gave way to approaches based on the participatory assessment principles (Chambers, 1997; World Bank, 2001), whereby attention was paid to the ways in which villages and communities in developing countries interpreted their needs. In countries like the UK, there were concerted attempts to ensure that large corporate-style local authorities consulted with local communities over planning proposals and housing policies, to institute forms of neighbourhood management and promote community-level initiatives for the management of social conflicts (Cockburn, 1977). Both these trends were double-edged: they had potential for democratising the interpretation of need, but they were also essentially top-down and technocratic in nature. Communities, as targets for intervention and actual or potential recipients of services, were required to participate, to collaborate with the state, to be willing consumers of essential services.

These technocratic tendencies gathered momentum towards the end of the 20th century and were increasingly inflected towards a more explicitly market-oriented form of consumerism, associated initially with attempts to 'marketise' social welfare provision, to make it more business-like and to subject it to market-like disciplines (Le Grand, 1990a). Increasingly, however, what has been described as 'new public management' (Hood, 1991; Clarke and Newman, 1997), sought to 'modernise' as much as marketise welfare services, a process that entails particular notions of partnership and participation. The principles of new public management can be seen at work in supranational bodies, such as the European Union (EU) and the World Bank (see for example Porter and Craig, 2004). The key to this 'modernising' trend is essentially de-politicising: insofar as social policies are a response to needs, needs are defined in partnership with a range of non-governmental, business, consumer and community organisations. The users of welfare services are constituted as 'customers' and the satisfaction of their needs can be guaranteed by customer charters, by quality assurance mechanisms, including complaints procedures, focus groups consultation exercises and customer satisfaction surveys. As with the more explicitly community-oriented approaches to participation, the techniques involved are double-edged: a well-informed and well-advised service user can make her needs known, but the participation of more vulnerable 'customers' may be at best tokenistic.

Table 3.2: *Expression through participation*

	traditional democracy	associative democracy	community consumerism	market consumerism
potentially empowering	mediated participation through elections	direct participation through self-help organisation	community self-governance/ service-user participation	customer charters and complaints procedures
ambiguous techniques	popular referenda/ citizen juries	participatory needs assessment		consumer focus groups
potentially disempowering	public consultation exercises	association membership/ passive participation	manipulation/ co-option	customer satisfaction surveys

The argument above, concerning the scope for the expression of need through participation, is diagrammatically summarised in **Table 3.2**. It may be seen that overlapping ideas about participatory assessment of need lie at the core of the argument, but that in the context of prevailing debates, they can as readily be inflected towards practices that co-opt, control and disempower as towards processes that liberate, enable or empower those whose needs are not met.

Social and symbolic constructions of need

Finally, there are social policy commentators who have sought to engage with social constructionist accounts of human need. I have referred to Baudrillard and Bauman's sociological accounts, which reduced human needs to mere constructs or symbols generated by a consumer society. Similarly, there are writers – in what is called the post-structuralist tradition – who have explored the ways in which the world around us acquires intersubjective meaning through the social discourses and practices of human beings, or, in other words, through the meanings that we generate and reinforce in the process of communicating with each other and acting on our interpretations of the world around us. We cannot understand the truth about the world – or so the argument goes – only the ways in which we and our forbears set about making claims about truth. The best known theorist in this tradition was Michel Foucault (1977, 1979; see also Fitzpatrick, 2005). Such theorists have done much to demonstrate the significance of social policies, institutions and the technologies of power and governance which underpin them, but they have tended not to focus, other than by implication, on concepts of human need.

There have, nevertheless, been attempts to apply Foucauldian thinking to the ways in which social policy does not so much respond to as continually define and redefine human need. Social policy is implicated in our understanding of human need. This is especially the case when tests of need become conditions of entitlement (Squires, 1990; Dean, H., 1991). The workhouse test under the Poor Laws – in Britain and across much of Western Europe – was based on the principle of 'lesser eligibility': only if supplicants' needs were so great that they were prepared to enter the workhouse and endure conditions less eligible (that is, more unpleasant) than those of the poorest independent labourer would they be allowed relief. As the Poor Laws were succeeded by modern social security systems means tests replaced workhouse tests. Means tests entailed more nuanced tests of need and more focused scrutiny of the supplicant. The specification of household requirements and conditions of entitlement entailed judgements about minimum living standards, living arrangements, familial dependency and work readiness. The making and administration of social policy confers the power to define need and to exercise control over the ways in which needs should be satisfied. It has been suggested that social policy that imposes constrained or alien interpretations of human need might more aptly be called 'anti-social policy' (Squires, 1990).

The social policy implications of the idea that human needs are socially or ideologically constructed have been considered in a rather different way by Martin Hewitt (1992). Hewitt draws on the ostensibly unlikely source of the psychoanalytical theorist Jacques Lacan (1977). Lacan's highly abstract argument is that as human individuals our needs and desires interact with one another. Our real needs are obscured by imaginary needs (ideological misrepresentations), but it is through the symbols we use in everyday communication that we can, in communion with others, discover an evolving awareness of our true needs. Hewitt draws parallels between this kind of argument and Habermas's (1987) notion of the 'ideal speech situation', the possibility that in genuinely un-coerced negotiation people would be able to recognise and agree on their own and each other's needs. The key point is that social policy cannot ignore the relevance of competing ideologies to the interpretation of human need and that it is only through a negotiated process that we can discover or agree the nature of inherent need. Hewitt acknowledges – albeit only in a footnote (1992, p 193) – some similarity between this argument and Nancy Fraser's notion of a 'politics of needs interpretation', a key concept to which this book will in fact turn in Chapter Nine.

Hewitt's contribution is important for the manner in which it reminds us of the importance of ideology and discourse, of the things people believe and the way they speak about human need. The notions of inherent need explored in Chapter Two require us to consider interpretive accounts and, in particular, the ways in which our view of inherent needs is mediated, obscured or distorted. And we are here concerned not only with the grand ideological narratives of liberalism, Marxism, feminism and so forth. It is in the 'moral repertoires' of everyday life that ordinary understandings of human need are generated (Dean, 1999). The anthropological theorist Mary Douglas (1977) has pointed to the natural symbols of everyday existence that are shaped over the course of history and within the individual life course. She explains these in terms of the reference 'grids' by which we classify the world and the strength of the social 'groups' to which we belong, develop and change. Douglas's grid/group analysis can be applied in ways that help us account for the complex and contradictory understandings of human welfare that are reflected in popular discourse in the UK (Dean, 1999; and see Chapter Seven, this book). All human beings are different, but they can be joined through what we call here 'discourse', through the language and forms of expression by which we achieve our view of social reality. And although they may interpret need differently, there is scope for shared and common interpretations of need.

Notes

[1] Experience suggests this is an analogy that makes sense for some people, but does not work so well for others. It is not essential, but I have included it for the benefit of those who might find it helpful.

[2] At the time of writing, this study has still to be completed.

Summary

- This chapter has discussed those understandings of human need that are based on the interpretation of social processes, on the ways in which need is experienced or constructed.
- Such interpretations may focus on needs that have been culturally constituted or in some way artificially created. We have observed that:
  - human societies evolve in ways that generate customary needs: observable norms and expectations about how people should live, what they should do and how they should appear;
  - capitalism has generated a distinctive set of expectations and perverse signals which, by some accounts, produce distorted understandings of need;
  - in particular, the kind of 'consumer society' that has developed in affluent countries attaches primarily symbolic meanings to the things people consume and so generates what may be regarded as illusory needs.
- Interpretive approaches within social policy have been examined, and we have observed that:
  - these have in the first instance been pragmatically focused on the ways in which policy makers and policy analysts can respond to social norms and expectations and how they decide which needs matter;
  - among the things to emerge has been debate concerning participatory approaches to human need and the extent to which people are able to give political expression to their own interpretations of need;
  - there are also related theoretical debates within social policy about the social construction of need. This final discussion has particular relevance insofar as different people's needs may be differently understood or constructed and there is an issue for social policy about how to achieve common and agreed understandings of human need.

Questions for discussion:

- What would you say is the difference and what is the relationship between inherent need and interpreted need? Is this a necessary or helpful distinction?
- If human needs are culturally relative, does that necessarily mean that they are no more than social artefacts or mere fictions of our imagination?
- How should social policy makers set about interpreting the needs of a human population?

four

Poverty, inequality and resource distribution

- This chapter considers the concepts of poverty and inequality, each of which is associated with the issue of human need and which, in their respective ways, offer a means to test for or to measure, on the one hand, the extent of unmet need and, on the other, the risk that needs may not be met.
- The ways in which poverty in its various manifestations has been debated is discussed, including:
  - issues relating to the definition and measurement of poverty;
  - issues relating to the meaning and consequences of poverty.
- Similarly, the chapter examines inequality and its relationship to the ways in which needs may be met or experienced, including:
  - issues relating to the definition and measurement of inequality;
  - issues relating to the meaning and consequences of inequality.

Our attention now turns from concepts and theories of need to the associated concepts of poverty and inequality. These are, at first glance, more practical or applied concepts that relate to the substantive issues of resource distribution. Having said that, poverty and inequality are in themselves both contested concepts precisely *because* they are inextricably connected with questions of human need.

Poverty – its definition and measurement, its relief and prevention – has been one of the central preoccupations of social policy. It provides an essential backdrop for any discussion of the relationship between human needs and welfare rights (Dean, 2002, p 20). The existence of poverty, however measured or defined, may be regarded as the 'limit case' for the effectiveness of social policy and social citizenship (Roche, 1992, pp 7 and

55). It is, metaphorically, the litmus test by which to establish whether human need has been met. The litmus test was developed by the earliest alchemists and uses the properties of a mixture of naturally occurring dyes extracted from lichens to determine whether something is acidic. A strip of litmus-impregnated paper turns blue under alkaline conditions, but red when exposed to acid. It is an apposite metaphor since poverty might be regarded as a danger signal that warns of the potentially corrosive effects of unmet human need.

Inequality is not the same thing as poverty, but it is related since it can be connected with the risk of poverty. The term 'inequality' is often too casually used and Sen famously asked 'inequality of what?' (see for example Sen, 1992). Human beings can experience unequal incomes or unequal material outcomes, unequal formal opportunities or unequal substantive life chances. We shall encounter Sen's own answer to this question in Chapter Five, but in this chapter I shall be discussing inequality of needs satisfaction. In any human society resources to meet need will never be completely equally distributed, but there comes a point at which inequality of distribution may become dysfunctional, unsustainable or simply morally unacceptable. If poverty provides a litmus test for the *presence* of unmet need, inequality warns us as to the *risk* that certain members of a society may be deprived of the things they need.

A discussion of human need, as we have seen, carries us into the realms of philosophical and ideological disagreement, but discussion of poverty and inequality opens up the possibility that we can *measure* the extent to which need is or is not met or the likelihood that certain members of society may be deprived of the things they need. Measurement matters for a number of reasons. I alluded to the issue of measurement at the beginning of Chapter Three, when I suggested that the connection between the observable and the natural properties of physical objects (their weight and mass) is, in a limited sense, analogous to the relationship between interpreted and inherent understandings of human need. Measurements of poverty and inequality similarly tell us not everything about human need, but important things about the extent to which it is met within human societies. They provide an indirect means of interpreting need, yet they entail implicit assumptions about the inherent nature of need.

Everyday measurements may be rough and ready: measurements of size and quantity may, for example, be based on customary estimations of the length of an outstretched arm or the capacity of an everyday cup. Scientific measurements are usually more precise: they are standardised in relation to the fixed properties of a specific artefact or phenomenon, such as a particular rod of metal or the oscillations of a particular kind of atomic particle. Measurements of poverty and inequality may rest on rough and ready political assumptions about the nature of human need, or on sophisticated social scientific methods. Measurement provides a way in which we can make comparisons and draw conclusions about the different needs of different social groups, of different localities and different countries. They enable us to make comparisons over time, to observe how needs change and the extent to which social policies succeed or fail in meeting needs within the life course of individuals or in the course of history.

There is a well-worn maxim 'to improve something, first measure it', of which a United Nations Children's Fund (UNICEF) report has said:

> Even the decision to measure helps set directions and priorities by demanding a degree of consensus on what is to be measured – ie on what constitutes progress. Over the long-term, measurement serves as the handrail of social policy, keeping efforts on track towards goals, encouraging sustained attention, giving early warning of failure or success, fuelling advocacy, sharpening accountability, and helping allocate resources more effectively. (UNICEF, 2007, p 3)

This is undoubtedly true, but it must also be remembered that the power to determine which measurements we use is a significant feature of any social order and can, to an extent, affect our understanding of our universe and of our human needs. What is more, those who are in the greatest need do not necessarily contribute to the 'consensus' by which their needs are estimated. When policy makers devise or adopt ways to quantify or estimate human need they can exercise considerable power over people's lives. An early illustration of this is provided in Box 4.1. One of the instruments of modern social policy, the means test, is rooted in decisions about how the needs of the most disadvantaged members of society are to be estimated.

Through the concepts of poverty and inequality we may articulate different meanings of human need. While poverty has meaning as a concept that is related to observable hardship, it is also a term with deep symbolic meanings associated with the blame or shame that may attach to our own and others' needs. While inequality has meaning as a concept associated with the measurable distribution of material goods and advantages, it is also a factor with fundamental relevance for our awareness of, and the meanings we attach to, social status and social difference. In the rest of this chapter, therefore, I shall discuss poverty and inequality in turn and in each case I shall consider first, issues of definition and measurement, and second, issues of social meaning.

> **Box 4.1: The Speenhamland means test and the measurement of need**
>
> Means tests are a way of measuring human need. The earliest systematic means test is thought to be that developed in 1795 by the magistrates of Speenhamland, a rural parish in Berkshire, England (de Schweinitz, 1961). The magistrates were responsible for the administration of poor relief and, at a time of economic recession when the cost of living was outstripping the level of agricultural wages, they elected to acknowledge the poverty of local farm labourers and their families by paying out of public funds a supplement to the labourer's wages. To this end they drew up a 'table of universal practice' under which relief could be calculated in accordance with the estimated requirements of a labourer's family. The difference between a man's wages and the minimum held to be necessary for his family's maintenance would be met from the poor rates. The scale on which relief was calculated was based on the cost of a gallon loaf of bread and upon the magistrates' assumptions as to how many multiples of that sum were needed to sustain a family of any given size.
>
> The system was imitated throughout much of England, but eventually abolished by the Poor Law (Amendment) Act of 1834. Nonetheless, the table of universal practice established a rough and ready method for the measurement of need and the fundamental basis upon which the 'low income families' poverty measure was developed later in the 20th century (see below).

The poverty debate and the meeting of needs

The distinction between absolute and relative need is reflected in a long-standing and rather tired debate about the nature of poverty (Lister, 2004; Alcock, 2006). Like need, poverty may be absolutely or relatively defined. In theory, an absolute measure of poverty is any measure that is determined without regard for the existing distribution of resources in society. In practice, absolute poverty is a term that is most widely used to refer to the condition of those who cannot meet their individual physical needs for food, clothing and shelter. In theory, a relative measure of poverty is a measure that is determined with specific regard for the existing distribution of resources in society. In practice, relative poverty is a term most widely used to refer to the condition of those who cannot achieve the living standards necessary for their acceptance into the society in which they find themselves. The distinction can never be hard and fast. George and Howards (1991) have argued that absolute poverty may be defined with reference to a strict 'starvation' standard or a more generous 'subsistence' standard, depending on what physical needs are to be taken into account. Relative poverty may be defined with reference to a strict 'coping' standard or a more generous 'participation' standard, depending on the extent of the social needs that are to be taken into account. While the victims of famine in sub-Saharan Africa may suffer the deepest forms of poverty, lone parents living on social welfare payments in the North American or Western European public housing developments suffer a qualitatively different kind of poverty. But it is still poverty nonetheless (Seabrook, 1985).

When Seebohm Rowntree (1901/2000) conducted the first of his pioneering studies of poverty in York in 1899 he applied an absolute standard which assumed anyone adjudged to be in 'primary poverty' must be unable to afford a weekly basket of goods which, according to expert opinion, they needed to maintain 'bare physical efficiency', a basket that expressly excluded such things as a newspaper, let alone such wasteful luxuries as beer or tobacco. And yet, when he repeated the study in 1936, Rowntree (1941) decided to make allowance for some such items. Had Rowntree simply changed his mind about what was absolutely necessary? Or was it changes in social customs, cultural expectations and relative living standards that had necessitated this re-evaluation? Rowntree also made a distinction between 'primary poverty', which he attributed to low wages, and 'secondary poverty', which arose in households that had sufficient income but in which that income was inefficiently or improvidently spent. (It was a distinction similar to that made by another pioneer of poverty research, Charles Booth – see **Box 4.2**.) Rowntree himself fully recognised the frugality of the living standard imposed by his measure of primary poverty. His purpose was to demonstrate the extent and the inequity of 'primary poverty' (Kincaid, 1975, pp 49-56; Veit-Wilson, 1986).

These early attempts to define and measure poverty nevertheless demonstrate two underlying contradictions: first, a contradiction between definitions of poverty based on physical sufficiency standards as opposed to definitions based on socially acceptable living standards; second, a contradiction between meanings that attribute poverty to an insufficiency of resources as opposed to meanings that attribute it to problems of economically dysfunctional and/or socially unacceptable behaviour.

Box 4.2: Charles Booth's classes of poor

Booth's study of poverty in London conducted between 1886 and 1903 did not use the same precise method of quantifying human need as Rowntree, but relied on classification of households, drawing upon School Board records, police notebooks, interviews with employers, trade union officials and ministers of religion and the judgements of survey assistants who visited individual households. He divided the people of London into eight classes of which the lowest four classes, comprising some 30% of the London population, rising to 35% in East London, he defined as poor:

Class	Description	% of East London population
A.	The lowest class of occasional labourers, loafers and semi-criminals	1¼
B.	Casual earnings – 'very poor'	11¼
C.	Intermittent earnings } together the 'poor'	8
D.	Small regular earnings }	14½

Booth recorded that:

> My 'poor' [Classes C and D] may be described as living under a struggle to obtain the necessaries of life and make both ends meet; while the 'very poor' [Class B] live in a state of chronic want. It may be their own fault that this is so; that is another question.... The lowest class [Class A] ... render no useful service, they create no wealth: more often they destroy it.

Source: Booth (1889) (extract in Court, W. (1965) *British Economic History 1970–1914*, Cambridge: Cambridge University Press, pp 288-94) (see also the Charles Booth Online Archive at http://booth.lse.ac.uk)

Definition and measurement of poverty

The well-worn distinction between absolute and relative poverty and their connection to differing conceptions of need are reflected in even the most recent definitions adopted by the United Nations (UN) (see **Box 4.3**).

These definitions can be operationalised in various ways in order to produce methods for measuring poverty. This book is not the place to consider these at length, but I shall outline the principal methods that are of contemporary relevance.

> ### Box 4.3: United Nations' definitions of poverty
>
> **Absolute poverty**: 'a condition characterised by severe deprivation of basic human needs'.
>
> **Overall poverty**: 'has various manifestations, including lack of income and productive resources to ensure sustainable livelihoods ... Also characterised by lack of participation in decision making and in civil, social and cultural life.'
>
> *Source:* UN (1995)

In practice, most widely used measures of poverty are based on people's incomes. But any such measure begs the question, how much income is enough? The crudest measures in general use are the $2 and $1 a day standards applied by the UN:[1] the former is used as a measure of 'poverty' in developing countries, the latter as a measure of 'extreme poverty'. By these standards almost half (46%) of the world's population were in poverty and around a fifth in extreme poverty at the turn of the millennium (Pogge, 2002, p 2). There are, however, infinitely more complex ways to determine what constitutes a poverty income level.

I have already mentioned the approach adopted by Rowntree, which used the cost of a virtual basket of necessaries to determine a poverty level. Rowntree himself was called on to advise as to the level at which the means-tested social assistance or safety-net benefit should be set when the modern welfare state was created in the UK. Although his advice was not exactly followed it eventually provided the basis for the post-Second World War equivalent of the 'table of universal practice' devised back in the 18th century for Speenhamland (see ***Box 4.2***). Since then, the level of means-tested social assistance in the UK has been periodically up-rated, but on an unscientific and haphazard basis (Veit-Wilson, 1999). It currently falls well short of the 'low cost but acceptable' living standard determined by contemporary experts (Parker, 1998). Nevertheless, for many years this arbitrarily set household income level, determined as sufficient for the purposes of the social assistance means test, was treated as a poverty income level and used to calculate the numbers of people living in 'low income families' (the LIF statistics). Similar approaches have been used elsewhere, although some developed countries, such as the US and Australia, have determined official poverty lines using some variation of a budget standards approach.

However, the measure that is now most widely used in the developed world is one that counts the number or the proportion of households who fall beneath a certain percentage of national average income. This is, clearly, a measure of relative poverty and it is capable of generating quite different results depending on a variety of factors, including:

- what percentage of average income is used (for example 50% or 60%);
- how incomes are averaged (for example by the mean or the median);
- the assumptions that are made about how income is allocated to the needs of different household members, including children and other dependants (that is, how to 'equivalise' for differently constituted households);
- the accuracy and inclusiveness of the survey data on which such measures depend.

What is known in the UK as the Households Below Average Income (or HBAI) measure has now replaced the old LIF measure and similar kinds of measure are employed, for example, by the European Union (EU) and, when measuring poverty in developed countries, by the United Nations Development Programme (UNDP) (see *Table 4.2*, which appears later in this chapter).

Other more sophisticated ways of measuring poverty have been under development since the 1960s. Such methods have stemmed from the groundbreaking work begun in the UK by Peter Townsend. Townsend (1979) sought to establish an income threshold beneath which a household could be shown to be disproportionately likely to experience deprivation. His concept of deprivation was extensively drawn and was based not on a basket of goods approach so much as a living standards approach encompassing housing, employment, health, lifestyle and access to services. This approach was later built on by the Breadline Britain studies (Mack and Lansley, 1985; Gordon and Pantazis, 1997) and the Poverty and Social Exclusion Millennium Survey (Pantazis et al, 2006). At the core of this latest approach – which has been attempted in several other countries (Gordon, 2006, pp 44-5) – lies a 'consensual' method by which to determine what the majority of current public opinion considers the necessities of life to be and how many people and what kinds of people are involuntarily deprived of such 'socially perceived necessities'. In 1999, at a time when 23% of British households were estimated to be 'poor' in the sense that they enjoyed less than 60% of median household income (after housing costs, AHC; see DWP, 2001), it was estimated that 26% of the British population were poor in the sense that they were deprived of two or more socially perceived necessities. What is especially interesting for our purposes, however, is the way in which successive surveys reveal the evolving nature of social perceptions of what amounts to human need (see *Table 4.1*).

Table 4.1: Socially perceived necessities: the percentage of participants in 'Breadline Britain'/consensual method studies identifying items as necessities (i.e. goods, facilities or activities that people should be able to afford and not have to do without)

	1983	1990	1999
Items consistently identified by more than 50% of participants			
heating in living areas of home	97	97	95
a damp-free home	96	98	94
refrigerator	77	92	89
celebrations on special occasions	69	74	83
washing machine	67	73	77
annual holiday	63	54	66
presents for friends/family	63	69	58
Items recently identified by more than 50% of participants			
telephone	43	56	72
having children's friends round for tea	37	52	59
Items consistently identified by less than 50% of participants			
car	22	26	36
holidays abroad	–	17	20
home computer	–	5	11
dishwasher	–	4	7

Note: this is a small selection of the items covered in the studies. Only items identified by 50% or more participants are regarded as socially perceived necessities.

Source: Pantazis et al (2006, p 108)

What these data disclose is changing expectations as to what constitutes an acceptable living standard in a developed country. Critics complain that they reveal only people's preferences, rather than their needs. It might be the case, for example, that some people spend their money on what society judges to be 'non-necessaries' in preference to 'necessaries' (McKay, 2004), but this is an issue we have already discussed. The point is that the data reflect complex and differing interpretations of need. What is clear is that public opinion is neither wholly stable, nor by any means unanimous. Nonetheless it is also clear that public opinion in Britain consistently accords greater priority to certain *social* needs (such as the need to celebrate special occasions and give presents to friends and family) than to certain *material* needs (such as for motor cars or home computers).

There are yet more ways of measuring poverty, and although not all measures will count the same people as being poor (Bradshaw and Finch, 2003; Dorling et al, 2007), there is a significant degree of overlap.

There are also certain forms of composite indicators that may be used to measure poverty. In order to identify and compare the needs of individual neighbourhoods, for example, the UK government uses a local Index of Multiple Deprivation (IMD) based on seven domain indices relating to income, employment, health, education, housing, crime and environment. At a global level, the UN uses two kinds of composite human poverty indicator (see UNDP, 2008):

- Human Poverty Index-1 (HPI-1) for developing countries, based on probability at birth of an inhabitant surviving to age 40, adult illiteracy levels, proportion of households with access to clean water and proportion of underweight children.
- Human Poverty Index-2 (HPI-2) for developed countries, based on probability at birth of an inhabitant not surviving to age 60, functional illiteracy levels, proportion of households with less than 50% median income and long-term unemployment rates.

The Human Poverty Indices compute a single score for every country, by which it is possible to rank the countries of the world by their performance in combating poverty (see *Table 4.2*, which appears later in this chapter).

Beyond measurement: questions of meaning

The measurement of poverty depends on various notions of sufficiency and insufficiency. But running alongside these notions, as I have already pointed out, are notions of acceptability and unacceptability. Consensual methods of poverty measurement go some way towards addressing what constitutes an acceptable living standard. This, however, tells us nothing about what it means to experience an unacceptable living standard (that is, to be poor) or the senses in which poverty may be regarded as unacceptable. To be poor is to be different from others in terms of the acceptability of one's living standards or in terms of the acceptability of one's appearance or behaviour.

In Chapter Three we discussed symbolic meanings of human need and the idea that need is socially constructed, but in the case of poverty symbolic meanings and processes of social construction are not merely conceptual, they have tangible consequences. If poverty is the result of unmet need, the discourses through which, in the course of human history, poverty has been identified tell us something about changing perceptions of human need. Jesus is reported to have said, 'ye have the poor always with you' (Matthew 26: 11), implying that in 1st-century Palestine a certain level of unmet need was ever present. In mediaeval Europe the poverty of mendicant friars, pilgrims and scholars was respected and even that of the honest labouring poor had a kind of sanctity (Lis and Soly, 1979). For the most part, however, although life for the majority of the population was in reality 'nasty, brutish and short' (Hobbes, 1651), poverty was quite simply normal. Modernity – the advent of industrial capitalism – constituted poverty as a new kind of problem. The displacement of agricultural labourers from the land and the burgeoning of slums in the new industrial conurbations posed an all too obvious threat to social order and public health. The extent of unmet human need became visible in a way that it had not been before. Poverty became a problem that had to be managed through the intervention of the modern state (Dean, H., 1991; Dean, M., 1991). More recently, in an age of global communication technologies, we are surrounded by multifarious and proliferating images of poverty, and yet paradoxically, despite rhetorical commitments to address the unmet needs of humanity (UN General Assembly, 2000), there is a tendency at the global level to acquiesce to world poverty (Pogge, 2002).

In the rich countries of the world poverty is widely regarded, even among poorer inhabitants, as something that happens to other people (Dean, 1999, ch 2). Poverty may be a distant spectre: perhaps spatially different in the sense that it reflects the unmet needs of unfamiliar people in foreign lands, or temporally distant in the sense that it relates to needy historical characters portrayed in tales of past times, or possibly just socially distant in the sense that it reflects the needs of those portrayed as, or popularly imagined to be, excluded from the social mainstream by reason of their homelessness, their unemployment, their welfare dependency or simply where they live. When poverty is not so remote, it tends to be a pejoratively regarded spectre, representing something beyond objective neediness; it is something contaminating, hazardous and blame-worthy. The nature of contemporary poverty is captured by Ruth Lister (2004, p 8), when she envisions what she calls a 'wheel of poverty', with a hub representing a material core of practical hardship and a rim representing the relational and symbolic aspects of poverty as a status associated at best with 'otherness' and at worst with stigma.

There is, inescapably, a moral element to poverty that is not adequately captured by scientific attempts to quantify it (Piachaud, 1981). In Chapter One we identified four broad kinds of response to human need: the economistic, the moral–authoritarian, the paternalistic and the humanitarian. These various responses translate into four distinctive understandings of poverty, grounded in four different kinds of moral thinking. The distinctions between these different kinds of understanding are conceptually drawn, but they can and have been identified empirically in studies of popular thinking or 'discourse' (Dean, 1999):

- *Economistic* responses to need draw on what might loosely be called an 'entrepreneurial' moral discourse. Within this discourse, while it is supposed that each of us has a civic duty so far as possible to meet our own needs, what is important is that we have the opportunity to do so, the opportunity to learn, to work and to succeed. To the extent that some people's needs are not met, their poverty stems from performative failure. For whatever reason, they have failed as actors to perform in such a way as to meet their own needs. Either they have been prevented from succeeding because of a lack of opportunity, or else they have failed to make good use of opportunities that have been available to them.
- *Moral-authoritarian* responses to need draw on what might loosely be called a 'survivalist' discourse. Within this discourse it is supposed that at the level of practical reality and everyday 'common sense' we must each of us attend to our own needs. To the extent that some people's needs are not met, their poverty stems from either their bad luck or their bad behaviour. Good people deserve to have their needs met. Bad people do not. But life isn't fair. Whether we get what we deserve depends on an unpredictable mixture of fate and moral justice. We all have to go by the rules while competing to survive as best we can.
- *Paternalistic* responses to need draw on what might loosely be called a 'conformist' moral discourse. Within this discourse it is supposed that we must each of us comply with the moral obligations of the social order, while trusting in its capacity to ensure that human needs will ultimately be met. It is unfortunate but inevitable that sometimes some people's needs will not be fully met, and their poverty may rightly give cause for social concern, compassion or beneficence.
- *Humanitarian* responses to need draw on what might loosely be called a 'reformist' moral discourse. Within this discourse it is supposed that we each of us as human beings have a right to the satisfaction of our basic needs, while collectively we are responsible for each other's welfare. To the extent that some people's needs are not met, their poverty stems from a failure of social organisation and social justice.

In each response, 'the poor', whether they be constituted as failures, reprobates, unfortunates or victims, are seen as different, not simply because of their unmet needs, but because of the ways in which human needs in general are constructed and understood.

Inequality

In one sense, it has been suggested, poverty represents no more and no less than the unacceptable face of inequality (Tawney, 1913). There are degrees of inequality in every society, but there comes a point at which inequality becomes either morally unconscionable or socially unsustainable. If human needs are unequally met this may invoke the range of moral discourses outlined in the section above. But inequality, it may be argued, is not necessarily morally objectionable, and another quite different concern is whether, or at what point, inequality can become dysfunctional.

Certain inequalities, it might be supposed, are an inevitable consequence of human diversity and to an extent they may even be desirable in any complex society. Some would say that inequality is functional and necessary to human society, since it fuels the motivation for self-improvement upon which innovation and enterprise depend (Davis and Moore, 1945). But equally it may be contended that the resentment inequality can cause and the damage it may do to people's self-esteem may also have enervating or destructive effects (Wilkinson, 1996). If we accept that human needs may be socially constructed, then systemic inequalities in need satisfaction may play a part in expanding or limiting understandings of need. Social inequalities can provide the basis on which people's identity, status or place in society are defined and fixed. The way that we understand and manage inequalities is critical to the maintenance of social order and social cohesion.

Measuring inequalities

First, let us consider the main ways to quantify social inequalities. As with the above discussion of poverty, this is not the place for an extensive explanation of the various techniques that can be employed. It should be clear from what has already been said (and the fact that I am now discussing inequalities in the plural) that this is potentially a complex topic. Most measurement techniques relate to economic inequality, but the sources or 'generative causes' of inequality include cultural, political and affective dimensions which are interdependent with the economic dimension, but are far harder to quantify and to measure (Baker et al, 2004, ch 4). Our focus is on inequality of resource distribution and inequality of access to resources for the satisfaction of need.

The two simplest and most widely used measures of inequality of distribution are the Gini index (often also called the Gini co-efficient) and the decile distribution ratio, for which simple explanations are provided in *Box 4.4*.

Box 4.4:   Measures of inequality

Gini index

This measure of equality or inequality is based on a method devised by an American economist, Max Lorenz, for representing cumulative distribution within a population.

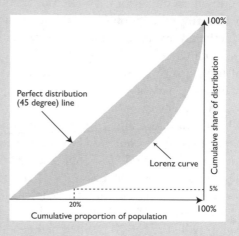

If a graph is drawn to compare the shares of income, wealth or of a particular good that are held by different proportions of a population with the overall distribution of income, wealth or of that particular good, the result is a curve as shown in this diagram; the Lorenz curve. The illustrative curve on this diagram shows, for example, that the least well endowed 20% of the population enjoyed only 5% of the overall distribution. If one could imagine a population in which income, wealth or the good in question were perfectly equally distributed this would produce a straight 45 degree line across the graph. The Gini index is the area enclosed by the perfect distribution line and the Lorenz curve as a proportion of the triangle defined by the perfect distribution line and the axes of the graph. In a population in which there is total equality of distribution, the Gini index would be 0. In a population in which there is total inequality, the Gini index would 100 (if expressed in percentage terms) or 1.0 (if expressed as a simple ratio).

Decile distribution (or '10/10') ratio

This measure represents the number of times the average share of income, expenditure, wealth or of a particular good that is held by the top (or richest) tenth (or 'decile') of a population is greater than that held by the bottom (or poorest) tenth of that population. A similar measure – the quintile distribution (or '20/20') ratio - compares the top and bottom fifth of a population. The ratio provides an indication of the gap between the top and bottom of the distribution.

Most usually, these measures of inequality are used to examine the distribution of income, expenditure or wealth, which are not indicators of need satisfaction, but important 'proxy' or indirect indicators that give us some idea of whether people's needs are being met. These two measures of inequality are both used in *Table 4.2*, alongside the two measures of poverty discussed in the preceding section of this chapter. *Table 4.2* allows us to compare poverty and inequality in the richest and poorest countries of the world, but also includes some other important countries. The countries are listed in order of their relative wealth, as measured by gross domestic product (GDP) per capita. The relationship between poverty and inequality is complex and the table reveals a great many things, but among them:

- the richest country in the world, the US, is a relatively unequal country, more so than some of the poorest countries in the world;
- while Brazil is a very unequal country it has a lower poverty rate than many other developing countries. Tanzania, on the other hand, has relatively low inequality (lower than the UK!) but with a very high poverty rate (more than half its people live below the UN's 'extreme poverty' level).

Comparing countries in this way does not necessarily give a picture of the overall extent of global inequality. It is estimated that the Gini index of income inequality for people of the world lies somewhere between 62 and 66 (Milanovic, 2007). Experts argue about the accuracy of data such as these and the ways in which they may be interpreted (Held and Kaya, 2007), but there can be little dispute that at the global level the needs of humanity are unequally met. The dynamic global trends that preceded the snapshot picture presented in *Table 4.2* are capable of competing interpretations that cannot be addressed in this short chapter, but it is clear that while economic development may combat absolute poverty, it does not combat inequality.

Development theorists have introduced the concept of 'sustainable livelihoods' (Chambers and Conway, 1992), to try and capture the resources that people need in order to sustain themselves from generation to generation. Unless they are wholly self-sufficient, people will usually need income, although income in itself is only a means to an end. Most fundamentally, people need sustainable supplies of food and water. They will need to have, or have access to, various kinds of assets or resources. Among these resources are health provision and basic education. And yet globally, inequality of access is staggering. In the richest countries of the world everyone has access to sanitation and clean water and only tiny proportions of the population (less than 2.5%) are undernourished; but

Table 4.2: Poverty and global inequality

		GDP per capita ($US at PPP 2005)	Poverty measures				Inequality measures	
			Poverty rate (% population **below 50% median income**)	HPI-**2** ranking (out of **19** countries with available data)	Poverty rate (% population **below $1US per day**)	HPI-**1** ranking (out of **103** countries with available data)	Ratio of income shares: richest 10% to poorest 10%	Gini index
The 'richest' countries with populations over 25 million*	US	41,890	17	17			16	41
	Canada	33,375	11	8			9	33
	UK	33,238	13	16			14	36
	Japan	31,267	12	12			5	25
	France	30,386	7	11			9	33
	Germany	29,461	8	6			7	29
Other major transition or developing countries	Russia	10,845			-	-	13	40
	Brazil	8,402			8	23	51	57
	China	6,757			10	29	22	47
	India	3,452			34	62	9	37
The 'poorest' countries with populations over 25 million*	Uganda	1,454			-	72	17	46
	Kenya	1,240			20	60	14	43
	Nigeria	1,128			71	80	18	44
	Ethiopia	1,055			23	105	7	30
	Tanzania	744			58	67	9	35
	Congo	714			-	88	-	-

Note: * The 'richest' country in the world in terms of GDP per capita is Luxembourg (but with a population of just 0.5 million this is smaller than most of the world's major cities) and in 2005 the 'poorest' country was Malawi. The country that ranked first on the HPI-2 index was Sweden and that which ranked bottom on the HPI-1 index was Guinea – each are small countries with populations of just 9 million. (This compares with the UK and France which have populations of around 60 million; Nigeria with around 140 million; the US with around 300 million; and China with 1.3 billion.)

Source: UNDP (2008)

across sub-Saharan Africa only 37% of the population have sanitation, only 55% have access to clean water and 32% are undernourished. The developed countries belonging to the Organisation for Economic Co-operation and Development (OECD) generally have well over 200 physicians per 100,000 population (and some have more than twice as many) and average primary school enrolment stands at 96%. However, there are sub-Saharan African countries such as Malawi and Tanzania that have only two physicians per 100,000 of the population and across sub-Saharan Africa average primary school enrolment stands at just 72% (and is less than 50% in some countries) (UNDP, 2008).

Such data tell us about human need at a very basic level. There is a considerable volume of more detailed data that tell us about inequalities of need satisfaction. There are, for example, data that tell us directly or indirectly about the particular experiences of children. Some of these data draw on conceptions of well-being that we shall be discussing in Chapter Six, but UNICEF (2007) have taken an extensive selection of such data in order to record not only inequalities of experience between children within countries but to rank 21 of the most economically advanced nations using composite indicators that measure well-being across six dimensions: material well-being; health and safety; educational well-being; family and peer relationships; behaviours and risks; and subjective well-being. In terms of average rankings across all six dimensions, the Netherlands and Sweden came top, the US and the UK came bottom.

Other measurement processes are concerned not with global or international comparisons, but more specifically with the ways in which unequal life chances may flow from inequalities of need satisfaction during childhood, even in highly economically developed countries such as the UK (Fabian Society, 2006). Children's physical development depends on their being adequately nourished, and their cognitive development on their having a secure and stimulating environment during their early years. Yet there is evidence from the UK of fundamental gaps in people's life chances depending on the extent to which their needs were met during and even before infancy. There is a variety of research indicating that low parental incomes correlate with:

- poor diet and maternal stress during pregnancy, with adverse consequences on foetal development and child health;
- poor housing conditions, poor nutrition and poor parental mental health during infancy, with adverse consequences for child physical and mental health;
- less supportive and stimulating environments during infancy, with adverse consequences for children's cognitive development;

- low educational test scores, early contact with police, which correlate in turn with adverse eventual outcomes for offspring in terms of income, employment and housing in adulthood. (See Hobcraft, 2002; Waldfogel, 2004; Fabian Society, 2006.)

These correlations conceal complex and multidirectional chains of causality, but illustrate the potentially pervasive consequences of inequality of needs satisfaction in the earliest years of a person's life.

Meaning and consequences

This leads us critically to consider not just the measurability of social inequalities, but their social significance. There are, broadly speaking, two kinds of interpretation of the meaning of social inequality: one derives from class analysis, the other from feminist and other new social movement analyses of social difference.

Class analysis is focused on labour market processes and the inequalities that flow from people's position in relation to the labour market. Implicitly it adopts a universalistic understanding of human need and attributes unequal needs satisfaction to occupational class differences. Human beings' needs, it is supposed, are basically the same, but the extent to which or the manner in which they are met relate to class position. One strand of class analysis has its origins in Marxist thinking. Marx had claimed that 'the history of all hitherto existing society is the history of class struggles' (Marx and Engels, 1848, p 16). His contention was that the wage labour system under capitalist relations of production was the realisation of a particular historical form of class exploitation: the exploitation of workers by capitalists. Characteristically, workers were unequally (and unfairly) rewarded for their labour. Inequality of needs satisfaction and living standards stems from this disparity of reward.

An alternative strand in class analysis has its origins in Weberian thought (Scaff, 1998), and is concerned with the interrelationship between socioeconomic and sociocultural differences. Occupational class differences are associated with inequalities of social status and power: the issue from this perspective is not so much inequalities in *living standards* as a diversity of *lifestyles* within the established social order. Some theorists have argued that class differences in developed welfare state societies are no longer associated with a person's social standing within the relations of production, so much as within relations of consumption. We considered one version of this theory when we discussed the work of Bauman (1998) in Chapter Three. A more contentious version was once advanced by Saunders (1984), who suggested that increasingly key social divisions in welfare state societies revolved around whether people were able to meet their needs (for housing, transport, healthcare and education) independently in the marketplace or whether they must depend on supposedly inferior forms of public provision.

An alternative interpretation of inequalities of needs satisfaction focuses on the substantive differences in human experience and life chances that result from human diversity. Human beings are characterised by biological differences in terms of sex, sexual orientation, phenotypical characteristics (such as skin colour, stature, facial features), age, state of health and functional abilities. These biological differences, however, assume social meanings that result in socially constructed differences and inequalities based on gender, sexuality, ethnicity or 'race', ageing and disability. Approaches based on such insights are not necessarily oblivious to the role of labour markets in driving inequality, but emphasise disparities of access to the labour market as much as disparities of reward. They also emphasise other sources of disparity that stem from an understanding of human need that is particularistic rather than universalistic. The focus, therefore, is on disparity of 'recognition' (Fraser, 1997, ch 1). The particular needs of subordinate social groups are not fully recognised and therefore not adequately met. The significance of this is considered in greater depth in the next chapter, but it is touched on here because, as is evident, inequality of recognition is associated with inequalities of resource distribution.

The origins of the central argument can be traced back to the 18th-century feminist Mary Wollstonecraft (1792), who argued that women were different from but equal to men. The dilemma for women in a society dominated by men is that demanding equal treatment with men neglects the fact women have different needs, but demanding that their particular needs be met means they will not be treated equally. Contemporary 'second-wave' feminists (see for example Pateman, 1989) have extended this argument and other new social movement theorists have adapted it to the analysis of the systemic disadvantages experienced by gays, lesbians, bisexuals and transsexuals, by minority ethnic groups, by older people and disabled people (Lewis et al, 2000). We have already touched above on the idea that it is the 'otherness' of people that may define them as 'poor', but the social processes by which people may be 'othered', excluded or discriminated against may lead to substantive inequality (Lister, 2004).

This can be illustrated with a set of statistics that demonstrate how in Britain, despite the redistributive and protective effects of a welfare state, women, minority ethnic groups and disabled people generally fare less well than men, white people and non-disabled people respectively (see **Table 4.3**). There is inequality in terms of the risk of poverty and both access to and remuneration within the labour market. The patterns of inequality are far more complex than is disclosed by this highly simplified set of statistics, not least because factors such as gender, ethnicity and disability may intersect with each other and with the effects of age, sexuality or other dimensions of inequality so that for some people the effects can be amplified. Such statistics cannot tell us about inequality between men and women within households, about the complex reasons why certain minority ethnic groups (such as Pakistanis and Bangladeshis in the UK) fare especially badly nor whether standard measures of poverty fully capture the material deprivation experienced by disabled people whose impairments increase their living costs. To understand these kinds of questions one must also address the meanings that attach to gendered interpretations of men's and women's respective claims on a household budget (Pahl, 1989), about the particular needs generated by the circumstances in which impoverished Pakistani and Bangladeshi communities have arrived in Britain (Law, 1996) and about the kinds of support that disabled people seek in order to lead fulfilled and dignified lives (Oliver and Barnes, 1998).

Inequalities manifest themselves in many other ways: in terms of health and educational outcomes; in terms of access to housing, transport and recreational facilities. The central issue, however, is that the ways that differences between people are socially constructed and popularly understood have consequences in terms of the inequalities that people actually experience. This is partly because they affect how people are treated both systemically, and in terms of the overt and covert discrimination they may suffer at the hands of others. But it is also partly because inequality can only have meaning for the people it affects if they are aware of it.

Elements of this last issue have been investigated through a classic sociological study of relative deprivation conducted in Britain by Runciman (1966) in the 1960s. Borrowing in part from the psychological literature, Runciman adopted the concept of 'reference groups' in order to show that the way in which people feel about the level to which their needs are satisfied depends largely upon with whom they compare themselves. If people's social horizons are limited and they tend to compare themselves only with groups in similar circumstances to their own, they will tend to be content with or resigned to the level at which their needs are satisfied. Runciman's findings (consistently supported in more recent social attitude surveys, such as the British Social Attitude Survey – see www.natcen.ac.uk/natcen/pages/op_socialattitudes.htm) is that people are seldom aware of the extent of the socioeconomic inequality that prevails in the society of which they are a part (see also Dean, 1999). It is to this ignorance that he attributed the fact that most people had little sense of injustice or resentment. Even those who were at or near the bottom of the economic class hierarchy did not necessarily *feel* deprived (Runciman,

Table 4.3: Inequalities in Britain (circa 2004–06)

		Gender		'Race'/ethnicity								Disabled people	
		men	women	white	mixed	Indian	Pakistani	Bangladeshi	Black Caribbean	Black other	Chinese/other	men	women
Risk of poverty % (UK)[1]		19	21	20	37	27	60		31	50	36	26	
Employment rate % (GB)		79	67	76	59	69	46	41	68	67	57	50	
Hourly pay £ (UK)	full-time mean	14.08	11.67	8.00	7.60	8.41	6.25		7.33		7.60		
	part-time mean	9.81	8.68										
	median											11.28	9.46

Note: [1] Risk of being in a household with less than 60% median income after housing costs.

Sources: These data are variously drawn from: DWP (2007); EOC (2006); CRE (2006) and DRC (2007). They have been derived in turn from various official sources relating in some instances to slightly different years and slightly differently defined populations. The broad comparisons they demonstrate are nonetheless indicative.

1966, p 192). It is this that makes inequality socially sustainable. In his study, nonetheless, Runciman did not find that everybody was satisfied with their lot and here he made a distinction between those who were dissatisfied with inter-reference group inequalities and those who were dissatisfied with intra-reference group inequalities. The former group he identified as working-class 'fraternalists', the latter as ambitious middle-class 'egoists'. Beneath this perhaps over-generalised analysis, however, we may infer that the inhabitants of economically developed societies do indeed have differing interpretations or constructions of need and that these depend on their awareness and perceptions of inequality.

A rather different understanding of the consequences of inequality of needs satisfaction is offered by the social epidemiologist, Richard Wilkinson (1996, 2005). Wilkinson's central thesis, simply put, is that health inequalities relate not simply to economic development, but to relative income equality and to the extent of social cohesion within a society. The inhabitants of rich countries undoubtedly experience greater life expectancy than those in poor countries but there is substantial evidence to show that among richer countries, those that are more equal generally have better life expectancy. Life expectancy is higher in Southern than Northern Europe, higher in Japan than the US. Overall mortality is lower in Sweden than in the UK. The reasons for this are complex. Wilkinson suggests that psychosocial factors are at work and that inequalities of social status are inimical to good health. This will in part relate to unequal experiences during critical development phases in childhood, as we have already discussed. But it is also likely to relate to the effects of stress or depression resulting, on the one hand, from lack of self-worth or diminished self-esteem associated with inequalities of social status, or on the other, from the ontological insecurity associated with relative social isolation and the lack of belonging that people may experience in an unequal society. Insofar as health should be construed as a basic need (Doyal and Gough, 1991), inequality is potentially inimical to human need fulfilment, although the mechanisms at work can be subtle.

Note

[1] The measures are calculated on the basis of the value of the US dollar at 'purchasing power parity' (PPP), although the methodology itself and its applicability (especially in non-cash economies) clearly has limitations.

Summary

- This chapter has discussed poverty and inequality quite specifically in relation to understandings of human need. There is a veritable plethora of literature relating to poverty and inequality, but here we have considered the extent to which poverty may be regarded as a manifestation of unmet need and we have considered inequality as an indication of a risk that some people's needs may not be met.
- The chapter re-examines the well-established distinction between absolute and relative definitions of poverty. Underlying the distinction are issues associated with sufficiency of resources on the one hand, and the acceptability of living standards and behaviour on the other. We have considered that:
  - there is an important distinction to be drawn between measures of poverty based on income and measures based on living standards;
  - at the same time, poverty, like need, may be understood as a social construct, a construct with particular meaning for the ways in which 'otherness' can be symbolised. The chapter has identified four different understandings of poverty with the four different approaches to need described in Chapter One; namely, the economistic, the moral-authoritarian, the paternalistic and the humanistic.
- Empirical measures of inequality reveal a complex relationship between inequality and poverty, both inter and intranationally. We have seen that:
  - of particular importance is inequality not just of incomes, but of livelihoods and life chances;
  - given the diversity of the human species, the meanings that attach to perceived social differences can and do affect substantive outcomes. The meanings that attach to social divisions – based on class, gender, ethnicity, disability, etc – are reflected in a range of social inequalities. At the same time people's subjective awareness of inequalities affects the extent to which they experience the inequality to which they may be subject as social deprivation. There is evidence to suggest that social inequality can have adverse effects on people's health and, to that extent, it is directly relevant to needs satisfaction.

Questions for discussion:

- Poverty and inequality are well-researched phenomena that, clearly, must be related to one another and to questions of human need. But how would you explain those relationships?
- Does the poverty experienced in the 'developed' countries of the global North relate to human need in the same way as the poverty that is experienced in the 'developing' countries of the global South? What is the difference?
- If everyone's basic human needs have been catered for, why should we be concerned about social inequalities?

five

Social exclusion, capabilities and recognition

- This chapter introduces three relatively recent concepts – social exclusion, capabilities and recognition – which are relevant to the issue of human needs and which in current debates may to some extent be replacing or displacing the concept of human need.
- The term 'social exclusion' relates to the ways in which people may be excluded from needs satisfaction. We will discuss different strands within the debate about social exclusion.
- The term 'capabilities' relates to the extent to which people have the freedom to meet their needs. We will discuss the impact of the capabilities concept and the ways in which it has been applied, and consider a critique of the concept.
- The term 'recognition' relates to the extent to which individuals and groups in society and their particular needs are recognised. We will discuss how misrecognition can deny people access to public deliberation as to their needs and consider how important recognition is to the meeting of our needs for care.

In the last chapter we considered the concepts of poverty and inequality, which are strongly associated with human need. In this chapter we shall turn to two further concepts – social exclusion and capabilities – and develop our discussion of the concept of recognition that was touched on in the last chapter. While the concepts of poverty and inequality can be directly connected to issues of resource distribution, the concepts of exclusion, capabilities and recognition are not so directly connected. They are all, however, critically relevant to human need:

- Social exclusion is a rather slippery concept that is concerned with the processes by which people may be excluded from various forms of social participation and, by implication, from having certain of their needs satisfied.
- Capabilities is a persuasive concept that is concerned with whether people are free to do and to be what they wish and therefore to meet their human needs in the way that they would choose.
- Recognition, as we have already seen, is a concept concerned with how people and their needs are recognised and with how human beings care for and about each other.

Social exclusion and the need for participation

The origins of the term and the concept 'social exclusion' are ambiguous. The term has several uses and meanings, but they all share some notion that human beings need to participate with one another, although the manner of that participation may be quite differently perceived. In Chapter One I outlined four different kinds of responses to human need: the economistic, the moral–authoritarian, the paternalistic and the humanistic. And in Chapter Four we saw how these four different approaches are reflected in different approaches to poverty. They can similarly be seen to be reflected in four different approaches to social exclusion.

The account that follows is not strictly a chronologically accurate narrative, nor is it intended to be. I want to suggest nonetheless, that the concept of social exclusion has emerged from two distinct directions: one concerned with moral–authoritarian and economistic understandings of social exclusion, the other with paternalistic and humanistic understandings of exclusion.

From moral-authoritarian to economistic understandings

Moralistic and economistic responses to human need (see **Table 1.2**, Chapter One) share a certain individualistic understanding of the relationship between the human individual and society. They regard human relations at worst as a war of all against all (cf Hobbes, 1651), and at best as an association between freely bargaining subjects (Smith, 1759). Social order depends, in the moral–authoritarian Hobbesian scenario, on moral obedience to rules imposed to protect the subject from the predations of others; in the economistic Smithian scenario, on the natural 'harmony of sentiments and passions' (Smith, 1759, p 72) that may be engendered within a free market economy. As a *failure* of the social order, social exclusion can be understood, in the moral–authoritarian scenario, as a failure to bind people to obey the necessary rules of society; in the economistic scenario, as a failure to integrate people into the productive social circuitry of a free economy.

The best example of a moral–authoritarian approach to social exclusion is to be found in the notion of 'underclass'. The concepts of social exclusion and underclass are generally regarded as quite different, the former being more commonly used in Western Europe, the latter in North America. In practice, however, they can sometimes share common assumptions. Although the term 'underclass' is relatively new there have been a variety of similar terms in the past, such as 'lumpenproletariat' (Marx and Engels, 1848), 'residuum' (Booth, 1889) and 'problem families' (see Macnicol, 1987). In every instance, the term has been used to refer to a morally degraded social stratum that was supposedly detached from society and whose existence was in some way dangerous or burdensome to the interests of the wider working class or the ordinary poor. When Myrdal (1963) reputedly first coined the term 'underclass' it referred quite specifically to the situation of poor black African Americans in the US, but when the term was later popularised by the US journalist, Ken Auletta, it had expanded to encompass long-term welfare recipients, street criminals, hustlers and 'the traumatized drunks, drifters, homeless shopping bag ladies and released mental patients who frequently roam or collapse on city streets', a mixture of delinquent and dependent social outcasts that constituted 'both America's peril and shame' (1982, pp xvi–xvii).

A similarly broad-brush definition of underclass was promoted in the 1980s by the ultra right wing political scientist, Charles Murray. Murray argued that a rising tide of labour market drop-out, 'illegitimacy' (that is, out of wedlock births) and criminality – all of which he blamed on the demoralising effects of the welfare state – had created an underclass that posed a threat to social order not only in the US (1984) but also in Britain (1990, 1994). Murray was accused of seeking to 'blame the victims', rather than the deep-rooted structural causes of the disrupted lives and unmet needs of those he condemned (see for example Walker, 1990). Murray unapologetically acknowledged that he wanted 'to reintroduce the concept of blame, and sharply reduce our readiness to call people "victims"' (1990, p 71). In a later publication, Murray referred to those he identified as the underclass as 'the new rabble' (1994, p 12). Although the concept of 'underclass' has been used in other ways by other writers (Field, 1989; Runciman, 1990), its dominant usage has been one that quite explicitly blames diverse minorities at society's margins – including some with very substantial unmet needs – for their own exclusion from society's protective norms.

However, at the same time as the notion of underclass was being born in and exported from the US, a very different concept of social exclusion was being generated in Western Europe, as we shall see shortly. For the moment, however, I want to focus on the way in which the term 'social exclusion' was received and adopted in the UK, where it was given a distinctly economistic 'spin'. It is generally acknowledged that the term 'social exclusion' was accepted into policy-making discourse in the UK in the early 1990s precisely because it could be used effectively as a synonym for 'poverty' at a time when the Conservative government refused to acknowledge its existence (Burchardt et al, 2002).[1] This in turn enabled the EU to employ the term and to facilitate the process that led eventually to the agreement of the Social Inclusion Process in 2000 (Marlier et al, 2007). The process absorbed and extended a previously existing anti-poverty policy agenda. An overview of the process is provided in *Box 5.1*.

Box 5.1:   The European Union Social Inclusion Process

- The process had its origins in the 1977 Amsterdam Treaty (which pledged to fight social exclusion) and the *European Social Agenda* that subsequently emerged under Commissioner Jacques Delors during the 1980s.
- The Social Inclusion Strategy was announced by 2000 Lisbon European Council, which pledged to eradicate poverty in Europe by 2010. To this end, priority was given to the development of 'a competitive and dynamic knowledge-based economy' across the whole of Europe.
- Original objectives:
  1. To facilitate participation in employment and access by all to resources, rights, goods and services.
  2. To prevent the risks of exclusion.
  3. To help the most vulnerable social groups.
  4. To mobilise all relevant bodies (governmental and non-governmental) so as to promote good governance.
- Implementation involved an Open Method of Co-ordination (OMC) under which member states produced biannual National Action Plans (NAPs), which were subject to a process of peer review through which 'good practice' could be shared between member states by way of a joint report.
- The strategy was reviewed in 2005. The OMC has been streamlined (and now requires 3-yearly NAPs) and the original objectives slightly reframed (so they are more generalised and place less emphasis on specific areas of policy intervention or specific vulnerable social groups). The dominant emphasis, however, is upon: labour market activation; eradication of child

---

poverty; promotion of 'decent' housing for all; combating discrimination against disabled people, ethnic minorities and immigrants; tackling financial exclusion and over-indebtedness.

- The social inclusion process has generated a battery of comparative outcome indicators which provide a valuable source of data relating to needs satisfaction across Europe. The original indicators agreed at the 2001 Laeken European Council have been subject to extensive refinement, and a streamlined set of social inclusion indicators was agreed in 2006, several of which are still under development. 'Primary' indicators include measures relating to:

1. Risk of poverty
2. Persistence of poverty
3. Intensity of poverty
4. Long-term unemployment
5. Population living in jobless households
6. Early school leavers not in education or training
7. Employment gap for immigrants
8. Material deprivation
9. Housing
10. Self-reported unmet need for healthcare
11. Child well-being

Source: Marlier et al (2007)

However, the term took on a protean quality. Insofar as it accommodated a common understanding, this constituted what Levitas (1996) termed a 'new Durkheimian hegemony': specifically, it allowed for common initiatives whose principal focus was on promoting social integration through individual labour market participation. By the time the EU Social Inclusion Process came into being, a 'New' Labour government had assumed control in the UK and in 1997 had established a cross-departmental Social Exclusion Unit (SEU) to address the issue of social exclusion. The definition of social exclusion it adopted was pragmatic, to the point of being almost tautologous:

> A short-hand label for what can happen when individuals or areas suffer from a combination of linked problems such as unemployment, poor skills, low incomes, poor housing, high crime environments, bad health and family breakdown. (SEU, 1997)

In effect, therefore, it was UK policy makers who would decide which particular social problems they would focus on under the 'short-hand label' of social exclusion. The initial focus was on highly marginalised and supposedly aberrant social groups, including rough sleepers, teenage mothers and young people not in employment, education or training. To an extent, it has been argued, elements of a 'moral underclass discourse' were absorbed into the social exclusion policy agenda (Levitas, 1998). At the same time elements of the social exclusion discourse were used to justify the development of a welfare-to-work strategy as a means of including people through paid employment. The language of social exclusion could be used to justify income redistribution, although in practice much of the redistribution was achieved through selective tax credits designed to reward lower-paid working families. Here was an approach to social exclusion that was seeking to engage the excluded as economically productive members of society. Elements of the approach have been influential across the EU and are reflected elsewhere in the design of active labour market policies and emergent tax credit schemes in several developed countries.

A related concept that has been powerfully linked to this particular application of the ideas of social exclusion and inclusion is the concept of social capital. Bourdieu (1997), an original proponent of the concept, had been engaged in a sociological analysis of the ways in which various forms of capital – financial, physical, infrastructural, human, cultural and social – could interact to create relative advantage or disadvantage. To what extent might deficiencies of social capital lead to social exclusion (see Piachaud, 2002)? Social capital has also become an increasingly economistic concept that seeks to account for the utility of the 'stock' of social networks or the milieu from which individuals draw for the norms that inform their preferences and for the trust that binds or connects them with the actors with whom they must deal (Becker, 1998). The greatest advocate of the concept, Robert Putnam (2000), has elevated it into a way of evaluating the quality of a community and the strength of civil society. Critics contend that the ascendancy of the concept amounts to an eclipse of social theory by economic theory (Fine, 2001). While the concept of social exclusion has different interpretations in different parts of the world, there appears to be a growing acceptance of the concept of social capital as a mutually agreed synonym for social inclusion and social cohesion, even at World Bank level (see Johnston and Percy-Smith, 2003). The economistic approach to social exclusion casts social capital as a constitutive human need.

From paternalistic to humanistic understandings

The paternalistic and humanistic responses to human need (see ***Table 1.2***, Chapter One) share a more solidaristic understanding of the relationship between the human individual and society. Human relations are regarded within the paternalistic tradition, on the one hand, as an ordered collaboration between vulnerable but cooperative beings struggling to survive in the face of adversity and external threats. Within the humanistic or humanitarian tradition, on the other hand, human relations entail a pooling of individual sovereignty through which to facilitate the fulfilment of mutual obligations and the promotion of collective well-being within a highly complex society. Social order depends, in the paternalistic scenario, on every individual belonging and accepting her lot within society; in the humanistic scenario, on every individual having an equal right to a share in the social product. As a failure of the social order, social exclusion can be understood in the paternalistic scenario as a failure of cohesion and as the alienation of the individual from society (cf Durkheim, 1893), and in the humanistic scenario as a failure of social justice and as the alienation of the individual from her social humanity (cf Marx, 1845).

Before the currency of the social exclusion concept, the term 'marginalisation' had been used, originally it seems by Park (1928), who coined the term 'marginal man' to characterise the way impoverished minority ethnic immigrants failed to assimilate within a predominantly white Anglo-Saxon protestant US. The same term later became popular, particularly in Latin America (for example Germani, 1980), as a term that captured the supposed 'backwardness', not of immigrants in developed countries, but of people in developing countries who fail to participate or are prevented from participating in economic, political and cultural progress. The term drew critical attention to the ways in which rural people and the urban poor were prevented by their subordinate status and cultural differences from assimilating to the formal economy or the political or social mainstream. More recently the term 'marginalisation' has been largely superseded by the term 'social exclusion' after it had appeared in Western Europe and had been promoted in global debate by international bodies such as the International Labour Organization (ILO). The expression *les exclus* was coined initially by Lenoir (1974) to describe the people who slipped through the net of the French social protection system. The characteristically continental European social insurance-based system had traditionally protected labour market insiders at the expense of people excluded from full protection. The expression *les exclus* and the notion of social exclusion that derived from it captured classic republican concern for the failure of the state to include every citizen. The concept, however, also resonated with European social democratic support for the idea of social rights and social citizenship. It was taken up by the ILO and also attracted attention within the UNDP as a way to emphasise how in many developing countries it is not vulnerable minorities who are excluded from social rights, but the majority of the population who are excluded from the right to the satisfaction of basic human needs (Rodgers et al, 1995).

The idea that it is exclusion from social rights of citizenship or from the social rights recognised within the international human rights framework (see Chapter Eight) that constitutes social exclusion is a long way away from the narrower definitions of social exclusion outlined above. This raises the question of whether the concept of social exclusion by itself is of any real value. It helps, however, to understand that the idea of social exclusion is inevitably connected to differing responses to human need and therefore different understandings of how members of different human societies may be excluded from the resources or the processes by which needs may be satisfied.

Capabilities and the freedom to meet one's needs

There is a sense in which the concept of capabilities – associated with Nobel laureate, Amartya Sen – represents a flip-side to the concept of social exclusion. If people are *excluded* from the resources or the processes by which needs may be satisfied, it follows, axiomatically that they are not *free* to access those things. If we think of exclusion as the denial of a person's freedom, this opens up questions of individual agency. The concept of social exclusion invites us to consider not only from *what* people are excluded, but *who* does the excluding (see for example Barry, 2002). But there is a deeper question: if people were truly free to live as they would wish, how might they define and fulfil their needs? In our discussion of inequality in Chapter Four I mentioned Sen and his question 'inequality of what?'. Sen's answer is that what matters is not equality or inequality of resources or outcomes, but of what he calls 'capabilities' (Sen, 1985, 1992, 1999, 2005).

Capabilities are more than mere opportunities. The term refers to a person's capacity to choose and to act. But capabilities are not the same as abilities. The term refers not to what people are able to do but to their freedom to lead the kind of lives they value, and have reason to value. Sen therefore re-defines poverty as an objective curtailment of a person's 'capabilities'. The central components of Sen's theory are crudely summarised in the diagram in *Figure 5.1*. The problem he addresses is that of how we as human beings are able to convert goods, services and other resources into doings and beings, into the valuable activities that characterise our humanity. In essence, therefore, Sen is distinguishing between the needs that exist within what he calls the 'space of commodities' from the needs that we realise in the 'space of functionings'. The former may be defined in terms of the characteristics of commodities; the latter in terms of valuable achievements and 'end states'. Between the space of commodities and the space of functionings lies the space of capabilities and it is within that space, we may infer, that the most essential of human needs – or substantive freedoms – may be defined.

Figure 5.1: *Locating the space of capabilities*

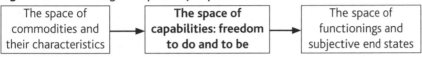

I shall briefly discuss first the impact and second the limitations of this abstract but beguiling concept.[2]

Impact of the capabilities concept

The concept has been influential, not least because it appears elegantly to transcend the distinction between absolute and relative needs.

Sen's contention is that while poverty may be relative in the space of commodities, it is always absolute in the space of capabilities. Equal resources do not necessarily give rise to equal achievements because people are not necessarily free to live as they might wish. The utility of commodities and the well-being to be obtained from their resultant functionings are determined or mediated by a host of intervening socioeconomic, cultural, historical, geographical and climatic factors, but human capability is an absolute imperative. The specific distinction between absolute and relative poverty was debated between Sen and Townsend in the 1980s (for a reprise see Townsend, 1993). Sen claimed that Townsend's concept of relative deprivation (see Chapter Four above) conflated poverty with inequality. Townsend claimed that Sen's insistence on identifying an 'absolutist core' of poverty perpetuated a narrow subsistence-standard conception of poverty. Neither claim stands up, but the debate is instructive. Townsend was seeking to define the point at which 'relative' deprivation leads to a person's *inherent* inability to participate in society. Sen, rather as Adam Smith had done (see **Box 3.2** above), was seeking to *interpret* the circumstances in which a person is 'absolutely' deprived of the ability to function 'without shame'. Both Sen and Townsend recognised the social nature of needs, but were adopting different understandings of 'absolute' and 'relative'. We have seen above that the distinction between absolute and relative needs intersects with another, more fundamental, distinction; namely that which may be drawn between inherent and interpreted notions of human need.

What is distinctive about Sen's capabilities approach is that it attempts to provide a single all-subsuming criterion of need: namely, whether a human being is substantively free to live as she would choose. As such, it offers an advance on other progressive liberal stances (see for example Rawls, 1972), which advocate an equal opportunities approach on the one hand, and a positive rights approach to basic necessities on the other. The capabilities approach, by focusing on the substantive freedom of the individual to do or to be that which she values, is better able to accommodate the diversity of human beings and the complexity of their circumstances (see Burchardt, 2006a). However, the concept has been interpreted and re-interpreted in a variety of different ways. Commentators and policy makers can adopt the language of capabilities without necessarily agreeing on what are the key drivers of poverty or inequality. This, as we shall see, is a fundamental weakness.

First, the concept of capabilities has been important within academic social policy. It was an explicit influence within Doyal and Gough's (1991) theory of human need (discussed in Chapter Three). In some respects, however, Doyal and Gough's specification of human needs tended in practice to focus on resources and functionings, rather than capabilities. The capabilities concept has been adapted and developed by Martha Nussbaum (2000b), a central figure in the Human Development and Capability Association (see www.capabilityapproach.com). Nussbaum has gone further than Sen in seeking to draw up a provisional list of human capabilities, an exercise that raises issues about the extent to which any particular list can ever be universally applicable. At the European level, the capabilities concept has provided a focus for an extensive debate under the auspices of the CAPRIGHT (Resources Rights and Capabilities: In search of social foundations for Europe) integrated project of the EU Sixth Framework programme (and see, for example, Salais and Villeneuve, 2004). Much of that debate, however, has been focused rather narrowly on issues of labour market activation.

Second, the concept has had some ostensible influence at the UN level, specifically in the context of the development of the Human Development Index and the promulgation of the Millennium Development Goals (UN General Assembly, 2000; UNDP, 2003). Sen has been a contributor to recent *Human development reports*. In the 2000 report (UNDP, 2000, ch 1), he argued that the process of human development amounts to and should be understood as the enhancement of human capabilities. However, the UNDP and the World Bank, for example, have not necessarily embraced this premise as fully as they might, since they tend to adopt the altogether more economistic assumption that the effective pursuit of human development amounts to the enhancement of 'human capital' (see also Dean, 2002, 2008a). Sen, for his part, is very clear that human capital and human capabilities are not the same thing, because 'human beings are not merely means of production, but also the end of the exercise'(1999, p 296). In practice, therefore, the capabilities concept is readily misinterpreted.

Third and finally, an attempt has been made in the UK to apply the capabilities approach to the construction of an Equalities Measurement Framework (Burchardt et al, 2008). This is being done under the auspices of the Equality and Human Rights Commission (EHRC), a quango (quasi non-governmental organisation) created under the 2006 Equality Act which has absorbed the separate functions of three previous bodies, the Equal Opportunities Commission (EOC), the Commission for Racial Equality (CRE) and the Disability Rights Commission (DRC), which had had powers respectively to promote sex equality, 'race' equality and equality for disabled people and to investigate complaints of sexual and racial discrimination and discrimination against disabled people. The new body has additionally been afforded powers in relation to the enforcement of equality legislation relating to age, religion or belief, sexual orientation and transgender status. To prepare the ground for the EHRC, the UK government had established an independent Equalities Review, whose final report explicitly drew for its definition of 'an equal society' on elements of a capabilities approach (Equalities Review, 2007; Burchardt and Vizard, 2007; Vizard and Burchardt, 2007). The EHRC is committed to developing 'an evidence-based understanding of the causes and effects of inequality for people across Britain' (EHRC, 2009, p 7). To this end the Commission is seeking to devise a way of monitoring a spectrum of inequalities using a capability measurement framework that attempts to operationalise 10 'domains of valuable capabilities', derived from the international human rights framework. At the time of writing it is not clear how broadly the EHRC's remit will be interpreted and whether, eventually, it will be able adequately to operationalise a capabilities approach.

Limitations of the capabilities concept

It may be argued that the capabilities concept has its own inherent limitations. Capability remains, fundamentally, an abstract liberal–individualist concept. It is possible to outline three potential criticisms. While capabilities relate to the liberty of the human individual to name and claim her needs,

- the naming and claiming of needs requires parity of participation in the public realm;
- human needs must be satisfied in the context of our interdependency with others;

- under capitalist relations of production the means by which needs may be satisfied cannot be wholly free from the direct or indirect consequences of the exploitation of human labour.

The first two of these three objections are concerned with the issues of mutual recognition and care, which will be discussed in their own right in the final section of this chapter. For a moment, however, let us expand on the implications these issues have for the concept of capabilities.

Sen acknowledged the role that 'public reasoning' must play in evolving definitions of capabilities (2005). The capabilities concept rests on the idea that there are things to do and be that the individual values and has reason to value. By implication, the individual must have 'good' reason to value such things. But who determines what constitutes good reason? How can recognition be afforded to the value that people may place on them? Such judgements are necessarily contingent and relative. If the capabilities concept is to inform public policy the liberal ideal requires that there should be a public forum in which to deliberate on the things we should value and to operationalise our capabilities. In the ancient democracies of Athens and Rome the public forum was quite literally a venue for debate. In modern liberal thought it is a metaphorical realm. Habermas (1962) argued that the public realm as a liberal ideal justified a social order in which the state was supposedly disengaged from the functioning of a 'free' market, yet made accountable before the metaphorical court of public opinion.

Sen himself was reluctant to engage in the listing of essential capabilities. Certain of his followers (Nussbaum, 2000b; Alkire, 2002; Burchardt and Vizard, 2007), however, insist that by public deliberative processes it is possible to determine what a list of central human capabilities should look like. Indeed, they include participation in public deliberation as a core capability. Nussbaum's list of central human functional capabilities includes 'Being able to participate effectively in political choices that govern one's life' (2000b, p 80). Yet, some would claim that we are witnessing a 'dissolution' of the public realm (Clarke, 2004). Even the most 'democratic' consensual agreements achieved in the process of public deliberation – through public consultations, citizens' juries, participative poverty assessments or focus groups – may elide fundamental social conflicts and hidden forms of oppression. Such deliberative processes seldom if ever achieve effective 'parity of participation' (Fraser, 1997). They may do nothing more than reflect prevailing hegemonic assumptions about what kind of a life any of us should value and what kinds of need should therefore be recognised.

Just as the forum of public deliberation and debate remains a metaphorical abstraction within liberal thought, so too is Sen's 'space of capabilities'. I mentioned in Chapter One that human need must be considered in the context of human interdependency. The liberal foundations of the capabilities concept frame the individual as an independent entity. Individualistic responses to human need tend to 'problematise' dependency: that is, they tend to regard the person as if axiomatically she were an individual actor functioning independently from others on life's stage; as an isolated atom unaffected by the gravitational forces of other particles or bodies around them. As a consequence, liberal attitudes tend towards ambiguity with regard to the ways in which people depend on each other. They find certain kinds of dependency (such as 'free-riding') morally objectionable, but perversely regard the dependency of individuals on their employers for the means of subsistence or on their families for everyday care as a form of 'independence'. Independence is equated, or rather conflated, with self-sufficiency. Contemporary Western societies are so imbued with the individualistic ethic that they become strangely blind to human interdependency, despite the inevitable dependencies associated with different stages of the human life course and despite the extensive social interactions that are essential to human survival. There is a tendency for people to condemn dependency on the part of others and to deny that they are themselves dependent, albeit that – paradoxically – they may celebrate their own *dependability*, especially for loved ones, neighbours or friends (Dean and Taylor-Gooby, 1992; Dean and Rodgers, 2004).

The consequences of this for the capability approach have been identified by Deneulin and Stewart (2000), who contend that social structures matter not only because they may enable or constrain what Sen calls 'capabilities', but because they are constitutive of our individual identities and the frameworks of meaning by which we value what Sen calls 'functionings'. A social being cannot wholly be free from others because the terms on which she belongs within a family, a community or a society will matter as much as her freedom to do or to be. Feminist supporters of the capability approach, in fairness, do not necessarily focus exclusively on the self-sufficient individual subject. For example, Nussbaum, in her list of central human functional capabilities, includes 'affiliation', which encompasses 'being able to live with and towards others' (2000b, p 79). She is clearly mindful of people's 'need for care in times of extreme dependency' (2000a, p 48), and that being wholly dependent on another need not subserve one's moral personality. To this end, she argues, the goal should be to create 'a space' within which even the most impaired and dependent individual can give and receive love and respect. In her list of central human capabilities, therefore, Nussbaum stipulates that a person should 'be able to imagine the situation of another and have compassion for that situation' (2000b, p 79). However, it seems that both the person and 'the other' are constituted as the abstract bearers of capabilities, not as what Selma Sevenhuijsen, for example, would term 'selves-in-relationship' (2000, p 10). To be capable of 'imagination' and 'compassion' for the situation of another implies disconnection as a starting point, not a substantive connection. The person and 'the other' interact in a metaphorical 'space of capabilities'. Human identity or moral personality depend in a very immediate and substantive sense on human association. In the final analysis an autonomous self-existing within an abstract space of capabilities must remain a conceptual illusion. Insofar as our humanity defines us, it places boundaries on our freedoms.

The third objection that can be made to the capabilities concept relates not to its abstract formulation but its silence regarding the systemic impediments to human freedom that are associated with capitalism. Sen is clear that hunger and poverty result from human not natural failures (1999), but he is not a critic of the capitalist mode of production. It may be argued that insofar as the capabilities approach would promote 'truly human functioning' (Nussbaum, 2006, p 85), it appears to resonate with the Marxist idea that work is constitutive of our 'species being' (see Chapter Two above; and see Bull, 2007). But the capability approach clearly departs from the understanding of capitalism to be found in Marx's later writings (see Chapter Three, this book), and is silent regarding the extent to which wage labour, as the dominant form that work takes under capitalism, may alienate us from our social humanity. The implication of the capabilities approach appears to be that human development and capitalist economic development are – potentially, at least – commensurable.

Whereas Marx's vision of communism was of a society in which there would be a unity of humanity and nature, Malcolm Bull (2007, p 25) has suggested that the capabilities approach has an equivalent vision of a path to human development, albeit one in which 'moving from bare capability to fully human functioning' will not necessarily be universal. Sen (1999, p 6) is anxious to defend the principles of free and fair market exchange, and markets for the exchange of goods and services clearly can serve human ends. But in a market economy there is no guarantee that human needs will adequately be met. Necessary and valuable functionings such as caring for children or for disabled relatives, studying, voluntary work or community participation have no marketable value and are not rewarded by the market (see for example Mooney, 2004).

Defenders of the capability approach will argue that it seeks to promote the 'value' of functionings that are not marketable. Nussbaum's list of central human functional capabilities includes, for example, 'Being able to use the senses, to imagine, think and reason … to laugh, to play, to enjoy recreational activities' (2000b, pp 78-9). Once again, however, the individual is constructed as an abstract bearer of freedoms and the capabilities that should ideally flow from these. The capability approach may demand substantive freedoms to choose, and offer an uplifting vision of what valuable capabilities might consist of, but it is an approach that must be accommodated with the imperatives of the market economy. Peter Townsend's original objection to the capabilities concept – from a non–Marxist perspective – reflected a fear that it could be used to justify a minimalist rather than an expansive conception of human need (see above). The objection may not have done justice to the logic of Sen's arguments, but the fear it reflected remains legitimate since there is nothing in the capabilities concept itself to challenge the ways in which a capitalist market economy can drive inequalities and impair as much as provide for the satisfaction of human need.

Need for recognition and for care

We saw in Chapter Four that economic inequalities impact on different social groups in different ways. We have seen in this chapter that inequalities can be interpreted as failures of social inclusion or as failures of individual freedom. To understand how such differences are associated with diversity and difference within human society, we have to return to the concept of recognition and the idea that disparity of recognition affects disparities of needs satisfaction. The concept of recognition and the 'struggle for recognition' dates back to Hegel (1821). His philosophy departed from the individualism of the Romantic philosophers by emphasising the intersubjectivity of human existence. We are defined by and through the recognition accorded or denied to us by other human beings; a premise that has been paraphrased as meaning we can none of us 'resign from society' (Gaarder, 1996, p 307). Contemporary authors have drawn on Hegel's notion of recognition to argue, for example, that colonial subjects and oppressed indigenous minorities are victims of 'misrecognition' (Fanon, 1967; Taylor, 1992).

If we are to draw the concepts of recognition and misrecognition into a discussion of human need we must nonetheless remind ourselves that human beings are defined in part by their biology. We are embodied creatures with bodily needs (Ellis and Dean, 2000). But while human beings share essential biological features, we also differ from one another biologically. This arises in part as we age. If we survive the varying degrees of physical risk to be encountered during our life course, we experience a protracted developmental stage in our early years and a period characterised by varying degrees of degeneration in later years. We differ from one another genetically: in terms of sex and sexuality; phenotypical characteristics; and physical and cognitive propensities or impairments. But we are only partly defined by our biology, because for human beings biological differences take on social meanings. We are *recognisable* according to the meanings that attach to difference. A simplified illustrative overview of the various intersecting ways in which this occurs is provided in ***Box 5.2***.

Box 5.2:   Social constructions of difference

- Because women have babies and men do not, women and men have tended to assume different social roles, with differing significance and degrees of power within society. The biological differences between men and women are subsumed by socially constructed conceptions of *gender*.
- Because sexual relationships are associated not simply with biological reproduction but the (re)generation of human ties and social relationships the differing sexual drives or orientations to which human beings are subject are subsumed by socially constructed conceptions of *sexuality*.
- Although phenotypical differences (for example skin colour) may have resulted from incidental or minor adaptive biological variations between different social groups of human beings in different parts of the world, they have assumed social meaning and significance in the course of human history through processes of migration and settlement, invasion and conquest, subjugation and slavery. It was once (and by some still is) mistakenly believed that phenotypical differences between humans signify that they belong to different 'races' and that some races are superior to others. Insofar as such beliefs are translated into discriminatory and oppressive practices, they can result in *racialised difference*.
- The genetic characteristics that human beings share with their immediate forbearers may differentiate them from other members of the human species, but such characteristics will invariably be accompanied and given context by social characteristics; by distinctive cultural, linguistic and, possibly, religious differences that together go to make up a person's *ethnicity*.
- Some people are born with genetic impairments. Others in the course of their lives experience illness, injury or degenerative conditions that impair their functioning. Impairment may be physical in nature or it may be associated with mental health problems or learning difficulties. The lives of some people are impaired by pain, physical discomfort and mental distress. However, while biological factors induce functional impairment, what constitutes impairment is also defined with reference to socially accepted or imposed standards of normality. People who cannot walk, see or hear or who have difficulty learning or relating to others are impaired as much as anything else by the norms of society around them. Biological effects are subsumed by socially constructed notions of disability.

> • The human life course entails growing up and, in time, growing old. However, while chronological ageing is a biological process, the meanings that attach to its various stages are shaped by social processes. 'Childhood' and 'youth' are not biologically defined. They are defined by social customs and practices, policy priorities and legal criteria. The notion of 'retirement' is a wholly modern policy construction and our understanding of what constitutes 'old age' is utterly dependent on social and cultural context. The biological basis of the relative vulnerability, strength and frailty that we can expect to experience in the course of a human life-span is overlaid with socially constructed (and often self-fulfilling) expectations and culturally specific assumptions concerning, for example, the relative immaturity, wisdom and senility of various age groups in society. Chronological ageing is subsumed by *social ageing*.

It may be argued that human beings have an overriding need to be recognised by other human beings in order to have their needs appropriately met. It may be seen, however, that women, gays, lesbians, bisexuals, transsexuals, members of racialised and/or minority ethnic groups, disabled people, young people and old can under certain circumstances or for certain purposes be recognised by their 'otherness' (Lister, 2004). In an important sense, therefore, as human beings with universal as well as particular human needs they are *mis*recognised. Given that we all of us experience shifting and overlapping social identities in the course of our lives, we are all vulnerable at some point to misrecognition. We can now reconnect with the first two of the critiques of the capabilities approach outlined above. People can be denied recognition in the public realm, so that they cannot name and claim their needs. People can be denied the mutual recognition on which personal identity and social caring depend.

Recognition within the public realm

This approach to recognition is associated with Nancy Fraser, who has argued at a normative level that the struggle for social justice necessarily encompasses both a struggle for the redistribution of resources *and* a struggle for recognition to ensure parity of participation by oppressed or excluded social groups. I shall return to the normative aspects of Fraser's writings in Chapter Nine. For now, however, I want to focus on her distinctive interpretation of the concept of recognition (Fraser, 1997, ch 1; Fraser and Honneth, 2003, ch 1). For Fraser, misrecognition is not a matter of impaired subjectivity, but a matter of injustice and 'status subordination'. 'Recognition is the remedy for injustice, not the satisfaction of a generic human need' (Fraser and Honneth, 2003, p 45). In this connection Fraser shares with many theorists an analysis that suggests that the nature of politics as we enter a post-industrial era has been changing. The shift, crudely put, is from a politics of class to a politics of identity.

What is currently happening is, on the one hand, a 'hollowing out' of the sphere of the public and of the state as in the developed economies of the world provision for human need is shifted increasingly from the public to the private and/or personal sectors (see for example Jessop, 2002), and on the other, a cultivation of the sphere of the private as the ethical space of the self-preoccupied, self-responsible individual citizen-consumer (Bauman, 1993). The public sphere in which the 'modern politics' of class and economic redistribution had been conducted is discredited and shrinking and so it is that a '*post*-modern' politics of cultural identity, recognition and respect appears to be emerging. This new politics is valorised within, and largely confined to, the personal or private sphere of the self (cf Taylor, 1998). It is a process driven from one direction by the resurgence of neoliberal ideology (Rose, 1999), but also from a completely different direction by the emergence of critical accounts emanating from second-wave feminism and from a range of new social movements, especially those concerned with combating racism, ageism and homophobia and those seeking to promote awareness of disability and ethnicity (see for example Annetts et al, 2009). A shift that addresses social differences other than class is clearly to be welcomed, but as Iris Young (2008) has pointed out, there is a distinction to be made between 'positional differences' that stem from the structural disadvantage experienced by particular social groups (see **Box 5.2**) and 'cultural differences'. Both surely matter, although Young laments the extent to which in recent times political preoccupations with the latter have tended to overshadow concerns about the former.

Nancy Fraser's contention is that the personal and the private are not properly connected and this she has pursued through her critique of the liberal ideal of the public realm (1997, ch 3). I have already drawn on this critique when drawing attention to the potentially problematic nature of the capabilities approach, which requires a process of public reasoning in order to define what constitutes valuable capabilities. The 'public realm' refers in a general sense to the space or spaces in which citizens supposedly deliberate their common affairs. Fraser's critique of the liberal ideal, as currently manifested by actually existing democracies, has four elements:

- First, the liberal ideal assumes that citizens are constituted as formally free and equal and that participation in the public sphere is open to everybody on the same terms. Fraser's argument is that it is impossible to ignore the effects of systemic inequalities in liberal societies that effectively exclude a variety of social classes and groups, or which compromise their participation. This applies especially to women who, throughout the world (with few exceptions), are systematically under-represented in formal democratic processes at both the legislative and executive levels (see *Table 5.1*). This, however, is only the tip of the iceberg. Disadvantaged social groups – including and especially poor people, minority ethnic groups and disabled people – are under-represented in positions of power at both formal and informal levels throughout most societies.

- Second, the liberal ideal assumes the existence of a single undifferentiated public; that for the purposes of public deliberation all citizens or participants are in the same mould, a mould that by default approximates to the characteristics of the dominant participants (who are characteristically male and middle aged, not poor, not from a minority group and not disabled). In practice, societies are composed of many publics, with competing and overlapping interests. The interests of powerful elites may be advanced in the name of defending the common interest, while the interests of subordinate groups go unheard or are ignored.

- Third, the liberal ideal seeks to distinguish between 'private' concerns and common concerns and to exclude consideration of the former. Inasmuch as economic and domestic concerns have been regarded as largely 'private', this has precluded or constrained debate about the nature of both class and gender oppression. The individual in the public realm is cast as an autonomous participant who leaves behind her personal unmet needs and vulnerabilities. Poverty is a state of private shame; cultural needs are a private concern. The business of intimate caring and of being cared for is something that goes on not in public, but behind closed doors.

- Finally, the liberal ideal has long sought a formal separation between state and civil society, between technical policy-making processes and the wider forum of public involvement and debate. To the extent that debate occurs at trade union or community association meetings, in pubs and cafes, waiting for the bus or at the school gate, in work places and living rooms, it is separable from formally legitimated debate that occurs within an elected legislature. The voices of what Fraser calls 'weak publics' (1997, p 90) are mere components of the background noise of public opinion and not part of public deliberation. The rigidity of this separation dilutes the accountability of the state as a provider of human services.

Table 5.1: Women's participation in formal democratic processes

	Women in parliament (lower or single house) circa 2007 (%)	Women in government at ministerial level circa 2005 (%)
Sweden	47	52
UK	20	29
US	16	14
Russia	10	0
Japan	9	13
Brazil	9	11
India	8	3
Nigeria	6	10

Source: UNDP (2008)

To an extent, of course, under liberal democracy it was ever thus. The implication, however, is that if post-industrial trends to post-Fordism, post-communism and globalisation are compromising the role of national welfare states and fuelling self-centred awareness of cultural diversity and identity, the liberal ideal of the public realm appears increasingly empty. At the heart of the analysis outlined above, as I read it, is a failure in the public realm to accommodate social diversity, to recognise status differences and particular needs. In later work Fraser contrives an alliterative distinction between maldistribution, misrecognition and misrepresentation, reflecting economic, cultural and political dimensions, respectively. She appears to capture elements of the above analysis under the heading of misrepresentation (Fraser, 2007). Clearly, however, the concepts of recognition and misrecognition are in themselves necessary to understand how human needs of particular human groups can go unmet.

Mutual recognition and social caring

A rather different understanding of recognition is provided by Axel Honneth (1995). Fraser and Honneth have debated their differences (Fraser and Honneth, 2003) and whereas Fraser argues that struggles for redistribution and recognition are necessarily intertwined, Honneth gives primacy to what Hegel called the struggle for recognition on the premise that recognition is the condition precedent for redistribution. His approach is a deliberate attempt to recapture and build on Hegel's early work in which he sought to characterise humanity in terms of the quest for intersubjective recognition. Hegel wrote of the family, civil society and the state as three 'spheres of recognition'. Honneth, drawing on social psychological influences from Mead (1934), reformulates this in terms of a claim that the three requirements for an 'ethical life' are to be found in three phases or modes of mutual recognition: love, solidarity and rights (see Dean, 2004, ch 10).

- All human beings need love. Love, Honneth claims, entails discovering and being oneself in and through another. It is necessary for self-identity. But as the emotional substance of our most intimate caring relationships, love also provides the basis on which we can come to recognise, accommodate and respect each other as *needy beings*.
- All human beings are capable of solidarity. It is through participation and solidarity with others in a community or social group that we establish who we are and what we can do, that we establish a collective identity and can achieve self-esteem. But, importantly, solidarity requires a sharing of goals and understandings with other members of society and enables us to apprehend our shared responsibilities to strangers as well as intimates. It provides a basis on which we can come to recognise, accommodate and respect each other as *beings defined by difference*.
- All human beings have rights. Through the processes by which we exercise rights for ourselves and respect the rights of others we are recognising each other as we ourselves would wish to be recognised. Possessing rights is necessary for self-respect. But to recognise each other as the possessors of rights requires an acknowledgement of each other's capacity to make claims against one another, a capacity that must be understood to be universal and constitutive. Rights provide the basis on which we can come to recognise, accommodate and respect each other as bearers of a universal capacity that characterises us as *human*.[3]

Honneth does not explicitly link his discussion of recognition to issues of human need, but the implication of his discussion is an acknowledgment of human interdependency: an acknowledgement that relates not only to an ontological need for self-identity, self-esteem and self-respect, but the conditions necessary for human beings to claim their existential needs. There are also resonances between Honneth's discussion and recent feminist theory concerning ethics and care.

The feminist ethic of care debate began with Carol Gilligan's (1982) claim that feminine moral codes of care were consistently subordinated to masculine codes of moral reasoning (see for example Ellis, 2004). Moral codes of care, she contended, were rooted in mutual responsibility and relationships, not rights and rules, in everyday reality, not abstract principles of justice and equality. Subsequent commentators (Friedman, 1993; Clement, 1998) expressed concern that in attempting to re-valorise an ethic of care one should not omit to embrace the interdependency of strangers as well as intimates. Principles of justice and equality are necessary if we are to have rights and rules by which to accord recognition and respect to distant others. Nonetheless, individuals can only exist through and with others within networks of care (Tronto, 1994; Sevenhuijsen, 1998). The meeting of human needs depends not just on how societies organise their means of production, but also how their members care for and about each other (Parker, 1981; Kittay et al, 2005). The insight is not necessarily new since it resonates with the premises of *ubuntu*, the ancient pan-African philosophy (Ramose, 2003). Nonetheless it reminds us of the concrete substance of human lives in which everyday relationships can entail conflict, negotiation and struggle. The ways in which we care for and about each other are, as often as not, socially negotiated within such relationships, across the generations and over time (see for example Finch and Mason, 1993). Substantive relations of care must be negotiated on the basis of mutual recognition between needy subjects with shared vulnerabilities.

Notes

[1] It is important to acknowledge that the flexibility of the term has been such that it has enabled many academics and poverty researchers to define social exclusion in terms remarkably similar to Townsend's (1979) definition of relative poverty (see Hills et al, 2002).

[2] A fuller account of this discussion may be found in Dean (2009), from which this discussion is partly drawn.

[3] In a previous work (Dean, 2004, ch 10) I suggested there was an affinity between this notion of the universal constitutive capacity of human beings and Sen's notion of capabilities. I am now less certain. Upon reflection, Honneth's conception of rights requires love and solidarity in a way that Sen's conception of capabilities does not.

Summary

This chapter has dealt with three different concepts, each with a direct bearing on human need.

- *Social exclusion* is a concept that addresses processes by which individuals or groups in society may be denied the satisfaction of certain needs. The concept is differently conceived depending on the approach that is adopted. Using the approaches to human need first identified in Chapter One it may be seen that moral-authoritarian approaches lead to concepts that associate social exclusion with notions of underclass; economistic approaches to concepts that associate social exclusion with a lack of social capital; paternalistic approaches to concepts that associate social exclusion with a failure of social cohesion or integration; and humanistic approaches to concepts that associate social exclusion with the denial of social rights. It is a contested concept.

- The concept of *capabilities* is concerned with the extent to which people are free to meet their needs. It is a concept that has influenced debates about poverty, which helped inform the UN's Millennium Development Goals and which has been applied, for example, in attempts to construct an equalities measurement framework. It has been argued here, however, that the concept neglects the limitations of liberal democracy's public realm as a forum for deliberation over the capabilities that are to be valued; the inherent tension between human beings' interdependency and the extent or nature of their autonomy; and the inherently or potentially exploitative nature of market relations under capitalism.

- The concept of *recognition* bears on how people's needs are recognised or mis-recognised. The issue relates to that of social difference that was considered in the context of the discussion of inequality in Chapter Four. It may be argued that the meeting of human needs depends not only on the distribution of resources, but also the recognition of the needs of oppressed minorities and the representation of those minorities in public deliberation. The fulfilment of human need depends on mutual recognition and relations of care.

The issue common to the discussion of these three concepts is that of human interdependency and the extent to which that interdependency is inimical to autonomous agency. Can human beings be socially included in ways that allow them effective participation? Can they ever be free to live as they would choose? Can they achieve mutual recognition on an authentically equal basis? We may be forced to conclude that, as Stenner et al have put it, 'we are neither as free as we might hope, nor as determined as we might fear' (Stenner et al, 2008, p 412). We have to situate our understandings of social need in relation to our identities as unique individuals and our interconnectedness as social beings.

Questions for discussion:

- Which, if any, of the various interpretations of the social exclusion concept do you prefer, and why? And which interpretations, if any, might you discount?
- What are the principal advantages and disadvantages of the human capabilities concept?
- What does the concept of recognition bring to our understanding of human needs?

six

The thin and the thick of human well-being

- This chapter introduces a particular distinction between 'thin' and 'thick' conceptions of human need.
- It links the idea of 'thin' needs to what may be called a *hedonic* concept of human well-being. To do this, it considers:
  - the development of philosophical utilitarianism and its expression in contemporary approaches to 'welfarism' and cost-effectiveness analysis;
  - the emergence in the social sciences of the study of happiness.
- It links the idea of 'thick' needs to what may be called a *eudaimonic* concept of human well-being. To do this, it considers:
  - the different ways in which philosophical notions of the 'good life' have been translated into policies intended to enable people not merely to survive, but to flourish;
  - explorations of the psychosocial dimension to human well-being;
  - attempts to generate a thicker interpretation of what human capabilities might consist of;
  - various analyses of the social context of human well-being.

In Chapters Two and Three we explored a distinction between inherent and interpreted need. In this chapter we explore a different distinction, between 'thin' and 'thick' interpretations of need (cf Soper, 1993). This might be regarded as just another way of distinguishing between absolute and relative need, or between basic and 'higher' needs, or between procedural and substantive definitions of need, or between what people need to survive as opposed to what they need to flourish. The distinction I seek to make resonates with that which ethnographic anthropologists make between thin and thick descriptions of human life (see for example Geertz, 1973). We should not assume that thick interpretations are always better than thin ones: they may be richer, subtler, more complex, but will not necessarily result in just outcomes and they are no less likely than other interpretations to be misguided. Michael Walzer (1994) draws on the same idea to distinguish between thin and thick moralities. He makes it clear that, in a pluralistic world, thin (or 'minimalist') moralities are important not because they necessarily lay the foundations for thicker (or 'maximalist') moralities, but for the contribution they make to different forms of human understanding and the pragmatic possibilities they create for agreed action among people with different moral beliefs. Insofar as there is a clear moral dimension to understandings of human need, this captures one of the ways in which we can consider the plurality of meanings attaching to concepts of need.

The depth of meaning I wish to bring to the distinction between thin and thick can most helpfully be achieved by linking it to yet another concept connected to human need, that of human *well-being*. There is a distinction to be made between being 'well enough' and being 'very well'. To be well enough is to be satisfied with what you can have and do in life. To be *very* well is, perhaps, to be 'truly' fulfilled as a human being. To be 'not well' implies some kind of deprivation. Significantly, of course, one cannot be 'excessively well' – this is a contradiction in terms. The notion of well-being is capable of invoking not just practical, but moral or ethical considerations about the extent and the limits of human need; not only a 'thin' conception of what the lives of human beings necessarily entail, but also a 'thick' conception of what a human life ought to or potentially could entail.

One recent introductory textbook has defined academic social policy as the study of human well-being or, more particularly, the social relations and systems that promote or impair human well-being (Dean, 2006). 'Well-being', although hardly a new concept, has become yet another in a succession of fashionable, insightful, yet slippery concepts relevant to human need (see for example Gough and McGregor, 2007; Jordan, 2008; Searle, 2008).[1] (In Chapter Five we have already considered some such concepts, namely 'social exclusion', 'capabilities' and 'recognition'.) The advantage of well-being as a term is that it can turn our attention to the positive aspects of social policy, as opposed to negative aspects relating to social problems. It is untainted by the pejorative connotation that attaches in certain quarters to the term 'welfare'. It also places the emphasis on human 'being' as opposed to 'having' or 'doing' (Fromm, 1976). It must be acknowledged nonetheless that as Gough and McGregor put it, 'wellbeing is still a novel category in applied social science, such that no settled consensus on its meaning has yet emerged' (2007, p 5). Well-being can be defined in relation to its opposite, depending on just how the opposite is conceived.

Gough and McGregor (2007) define well-being as the opposite of 'ill-being' or poverty. Jordan (2008) goes so far as to define it as the opposite of 'welfare': well-being he sees as the realisation of what he terms 'social value', welfare as the realisation of individual utility. Arguably, Jordan is drawing the same distinction as I am making between thick and thin conceptions of well-being, equating the former with a social or relational ideal, the latter with an economistic ideal.

This brings us to the essence of the fundamental distinction between the 'hedonic' and the 'eudaimonic'. The etymological origins of these two terms are to be found in classical Greek philosophy. Hedonism was concerned with pleasure; eudaimonia with spiritual well-being (see **Box 6.1**). The Socratic tradition recognised both, but the traditions have diverged. The Epicureans supposed that a good life entailed the pursuit of pleasure (mental as well as physical) and the avoidance of pain or discomfort. The Aristotelian tradition – as expounded in *Nicomachean ethics* and the *Eudemian ethics* (see Macintyre, 2007) – contended that leading a good life meant more than pleasure seeking; it entailed virtue (see also Fitzpatrick, 2008, ch 4). Self-realisation comes through the nature of our social relationships, civic duties and creative activities. I have attempted elsewhere (Dean, 2003, 2008b) to argue that the hedonic–eudaimonic distinction is reflected in the different ways in which post-Enlightenment concepts of citizenship and associated approaches in social policy have been constructed. I shall endeavour to develop that argument a little further in this chapter.

Thin needs and hedonic notions of well-being

In Chapter Two (see **Table 2.1**) it was argued that if the human subject is regarded as a utilitarian subject or as a market actor her needs may be understood in terms of her objective interests or subjective preferences, respectively. These are 'thin' understandings in the sense that the human subject is abstractly construed as a calculative actor without regard for her 'true self' or social identity. Such understandings are premised on assumptions about the nature of utility on the one hand, and of human happiness on the other.

From utilitarianism to welfarism

The hedonic approach to human well-being found expression in the 19th century in utilitarianism. And utilitarianism found its clearest expression in the work of Jeremy Bentham. As Eric Hobsbawm put it, arithmetic was the fundamental tool of the era and for Bentham and his followers, particularly:

Happiness was the object of policy. Every man's pleasure could be expressed … as a quantity and so could his pain. Deduct the pain from the pleasure and the net result was his happiness. Add the happiness of all men and deduct the unhappiness, and that government which secured the greatest happiness for the greatest number was the best. (Hobsbawm, 1968, p 79)

Box 6.1:   The etymological roots of the word *eudaimonia*

Historically speaking, the word 'daimon' (or its derivatives, such as *daemon* or *demon*) has referred:

* **either** to what might be called a person's own 'soul' or their true or 'noumenal' self (see Chapter 2 above)
* **or else** to an independent 'spirit' – whether good or bad – for example, a guardian angel on the one hand or an evil incubus on the other.

During the last few hundred years, it is this last mentioned imagery - of the evil demon - that has tended to hold sway. However, in Phillip Pullman's 'His Dark Materials' children's book trilogy (*Northern Lights* [1995], *The Subtle Knife* [1997] and *The Amber Spyglass* [2000], published by Scholastic Ltd) each of the human characters to be found living in a fictional world, parallel to our own, has a 'daemon' in the form of an animal familiar. Such daemons reflect or embody the noumenal self of the person to whom they are uniquely attached. They are essential to the integrity of that person as a human being and accompany her or him throughout that person's life. This is a contemporary example of a way of imagining our daimonic existence.

The prefix 'eu-' implies 'wellness' or 'goodness' and so exposes the supposed 'spiritual' dimension of our human existence to moral judgement as to the nature of human virtue. Axiomatically, this frames the person in her social context. Through the concept of eudaimonia this book will not concern itself with the many religious interpretations of spiritual well-being, but with secular interpretations bearing upon the social context through which personal identity and the human 'self' are ethically or morally constituted.

Such a calculus could by implication justify inflicting disutility (that is, pain) on any who threatened the happiness of the majority. So it was that in Britain a Benthamite approach to social policy resulted in the creation of the Victorian workhouse and the principle of 'lesser eligibility' (Fraser, 1984). The workhouse was deliberately contrived to be a place of wholesome horror compared even to the hardships endured by the poorest self-sufficient labourer. None but the most desperate would seek relief on such terms. In this way the pressure on the destitute to be self-sufficient was maximised and the cost of poor rates to be borne by property owners was minimised. The misery of the pauper would promote the greater happiness of the population in general (and property owners in particular).

This represents a draconian illustration of utilitarian or 'consequentialist' (see for example Bochel et al, 2005, pp 197-8) social policy. Nonetheless it encapsulates founding elements of a 'welfarist' approach that continues to inform social policy (Jordan, 2008). Welfarism here is taken to refer to a particular kind of thinking that assumes that social policy intervention should be judged by its aggregate effects, rather than the well-being of any particular individual. It is also premised on certain assumptions about what motivates people: pleasures or rewards provide incentives; pain or punishment provides disincentives. Policy may be used to induce or to reinforce the behaviour most likely to generate beneficial overall outcomes.

While this is indeed an illiberal approach, its origins lie perversely in liberal Enlightenment thinking about the nature of the human individual (King, 1999). The starkest of liberal conceptions of the social order regarded human relations as a war or competition of all against all (Hobbes, 1651). Dealings between people entailed various forms of bargaining – for goods, for land, for position. Citizenship could accordingly be construed in contractarian terms as a trade-off between the unrestrained pleasures of individual sovereignty or freedom in return for protection against the pain that may be occasioned through the predations or malfeasance of others. We trade the freedom to help ourselves to our neighbour's possessions for protection against our neighbour's propensity to steal from us. T.H. Marshall (1950), however, claimed that the modern welfare state provided far more than the legal rights entailed by an extension of civil liberties or the political rights bestowed through the extension of the franchise. Modern 20th-century citizenship in the developed world began to afford citizens a right to 'welfare', including healthcare, education, housing and social security. But rights to welfare can come with strings attached. Entitlement to various kinds of welfare has been and can still be subject to the good character, the good behaviour or the healthy lifestyles of recipients, or expressly conditional on the recipients' participation in training or work experience or on ensuring their children attend school. The extension of state administration into the field of welfare extended its capacity to control people's lives in the cause of the greater good (Garland, 1981; Dean, H., 1991; Dean, M., 1991).

The political calculus of utilitarianism has its counterpart in welfare economics. Passing reference was made in Chapter Two to Pigou (1928, 1965) and his attempts to bring neoclassical economics to bear on the analysis of human well-being. For Pigou, money was the measure of utility although he acknowledged that this approach was not adapted to investigate the costs of non-economic factors (see Jordan, 2008, p 201). Theorists of the 'new' welfare economics approach have been less reticent. The best known of these build on the work of Pareto (1909). Pareto's concern was with the extent to which the allocation and distribution of income, goods, services, jobs and life chances (not just money) in society are efficient. The optimum allocation is achieved at the point at which it is impossible to make any one person better off without making another worse off. Although such perfect equilibrium can never be achieved in practice, the Pareto principle has continued to inform cost-benefit or, more importantly, cost-effectiveness analysis in public policy making. Welfare economics assumes that, ideally, there should be some prospect that those who gain from social policy interventions should to some extent compensate those who have lost out. The compromises thereby achieved are leading to what may be described as a 'weak welfarism' (Adler and Posner, 2006; see also Jordan, 2008). This is characteristically evident in the 'creeping conditionality' of welfare provision that may be observed not just in developed countries, but in emerging economies, whereby social assistance to poor households may be conditional on the head of household's job-seeking efforts or on whether the children of the household are attending school (Dwyer, 2004a; Britto, 2006). We shall be returning to such issues in Chapter Seven.

Utilitarian forms of cost-effectiveness analysis can also be applied in healthcare policy. In Chapter Three I made mention of Forder's (1974) concept of 'technical need', needs that are generated by technological and medical advances, but whose cost may exceed the resources available. When public access to life-saving procedures is to be rationed, difficult decisions have to be taken. The best known example of how this might be done is the system of QALYs (quality adjusted life years), developed amidst some controversy in Oregon, USA (and once considered for use in the UK) (Bochel et al, 2005, p 203). QALYs can be used to evaluate whether the cost of surgery or some other form of healthcare intervention is justified, whether a person's life is 'good enough' to be worth saving. They indicate the length of time a patient can expect to achieve an acceptable quality of life as a result of treatment, but the measure of quality of life – the Rosser Index – is a classic example of a hedonic calculus. It evaluates degrees of disability in one dimension (ranging from 'none' to a 'state of unconsciousness') and degrees of distress in another (ranging from 'none' to 'severe') in order to compute a matrix score (ranging from

1 for 'healthy' to 0 for 'dead') (Kind et al, 1982; Gudex, 1986). Hedonic approaches to well-being have informed a succession of health-related quality of life measures that have in the first instance related wellness primarily to healthiness (Phillips, 2006, ch 2). But the utility or quality of life may be judged not simply in terms of healthy life expectancy, but happy life expectancy (Veenhoven, 1996).

Study of happiness

The ideal generally espoused by welfare economists is that the Pareto optimum (see above) would be best achieved under conditions of sustained economic growth and general affluence. In this way, everyone can be happy (provided they keep healthy). At any particular point in time there is a positive correlation between a person's happiness and her income (Di Tella and MacCullough, 2007), but there is a substantial body of evidence to suggest that economic growth does not necessarily promote additional happiness. In many countries, rising gross domestic product (GDP) does not correlate with increased well-being (Layard, 2003, 2005; Easterlin, 2005; Searle, 2008). The tiny, predominantly Buddhist, nation of Bhutan has decided it will no longer try to measure its success in terms of GNP, but GNH (gross national happiness) (see www.bhutanstudies.org.bt). Elsewhere, however, what has been called the 'Easterlin paradox' (crudely, that extra money does not always buy extra happiness) has become something of a preoccupation.

In recent years various kinds of social scientists have turned their minds to the measurement of happiness, life satisfaction or subjective well-being. It is possible to measure such things by asking people to say how happy they feel, how satisfied they are with their lives or to answer a battery of health-related questions to establish how 'well' they feel (mentally as well as physically). Whereas 'objective' measures of well-being might draw on indicators such as wealth or poverty statistics (see Chapter Three), welfare economists are now interested in 'subjective' well-being. They have concluded that people's replies to such simple questions as 'How do you feel about life as a whole?' are generally a good predictor of subjective well-being (Andrews and Withey, 1976; Searle, 2008).

It was Inglehart who first identified a cultural shift to what he called 'post-materialism' (1990). As advanced industrial societies became more affluent, he observed, the preoccupations of their inhabitants began to change. As material scarcity declined people became more individualistic and introspectively preoccupied (see also Beck and Beck-Gernsheim, 2001). Evidence from a variety of sources, including the World Values Survey, tended to indicate that as economic growth and personal incomes rose across the developed world, empirical measures of 'happiness', life satisfaction and subjective well-being had stalled. However, it is important to note: first, that the variation in happiness 'scores' within countries was less than that between countries, underlining the extent to which cultures are highly context specific; and second, that the latest time series data suggest that while overall trends in happiness levels in countries such as the US and the UK have indeed been flat or slightly downward in the past half century, there has been improvement in recent years. Furthermore, in a majority of countries – including rapidly developing countries such as India and China – the overall trend has been one of *rising* happiness (Inglehart et al, 2008). The trends are complex and interpretations of aggregated data of this nature are, inevitably, contestable (see for example Burchardt, 2006b).

There remain well-established doubts, for example, as to the *social* sustainability of continuous economic growth (Hirsch, 1977); as to whether success within a perennially competitive economic environment may fuel a culture of corrosive anxiety at the level of the individual actor (Pahl, 1995); and as to whether affluence undermines general well-being (Galbraith, 1958; Offer, 2006). The economist Richard Layard (2005) has joined those who claim that riches do not bring happiness. His analysis and prescriptions are described by Jordan (2008) as neo-utilitarian in nature. Layard draws his definition of happiness from the post-Enlightenment liberal tradition, explicitly rejecting any eudaimonic dimension (2005, p 22). He concludes that we should monitor GNP and GNH together; that we should constrain the effects of excessive inequality, exploitative work cultures and rampant consumerism; and that (in the UK) we should spend more on mental health provision. But he seeks nonetheless to maximise the sum of utility and to contain the process within the parameters of a cost-effectiveness analysis. He favours the retention of welfare-to-work sanctions and the extension of moral education in schools. The implication is that with better understanding, we can make more people happier.

Psychologists in particular have investigated happiness and have made a substantial contribution to the methodological development of the subjective well-being measures mentioned above. Ryan and Deci (2001) make a clear distinction between hedonic and eudaimonic approaches within the psychology discipline. It is what they call hedonic psychology that adopts subjective well-being as a *primary* indicator, rather than an operational or interpretive tool. This 'scientific' variant of psychology has its roots in medicine and biology and is concerned with the well-being of an essentially asocial human organism (Stenner and Taylor, 2008). From a hedonic perspective, the incidence of mental ill health – clinical depression, for example – is to be understood as a consequence of stress, in particular the stress of coping with the tribulations of a life in which pleasure may be hard to achieve and pain hard to avoid (Frost and Hoggett, 2008).

Welfare economists and hedonic psychologists can agree on certain kinds of explanation. To the extent that increasing levels of material consumption and wealth do not necessarily enhance subjective well-being, this may be understood in terms of the decreasing marginal utility of additional consumption on the one hand, and the effects of the 'hedonic treadmill' on the other (Offer, 2006). People adapt to rising living standards to the point that they no longer find them satisfying. And keeping up with the Joneses can be unsatisfying, exhausting or depressing. The utilitarian arithmetic alluded to by Hobsbawm gets more difficult. As Searle has put it, 'wellbeing is an entanglement of experiences, a process with no beginning and no end' (Searle, 2008, p 104).

The challenge is that of how better to regulate the hedonic treadmill and to govern the behaviour and preferences of those who turn it, so as to make their lives more satisfying. This book is being written at a time of global economic recession, when maybe the hedonic treadmill could be arrested. And yet interim findings from an ongoing study of unmet needs in the UK concludes that in this affluent nation:

> Psychological needs seem to be more likely to go unmet than material ones; our society, welfare systems and services are better designed for material than psychological needs. These could get worse during an economic downturn for example with greater unemployment and anxieties about finance. (Vale et al, 2009, p 21)

Happiness can be elusive and Tania Burchardt has suggested that although social scientific investigators of happiness might be 'barking up the right tree', they might be doing so 'in the wrong neck of the woods': 'the goal of social policy should be actual well-being, not just the cosy sensation of well-being' (2006b, p 157).

Thick needs and eudaimonic notions of well-being

Arguably, the aggregate measures of well-being derived from survey data as interpreted by welfare economists and hedonic psychologists do not fully engage with the social realities of individual lives. In Chapter Two I suggested that if the human subject is regarded as a psychosocial being or as a species member, her needs may be understood in terms of her inner drives or constitutive characteristics, respectively (see *Table 2.1* in Chapter Two). These are 'thick' understandings in the sense that the human subject is substantively construed as an embodied and socially situated being. The psychosocial being I had in mind owes more to what Ryan and Deci (2001) characterise as eudaimonic as opposed to hedonic psychology. And the species to which I refer is not *homo œconomicus*, but that of the *social* human being (Douglas and Ney, 1998). We shall now consider certain philosophical underpinnings, the emerging notion of a psychosocial dimension and related sociological/social anthropological accounts.

Philosophical underpinnings: in search of the good life

The Aristotelian conception of the 'good life' provides not necessarily a constitutive foundation, but the beginnings of a pathway or pathways leading to eudaimonic conceptions of human well-being. While the hedonic pathway led to utilitarianism, the eudaimonic approach has led in different directions. Elements of the approach translated themselves during the 18th century onwards into Kantian 'deontological ethics', that is to say, into notions of universal moral duty and the contention that not only does everybody have a right to well-being, but nobody should be treated as a means of achieving happiness for another. Such thinking opened the door to the social liberalism that informed the creation of modern welfare states, to liberal concepts of social justice, such as that espoused by Rawls (1972) and, for example, to Sen's capability approach, discussed in Chapter Five.

Paradoxically, the principal critique of the social liberal approach came from radical democrats or 'communitarians' (Sandel, 1982; Walzer, 1983; Macintyre, 2007), who also trace their thinking back to the Aristotelian tradition, and in particular to the idea that human knowledge and governance are fundamentally social or collective enterprises. Their objection was to the abstract nature of the individual 'self' that is posed in liberal deontology as opposed to a presumption that the mutual obligations human beings owe to each other are grounded in the realities of their social belonging. This particular brand of communitarianism[2] has much in common with the republicanism of Rousseau and Montesquieu and embodies tendencies, at least, to social conservatism. Post-Enlightenment republicanism favoured the Aristotelian rather than the Platonic tradition in that it envisaged a republic governed not by philosopher kings, but by the general will of the people. The republican approach was by implication more eudaimonic. It assumed that human relations amount to a collaboration between vulnerable but cooperative beings, that dealings between people entail various forms of interpersonal attachment or belonging. Citizenship is therefore construed in solidaristic terms as a pooling of individual sovereignty and the promotion of social order, existential security and collective well-being.

Social liberalism and social conservatism each, therefore, embody a potentially eudaimonic interpretation of the good life, the former premised more on abstract philosophical doctrine, the latter more on a concern for cultural norms. The former as it evolved became increasingly associated with the politics of social democracy, with its emphasis on promoting social justice.[3] The latter, as it evolved, became increasingly associated with the politics of Christian democracy, with its emphasis on preserving the traditional social order. Both, however, attached value to solidarity and the idea that there is virtue in sharing risks and responsibilities. For example, social liberalism and social conservatism have each embraced social insurance and/or social protection principles (which will be further discussed in Chapter Seven). Forms of social provision premised on social insurance or universalistic social protection entail solidaristic notions of risk sharing: they are consistent with a 'eudaimonic ethic' (a concept to which we shall return in Chapter Nine). They imply a concern that human society should do more than avoid the suffering of its members, but enable them, notwithstanding the vicissitudes of the life course, to participate and to flourish.

At a global level, while some UN agencies remain under the sway of a neoliberal 'Washington Consensus' that favours a hedonic calculus of free trade, mitigated by welfare safety nets (Deacon, 2007), agencies such as the ILO favour insurance-based or universal social security (ILO, 2006), and the World Health Organization (WHO) – in contrast to the Rosser Index mentioned above – has been seeking to define and to monitor quality of life in distinctly eudaimonic terms, as:

> ... an individual's perceptions of their position in life in the context of the culture and value systems in which they live, and in relation to their goals, expectations, standards and concerns. It is a broad ranging concept affected in a complex way by the person's physical health, psychological state, level of independence, social relationships and their relationship to salient features of their environment. (WHOQOL Group, 1995, p 495; see also the discussion in Schmidt and Bullinger, 2008)

Psychosocial dimension

Eudaimonic as opposed to hedonic psychology is sceptical about the application of subjective well-being measures or else it is concerned to incorporate additional dimensions such as 'personal expressiveness' and 'self-determination' (Ryan and Deci, 2001, p 146). Psychologists, such as

Raphael et al (1998), have sought to define and to measure quality of life in terms of such dimensions of 'being', 'belonging' and 'becoming'. Ryan and Deci's own contribution has been the development of self-determination theory (SDT), which posits three requirements for psychological growth: autonomy, competence and relatedness. SDT presents these as basic and universal needs on which psychological health and well-being depend. Autonomy is concerned with the authenticity and integrity of the self and is measurable with reference to one's self-motivation and feelings of self-endorsement and personal value. Competence is concerned with effective functioning and the internalisation of cultural values and is measurable with reference to one's confidence in one's ability to attain outcomes. Relatedness is concerned with social integration and connectedness and is measurable with reference to one's feelings of belonging. Unlike the hierarchy of needs defined by Maslow (see Chapter Two above), these needs are equally and indivisibly integral to a person's well-being. The focus is on preconditions for life as an 'inherently active, relational being' (Ryan and Sapp, 2008, p 73).

Ryan and Deci would acknowledge that 'specification of basic needs defines not only the minimum requirements of psychological health but also delineates prescriptively the nutriments that the social environment must supply for people to thrive and grow psychologically' (2001, p 147). Social environment and, by implication, social policy are critical to well-being. We are drawn back to our discussion in Chapter Four of Richard Wilkinson's work. Wilkinson's evidence suggests that unequal societies, however affluent, do not nourish people in the sense that Ryan and Deci describe. For Wilkinson, however, it is not necessarily affluence but social inequality that is the problem. In earlier work Wilkinson places the emphasis on the damage that is done by 'chronic stress'. Relative deprivation makes people feel:

> ... depressed, cheated, bitter, desperate, vulnerable, frightened, angry, worried about debts or job and housing insecurity; to feel devalued, useless, helpless, uncared for, hopeless, isolated, anxious and a failure. (Wilkinson, 1996, p 215)

To an extent Wilkinson is alluding in a hedonic sense to the pain and unhappiness that can result from systemic inequalities, but in another sense he is grounding his explanations in a social context. This is clearer in later work in which Wilkinson adopts elements of the social capital concept (for a critical discussion see Chapter Five), and emphasises that it is because egalitarian societies have higher levels of social cohesion that they are healthier than inegalitarian societies.

Other levels of explanation are offered by emerging psychosocial approaches in social policy (Stenner and Taylor, 2008). Frost and Hoggett acknowledge that studies which draw on a hedonically conceived 'stress and coping model' can disclose the 'massive psychical effects of social justice' (2008, p 442), but they call for a deeper understanding of people's lived experiences. They draw on Bourdieu's notion of 'social suffering' (1999). Just as I have drawn in Chapter Five above on feminist perspectives in a critique of the liberal subject envisaged by the capabilities approach, it is argued that the 'post-liberal' subject may be understood in terms not of her autonomy, but her relationality; in terms not of capability deficits, but of the social space she inhabits and the structures of oppression she experiences. Social suffering may be inflicted through the 'hidden injuries' of social inequality, the injury caused by such things as class or racialised differences or the social construction of ageing and disablement. Experiences of social stigma and shame inflict trauma and loss on individual identity. In some instances this may be acted out through violent or anti-social reactions, but it will, in any event, be reflected in somatic outcomes and health-related inequalities.

This 'thick' psychosocial approach, like the communitarian approach, is sceptical of liberalism, but draws, albeit implicitly, on a eudaimonic sense of the human self.

The thickening-up of capabilities?

In a very different vein, Martha Nussbaum's development of the capabilities approach, discussed in Chapter Five, involved the elaboration of a list of 'central human functional capabilities' which represents, undoubtedly, the 'thickest' and most explicit attempt to specify what human capabilities should consist of (Nussbaum, 2000b, pp 78-80). The list is summarised in *Box 6.2*, and encompasses hedonic and eudaimonic elements. The hedonic elements are richly drawn and can in one sense clearly be said to be more thick than thin. However, while capability to laugh and to play, for example, is a notion that extends beyond the grimness characteristically associated with utilitarian thinking, it is still fundamentally concerned with the maximisation of pleasure, albeit in a qualitatively different dimension. The eudaimonic elements include capabilities associated with participation, affiliation and relationships, but as suggested in Chapter Five, there is a degree of 'thinness' to the way these capabilities are drawn. The possessor of such capabilities is constituted not through her interconnectedness, but by her capability as a free actor to connect with others. This impression is reinforced by the terms in which, controversially, a capability to live in relation to other species is included: human beings most certainly need to live in harmony with the planet, but if this were to imply, for example, a moral claim for species equality,[4] this would not sit comfortably with those elements of eudaimonic thinking that consider the human species (with all its ethical responsibilities) to be uniquely constituted by virtue of its sociality.

Box 6.2: Nussbaum's list of central functional capabilities: a summary

1. **Life**. Being able to live to the end of a normal human life.
2. **Bodily Health**. Being able to have good health.
3. **Bodily Integrity**. Being able to move freely from place to place and to be safe from assault.
4. **Senses, Imagination, and Thought**. Being able to use the senses, to imagine, think, and reason in a way informed and cultivated by an adequate education, with freedom of expression and religious observance.
5. **Emotions**. Being able to have attachments to things and people outside ourselves, to love and to grieve and to be safe from trauma, abuse and neglect.
6. **Practical Reason**. Being able to form a conception of the good and freely to engage in critical reflection.
7. **Affiliation**. Being able to engage in social interaction, to have compassion and friendship with others and to be safe from discrimination and disrespect.
8. **Other Species**. Being able to live with concern for and in relation to animals, plants, and the world of nature.
9. **Play**. Being able to laugh, to play, to enjoy recreational activities.
10. **Control over One's Environment**. Being able to participate effectively in political choices that govern one's life and being able on equal terms with others to own property and seek employment.

Source: Nussbaum (2000b, pp 78-80)

Ian Gough has emphasised the need to distinguish thinly drawn notions of autonomy of agency from the concept of critical autonomy (Gough, 2003, p 19). Liberal conceptions of autonomy entail a thin conception of the human subject and although this is less pragmatically or austerely conceived in Nussbaum's work than that of other theorists, it is still – in the sense that I am using the term – thin. Doyal and Gough's (1991) notion of 'critical autonomy' (to be discussed later in Chapter Nine) is more elusive. It hints at a human subject who is more 'thickly' bound by her interconnectedness, but who critically engages and negotiates as to her needs and the needs of other humans.

Nussbaum, like Doyal and Gough, recognises the importance of societal conditions for the realisation of human needs or functional capabilities. Capability refers to freedom to choose and Nussbaum clearly acknowledges that the realisation of such freedom depends on personal endowments and institutional contexts. She speaks of 'combined capabilities', referring to factors that are both endogenous and exogenous to the person: the abilities and freedoms of the individual and the characteristics of the market, civil society or state-based systems by which these are converted into valuable functionings (Nussbaum, 2000b). To this extent, it can be agreed that social context matters.

Social context

In this final part of the chapter I consider three quite different attempts to address the way in which social context matters: the social quality approach, the well-being in developing countries (WeD) framework and Bill Jordan's conceptualisation of social value.

First, the idea that quality of life necessarily has a social dimension has been captured in the concept of 'social quality'. It is a concept that had its beginnings in a declaration by a group of academics – The Amsterdam Declaration on the Social Quality of Europe – issued in 1997 to coincide with an EU summit at the time of the Dutch presidency. The concept was intended explicitly to capture the intention expressed in Jacques Delors' call for a social dimension to the EU and to establish a dialogue or *dialectique* between economic and social policy concerns (Beck et al, 1997). Social quality was to be a multidimensional concept and was defined as:

> ... the extent to which [European] citizens are able to participate in the social and economic life of their communities under conditions which enhance their wellbeing and individual potential. Thus the social quality experienced by citizens rests on:
>
> * the degree of *economic security*
> * the level of *social inclusion*
> * the extent of *social cohesion* or solidarity
> * the level of autonomy or *empowerment*. (Beck et al, 1997, p 3; emphasis added)

The theoretical and empirical development of the concept has been furthered by the European Foundation on Social Quality (EFSQ). The theoretical elaboration of the concept has become extremely complex (Baers et al, 2005; Phillips, 2006, pp 175-89). The four components of social quality identified above were conceptualised in relation to 'two sets of tensions' (Beck et al, 1997, p 320): between macro and micro level concerns on the one hand, and between the organisational and the community level on the other. Socioeconomic security is a macro concern, involving social processes, and is addressed organisationally. Social inclusion is a micro concern, involving individual biographical processes, but is also addressed organisationally, through policy, at an institutional level. Social cohesion is once again a macro concern, albeit one that is addressed by citizens through group action. Empowerment or competence is a micro concern, but is also addressed at community level. However, the two sets of tensions tend to overlap, since the definition of each of them appears to have been expressly informed by Jürgen Habermas's celebrated distinction between system and life world (Habermas, 1987). Later analysis (Baers et al, 2005) has sought to develop an additional layer of social constructs mapping on to the four components of social quality. This focuses on the 'constitutive interdependency' of the social actors (cited in Phillips, 2006, p 182). Thus socioeconomic security becomes a matter of social justice, social inclusion a matter of participation, social cohesion a matter of social recognition, and empowerment a matter of compassion and social responsiveness. There is richness to this analysis, but also confusion. Social quality does not of itself appear to be a unitary concept. It is not so much that as an account of human need it is too thick, it is simply that it has in its complexity, perhaps, lost coherence. We shall nonetheless return to the EFSQ social quality model in Chapter Seven.

Second, a similarly multidimensional and indeed multidisciplinary conceptual framework has been adopted by the ESRC's Well-being in Developing Countries Research Group at the University of Bath. Central to their framework are five 'key ideas':

1. The centrality of the social human being
2. Harm and needs
3. Meaning, culture and identity
4. Time and processes
5. Resourcefulness, resilience and adaptation. (McGregor, 2007, p 321)

Here is a set of concerns that may be held in common by different disciplines from across the social sciences and which can all be encompassed by a term such as 'well-being'. However, the resulting approach, like that used to define social quality, is complex. It lacks the parsimony or elegance to be hoped for in an effective or enduring theoretical framework. It turns 'well-being' into a convenient but loosely defined portmanteau term. Nonetheless, the first of the five key ideas – the centrality of the social human being – explicitly emphasises relational as opposed to individualistic approaches and the sense in which it is through social being that the wholeness of the person is established. It is on this point that McGregor calls on the argument made by the anthropologist Mary Douglas in her book with Steven Ney, *Missing persons* (1998). The argument is that much social science is premised paradoxically on the asocial individual person. The whole person – the locus of human transactions and the constructor of myth and meaning – is missing, replaced by a 'choosing machine' (Douglas and Ney, 1998, p 184). Douglas and Ney acknowledge that, potentially, this argument is 'implicitly reactionary yet radical at the same time' (1998, p 4). They recall Sahlin's celebrated claim that pre-modern hunting and gathering societies are not poor, because their wants are scarce and their means plentiful (Sahlins, 1974). But Douglas and Ney clearly do not advocate an enforced return to a supposedly carefree Stone Age existence. They acknowledge that poverty is not about lack of material goods or asymmetry of distribution; it also involves people as cultural and political creatures, whose prime need is to communicate with others and who, in communication with others, make moral judgements.

Third, we return to Bill Jordan's notion of 'social value' (2008), to which passing reference has already been made. This concept is more vaguely specified yet more encompassing than that of social quality. Jordan's argument is that the ascendancy of an economic model of welfare, the marketisation of public service delivery and the promotion of self-provisioning – especially in the Anglophone countries – have crowded out the socially valuable personal relationships, the trust and the participation that sustain the quality of people's lives. Economic theory reinterprets and remoulds the functioning of social institutions and cultural traditions as contracts for individual utility maximisation. Utility becomes 'a single calculus, and a single currency for exchange' (Jordan, 2008, p 62). In this context Jordan advances his own critique of the increasingly hegemonic concept, social capital (also touched on in Chapter Five). Social capital theory blames the Easterlin paradox (see p 105 above) on deficiencies of social capital, whereas Jordan blames it on the destruction of social value. Social value is presented as an alternative to social capital and the source of human well-being. There are resonances between Jordan's arguments and those of other thinkers referred to at various stages throughout this book, including:

- Marx and what he would have referred to as the suppression of 'use value' through 'commodity fetishism' (whereby capitalism achieves material or contractual relations between people and social relations between things);
- Baudrillard and what he would have called the ascendancy of 'sign value' (whereby the symbolic exchange between people of meaningful acts has been reduced to a system of culturally constructed but otiose signs);
- Honneth and what he would identify as the enduring prerequisites of human well-being (described by Honneth, 1995, as 'love, solidarity and rights', but by Jordan as 'intimacy, belonging and respect').

Jordan also draws on the work of Mary Douglas in order to contend that it is social not market relations that provide the cultural symbols and the meanings that underlie all human exchanges. The analysis shares the ambiguity identified by Douglas and Ney (see above) in that it is by implication potentially Luddite rather than transformative. As may be seen, there is a tendency for communitarian versions of a eudaimonic approach to conservatism. This, however, is another issue to which I shall return in Chapters Eight and Nine, when we shall consider ways of re-thinking autonomy and personhood in a dynamic and shifting social context and whether it is possible to defend and promote the good life when notions of virtue and value are eroding or changing.

Notes

[1] I have written a review of these three books for *Social Policy and Administration*, vol 43, no 3, pp 311-16, and have drawn on elements of that review in this chapter.

[2] There is a problem here with terminology since 'communitarianism' is a label that has been attached to some very different ideas. Philosophical communitarianism may be and has been drawn on by liberals, by socialists or indeed by those who seek alternative ideological narratives. In this light, Sandel, MacIntyre and Walzer have been described (some might say inaccurately) as 'left' communitarians or 'radical democrats'. However, the term 'communitarianism' has also been claimed by or attributed to New Right and Third Way thinkers, including, on occasions, the proponents of social capital theory such as Putnam, discussed in Chapter Five.

[3] Social democracy, I would argue, is very much a hybrid ideology. It has also drawn on Fabian or reformist strands of socialist thinking. In practice, however, social democratic policy has tended to reflect Kantian moral assumptions, rather than modified neo-Marxist ambitions.

[4] In fairness, this may not have been Nussbaum's intention: see *Frontiers of justice* (2006).

Summary

- This chapter has proposed a distinction between 'thin' and 'thick' conceptions of human need or human well-being. It is a broadly drawn distinction that rolls together a number of ways in which the metaphors of thin and thick may be applied. But it is a peculiar (in the literal sense of that word) adaptation. The sense that best captures this is provided through discussion of the distinctive hedonic and eudaimonic notions of well-being. The hedonic is 'thin' insofar as it may be individualistic, utilitarian and/or abstract. The eudaimonic is 'thick' insofar as it may be solidaristic, in some sense spiritual and/or organic.
- It has been argued that thin or hedonic notions of need are implicated not only in the classically utilitarian social policies of the 19th century (of which more will be said in the next chapter) but in the emergence of a form of welfare economics premised on cost-efficiency analysis. However, recent developments within certain branches of economics and psychology have focused on the Easterlin paradox, which suggests that rising affluence and state welfare provision in modern developed economies are not necessarily making people any happier. The challenge is that of ensuring that economic development and human happiness remain in step with each other.
- It has been argued that thick or eudaimonic notions of need are implicated in potentially contradictory ways both in liberal conceptions of social justice on the one hand, and in post-Enlightenment republicanism and more recent radical strands of communitarian thinking on the other. Recent developments within the social sciences have elaborated on the psychosocial dimension to human well-being – the focus is on the self-determination of the human individual within her social context, but at the same time the social suffering that may be inflicted by social inequalities and injustices. Other accounts have focused on aspects of the quality of human lives, with attempts to specify richer accounts of what human capabilities might encompass, new conceptions of 'social quality' and new arguments about the promotion and production of 'social value'. The challenge is to restore some priority for the constitutive social dimension of human life. These differently conceived challenges imply different approaches to social policy.

Questions for discussion:

- What would you say is the difference and what is the relationship between 'thin' and 'thick' needs? Is this a necessary or helpful distinction?
- 'The most practicable and worthwhile test of a good social policy is whether it succeeds in maximising human happiness.' Explain whether and why you might agree or disagree with this statement.

- What constitutes a 'good life' and what business is it of social policy to make sure we lead one?

seven

Human need and social policy

- This chapter will introduce a taxonomy or model, the aim of which is to simplify the discussion of human need. The model is constructed around the two key distinctions developed earlier in the book: between inherent and interpreted need on the one hand, and between thin and thick need on the other.
- The four broad categories of human need that constitute the model are outlined and explained, namely, circumstantial, particular, common and universal needs.
- The model is related to similar ones and each category related to the different approaches and traditions that have been developed or applied in social policy.
- The scope and limits of the model are briefly discussed.

In this chapter I shall endeavour to bring together the threads of the various arguments about human need that have been presented so far, and I am doing so for a particular purpose. Our interest in this book is to relate different approaches to our understandings of human need to social policy. To do this I shall present a simplified taxonomy or classification of different approaches to human need. This will encompass the range of approaches so far discussed within just four broad categories. I shall then examine each of those categories in relation to its application within social policy.

Insofar as I shall draw on specific historical and contemporary examples of social policy provision, these will be illustrative, rather than exhaustive.

A taxonomy of needs-based approaches

My taxonomy is outlined in *Figure 7.1*. The object is not to add another layer of complexity so much as simplify or at least clarify the variety of conceptual distinctions already discussed and to locate them in relation to each other. The taxonomy is no more than a model. Although it is reductive, its purpose is heuristic: to help us make sense of an otherwise bewildering plethora of intersecting ideas and debates. In real life, many approaches to human need do not neatly fit into one of the categories defined here: they are likely to straddle more than one. The categories are ideal types, and not necessarily accurate descriptions of any particular approach.

Figure 7.1: A taxonomy of needs-based approaches

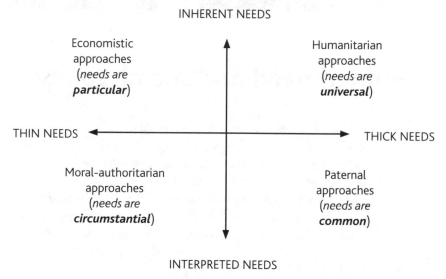

It may be seen that I have already introduced the four broad categories – the moral-authoritarian, the economistic, the paternalistic and the humanistic approaches – in Chapter One (see **Table 1.2**), when we first addressed the significance that may be inferred from different responses to need, and also in Chapters Four and Five. Now, however, I have ordered these four approaches around two axes, to provide a two-dimensional schema or model. The first, the vertical axis, represents the distinction I drew in Chapters Two and Three between inherent and interpreted conceptions of need. The second, the horizontal axis, represents the distinction I drew in Chapter Six between thin and thick conceptions of need. It is important to emphasise that both axes represent continua or spectra of interdependent understandings and for the purposes of the discussion in this book each has been quite particularly drawn.[1]

There are at least three other two-dimensional models or schema with which the taxonomy in **Figure 7.1** may be compared. The first is the cultural theory model of the anthropologist, Mary Douglas (1977; Douglas and Ney, 1998). The second is the liberally inspired typology of human need devised by Johan Galtung (1994, ch 3). The third is an essentially social-democratically inspired model relating not to human need but the components and constructs of 'social quality', as advanced by the EFSQ, discussed in Chapter Six (Beck et al, 1997; Baers et al, 2005; and see Phillips, 2006, pp 175-89). The EFSQ model represents, I believe, an unduly complex and somewhat clumsy model, but it is widely respected and I include it in this analysis because it provides an illustrative counterpoint to the Galtung model. None of the three models equates directly with my taxonomy. Nor is it intended that the taxonomy in ***Figure 7.1*** should in any way supersede these alternative models. Nonetheless, in the following discussion I shall briefly contrast the various models, because it may be useful to mention the resonances between these taxonomies and my own.[2]

Inherent–interpreted continuum

The inherent–interpreted distinction is intended to capture the difference between the idea that human need vests in the person and the idea that human need can or should be defined independently of the person. The two can seldom be completely dissociated since they will inevitably feed off each other.

Mary Douglas's influential concept of 'grid', which captures the relative extent to which people in any culture may be bound by shared classifications and structures, equates, albeit only loosely, with the inherent–interpreted continuum. Inherent conceptions of need implicitly or explicitly require some theory or doctrine of personhood, while interpreted conceptions are more pragmatic or grounded in everyday human experience. Habermas (1987) similarly distinguishes between system and life world and Galtung (1994, p 57) between 'structure-dependent' and 'actor-dependent' human needs. These equate, albeit with some degree of ambiguity, to our distinction between inherent and interpreted conceptions of need: the former are premised on an element of abstract or systemic understanding; the latter on perceived realities or received wisdom. Finally, the EFSQ (see above) draws a similar distinction between the realm of systems, institutions and organisations on the one hand, and communities and groups on the other. In some instances the correspondence between these various conceptually drawn dimensions and the inherent–interpreted dimension is not intuitively evident. This is partly because there is a mistaken tendency to assume that – whether for good or for ill – a fixed hierarchy exists between the opposing poles of the continua involved: a weak grid is subordinate to a strong one; the life world is dominated by systems, the actor by structures and communities by institutions. However, particularly in the case of the inherent–interpreted continuum this does not apply.

Inherent conceptions of need can, although abstract, be simplistic or naïve; interpreted conceptions, although pragmatic, can be elaborate and conceptually sophisticated; and, of course, vice versa. In a historical sense there is fluidity of meaning between the poles of the inherent–interpreted continuum and each kind of conception has been or may become indebted to the other for its own meanings.

Thin–thick continuum

The thin–thick distinction, as here conceived, is intended to capture the difference between the instrumental needs that may be ascribed to the human individual and the experiential needs that may be ascribed to human beings in their social context. Once again, it is a conceptual distinction that is not always easy to sustain because the opposite poles of the continuum are often informed by or interact with each other. It is a conceptual distinction that is consonant with other conceptual insights, such as the classic distinction between *hedonia* and *eudaimonia* and Walzer's distinction between minimalist and maximalist moralities (Walzer, 1994). These have been adequately discussed in Chapter Six. However, the thin–thick continuum also resonates with dimensions defined by some other two-dimensional conceptual schema.

The second influential concept developed within Mary Douglas's cultural theory is that of 'group', which captures the relative extent to which people in any culture are socially incorporated. This equates with the thin–thick continuum (at least so far as I have chosen to define it), in as much as thin conceptions of need are characteristically individualistically drawn, whereas thick conceptions may accommodate more solidaristic understandings. The second dimension in Galtung's typology of human need contrasts material and non-material needs. This equates, in part, with the thin–thick continuum in as much as it captures key elements of the same hedonic–eudaimonic distinction as the thin–thick continuum. Finally, the second dimension envisaged for the purposes of the EFSQ's conceptual model entails a distinction between micro-biographical processes and macro-societal processes. This also equates, in part, with the thin–thick continuum in as much as it captures a distinction between individual and social levels of analysis.

Circumstantial needs

We turn first, therefore, to the bottom left-hand quadrant in *Figure 7.1*, in which human need is thinly conceived and interpreted. This encompasses what I have previously referred to as moral–authoritarian approaches. They are moral–authoritarian (rather than 'ethical'[3]) in the sense that they assume first, that the baseness (actual or potential) of human nature must be constrained by authority and second, that judgements must be made about what people deserve. They are quintessentially hedonic and utilitarian. They entail interpretation in the sense that needs are seen to arise and are evaluated in relation to the specific context and an individual's personal circumstances. Needs are circumstantial.

Locating circumstantial needs in relation to other models

People who satisfy circumstantial needs are survivors. In a study of popular discourse that explored the ways in which a diverse sample of individuals made sense of and talked about their place as citizens in a highly unequal society (in this instance, the UK),[4] one of the discursive 'moral repertoires' on which people were observed to draw was the *survivalist* repertoire (Dean, 1999). The survivalist moral repertoire assumes that those in society who are deprived have experienced bad luck. The maxim is 'Everyone for her or himself'. Everybody must get by as best she can. To survive you have to be strong, smart or street-wise. But bad things happen. And although survivalism is fatalistic in terms of its attitude to the vicissitudes of everyday life, it is also morally authoritarian. In the struggle for survival there have to be rules, and if you or I must go by the rules, so must everybody else. Rules should be enforced.

As indicated, there are other two-dimensional conceptual schema to which the taxonomy represented in *Figure 7.1* has varying or passing degrees of similarity:

- The corresponding quadrant in Mary Douglas's cultural theory schema is the *weak grid/weak group* quadrant that is inhabited in some versions of her scheme by the 'robust' person (Douglas and Ney, 1998, p 109). We can infer that the robust person is a survivalist who adapts to changing circumstances.
- The corresponding quadrant in Galtung's typology of need is the *material need/actor-dependent* quadrant that is characterised by 'survival' needs. Although this appears at first sight to be closely resonant with the taxonomy in *Figure 7.1*, Galtung's antonym for survival is 'violence', reflecting a somewhat starker focus, but one that nonetheless retains some resonance with the idea that circumstantial needs are defined in relation to external hazards.
- The corresponding quadrant on the EFSQ model – relating to components and constructs of social quality (Beck et al, 1997, p 321;

Baers et al, 2005) – is the *micro-biographical/groups and communities* quadrant in which references are made to 'empowerment' on the one hand, and 'compassion' and 'responsiveness' on the other. This may seem confusing, but the dimensions around which the taxonomy is built involve an inverted emphasis. It is addressing alleged deficits. It is possible to see, from the normative premises of the social quality approach, that the achievement of social quality rather than individual survival would indeed require some form of *social* empowerment and the realisation or injection of the kind of compassion and responsiveness that may be weak or absent in the context that this quadrant is supposed to represent.

From these contrasting theoretical perspectives it may be deduced that the space in which the strong can survive in spite of the hazards of the world can be unforgiving so far as those who fail or are prevented from meeting their circumstantial needs. To what extent has social policy responded?

Responding to circumstance in practice

Such responses are those which pre-dated the 'modern' welfare state, but which are still present in various aspects of contemporary social policy. The origins of such responses go back to the era of the Poor Laws.

Laws relating to the control of the poor had been developed across medieval Europe and were subsequently adapted to accommodate the advent of industrial capitalism. As the role of the administrative state began to develop, such laws were intended to supplement or to regulate the provision of charity to people who, through dispossession or destitution, faced adverse circumstances. Although the exact provenance of the expression 'cold as charity' is unclear, its meaning is more than clear. It bespeaks a response to circumstantial need that is borne not out of love, warmth or compassion, but cold calculation. In this respect there were in the 19th century two distinct policy innovations whose legacy endures. They are exemplified by the development in England of the Victorian workhouse under the 'New' Poor Law of 1834, and by the subsequent emergence of the social casework method pioneered by members of the Charity Organisation Society (COS), founded in 1869.

The workhouse was not a 19th-century invention since it had existed in a variety of guises under older versions of the Poor Laws. The agrarian revolution, by displacing people from the land, created circumstantial need in a highly visible form and workhouses were one way of containing that need by hiding the poor from view under conditions that were sometimes compassionate and secure, sometimes punitive and squalid. However, the function of the workhouse under the New Poor Law was neither compassionate nor punitive, but the application of a coldly utilitarian logic. This has already been alluded to in the discussion of Benthamite utilitarianism in Chapter Six. The new workhouse regime was centrally regulated and contrived to ensure that paupers be adequately nourished and hygienically accommodated, but that their lives should be harsher than the lives of those who were managing to survive outside the workhouse. This was achieved by way of forced (and sometimes wholly unproductive) labour for the able-bodied; by the separation of children from parents and wives from husbands; and by the imposition of a Spartan environment and unremitting daily routine (de Schweinitz, 1961).

Although the workhouse shared with the prison certain forms of disciplinary 'technology' (Foucault, 1977), the workhouse was *not* the prison. Utilitarian logic entailed certain key binary distinctions, between the perishing and the dangerous on the one hand (Morris, 1994), and between the deserving and the undeserving on the other (Fraser, 1984). Prison was for the dangerous, the workhouse for the perishing, that is to say, for the circumstantially needy. But among the perishing classes, those who were undeserving were to be put to work, while those who were deserving of relief might, under certain circumstances, be considered for 'out-relief' (for assistance, that is, outside the workhouse).

The job of distinguishing between the perishing and the dangerous (the innocent and the guilty) belonged to the criminal justice system. The job of distinguishing between the deserving and the undeserving required a different kind of system, based on a new method. Such a method was found in a special kind of social casework developed by charity organisation societies, which sprang up not only in England, but in other European countries and the US. The object of charity organisation societies was to systematise charitable giving and ensure that philanthropic relief was efficient and effective, not indiscriminate. To this end, the middle-class volunteers of the English COS worked not only to root out scroungers, but also to identify families that could be saved from destitution by judicious intervention. The COS, it has been said, was primarily concerned to prevent 'not suffering, but sin' (Stedman-Jones, 1971, p 271), to ensure that profligacy and idleness (among the poor) should never be rewarded and that even those in the most precarious of circumstances should be kept honest, thrifty and industrious. This was achieved by rigorous scrutiny, through visiting, interviewing and meticulous record keeping. These methods laid the foundations of social casework, a set of processes that could be applied to the provision of state-administered as much as philanthropic relief, and a set of skills on which the modern social work profession would in time be built (Younghusband, 1964).

The workhouse is now a thing of the past and social work is identified as the quintessential *caring* profession. And yet, certain of the social policy principles of the Poor Law era are enduring (Harris, 2007). Especially since the 1970s 'crisis' of the modern welfare state (Mishra, 1984), moral-authoritarian approaches to need as a circumstantial phenomenon have been increasingly in evidence. Now, as then, there are two aspects of a person's circumstances that are taken into account: work status and/or dependency status. In this context 'work' means labour market participation and 'dependency' refers to state support.

The centrality of work status is manifest in the mantra of the so-called Third Way, as coined by the UK's New Labour government in the late 1990s: 'work for those who can, support for those who cannot' (DSS, 1998, p 3). The growing emphasis on 'work for those who can' and on welfare-to-work policies in many of the world's developed economies (Lødemel and Trickey, 2001) has led some critics to suggest we are witnessing a transition from the welfare state to the 'workfare state' (for example Jessop, 2002). The transition, however, is complex and it encompasses different approaches. Most importantly, there is a distinction between 'work-first' and 'human capital' approaches to welfare-to-work. The latter we shall consider in relation to particular needs in the next section. The former, however, is an approach that insists that welfare recipients should work for their relief, or else that they should take any job – however poorly paid and uncongenial – or be denied relief. It entails a coercive form of conditionality. The approach is most commonly associated with workfare arrangements in the US, but elements of the approach are clearly in evidence elsewhere (Peck, 2001). The work-first approach addresses nothing but a person's work status and may potentially be as coercive as the workhouse.

The centrality of dependency status is evident in several contexts. In some countries of the developed world (Gough et al, 1997) and in the developing world (Hall and Midgley, 2004) the administration of means-tested social assistance is still locally regulated and undertaken by professional social workers. People whose circumstances are such that they must depend on a state safety net are still subject to scrutiny by variations on the social casework method. In other parts of the world (especially Anglophone countries), however, social work professionals are not concerned with the administration of social assistance, but the provision of personal social services for the most vulnerable and dependent people. While state provision for health, education and pensions, for example, are bedrock services to which all or most citizens are entitled, the personal social services are reserved for the more highly dependent: for children at risk and disabled or frail elderly people in need of care from the state. In these countries social work has or had attained a particular professional status, based on training that included, among other things, a grounding in psychotherapeutic methods concerned not with purely circumstantial needs but needs inherent to the individual (Halmos, 1973). More recently that status has been to some extent compromised by the advent of a new managerialist approach to the administration of public services (Clarke and Newman, 1997). This managerialism can have a tendency to refocus the attention of the personal social services on circumstantial needs. In certain branches of the profession, social workers have been effectively reconstituted as 'care managers', responsible primarily for devising efficient care packages appropriate to the circumstances of the client and what she needs to survive.

Particular needs

Second, we turn to the top left-hand quadrant in *Figure 7.1*, in which human need is thinly conceived but regarded not as circumstantial but as inherent to the human subject. This encompasses what I have previously referred to as economistic approaches. They are economistic in the sense first, that the human subject that is envisaged is *homo œconomicus* (see Chapter Two), and second, because they take seriously the wants and preferences that people express, given the freedom to choose. They are not utilitarian approaches in the Benthamite sense, precisely because they demand the freedom of the subject, but they still assume that people are hedonically motivated. They entail inherent conceptions of need in the sense that the individual is constructed as an economic actor who functions as a producer and consumer of goods (in the broadest sense of that term). The person is defined by her individuality and needs are particular to the individual.

Locating particular needs in relation to other models

People who satisfy particular needs are economic actors, but also unique individuals. In the above-mentioned study of popular discourse, another of the 'moral repertoires' on which people were observed to draw was the *entrepreneurial* repertoire. The entrepreneurial moral repertoire assumes that those in society who are deprived have experienced performative failure. Some people will fail because they are less able or less hard working than others, others because they are denied the opportunity to develop their unique skills or abilities. The maxim is 'May the best person win', but competition should always take place on a level playing field. Everybody should have the chance to succeed. Entrepreneurialism is liberal individualist.

Once again we can contrast the taxonomy presented in *Figure 7.1* to a related two-dimensional conceptual schema:

- The corresponding quadrant in Mary Douglas's cultural theory schema is the *strong grid/weak group* quadrant that is inhabited in some versions of her scheme by the 'unpredictable' person. We can infer that the unpredictable person is an entrepreneur, or potential entrepreneur, an individualistic calculator, responding to opportunities as they present themselves in order to satisfy her particular needs.
- The corresponding quadrant in Galtung's typology of need is the *material need/structure-dependent* quadrant that is characterised by 'well-being' needs. At first glance the resonance with the taxonomy in *Figure 7.1* is obscure, but Galtung's antonym for well-being is 'misery', reflecting that it is a distinctively hedonic interpretation of well-being that is implied. Particular needs are defined in relation to a hedonic calculus.
- The corresponding quadrant on the EFSQ taxonomy – relating to components and constructs of social quality – is the *micro-biographical/ institutions and organisations* quadrant in which references are made to 'inclusion' on the one hand, and 'participation' on the other. Recalling that the EFSQ's critical aim is that economic growth should go hand in hand with social quality, the emphasis on social inclusion and social participation is presented as the necessary corollary to economic inclusion and/or labour market participation. It is important to those who propose this model that entrepreneurialism and economic opportunity should not squeeze out the opportunity for meeting social needs.

From these contrasting theoretical perspectives it may be deduced that the space in which the enterprising must compete in order to pursue their well-being is a risky one and that those whose particular needs are not met face exclusion. Once again, to what extent has social policy responded?

Promoting particularity in practice

There are, broadly speaking, three responses attuned to particular need: means testing, which has a long history; policies to promote what in current jargon is called 'human capital development', although such policies also have a history; and, more recently, equal opportunities policy.

The beginnings of systematic means testing may arguably be traced to the Speenhamland system in late 18th-century England. This has already been encountered in Chapter Four as an illustration of the ways in which policy makers have sought to measure the particular needs of particular households. The Speenhamland system entailed a crude measure based on the number of loaves of bread a family of any given size might need in order to survive. However, as a way of 'targeting' assistance where it is most needed, means testing has developed into an often finely-tuned technique and an essential feature of social policy intervention (Dean, 2002). Means testing is generally associated with the administration of social assistance safety nets (Dixon, 1999; Walker, 2005), although it is also widely used as a method of rationing the distribution of other sorts of assistance, whether in cash (examples range from student maintenance to home improvement grants) or kind (examples range from free medical prescriptions to social care provision). Means testing attracts a variety of criticisms. In practice it can be deeply unpopular because it is tainted by association with the circumstances under which the technique has been developed. Modern social assistance schemes are the direct successors of the Poor Laws and in some countries the transition has been partial or incremental. In many instances the application of a means test to determine eligibility for social assistance could not easily be dissociated from the application of a workhouse test to determine whether a supplicant deserved to receive relief without admission to the workhouse. A test to ascertain particular needs can be made to look just as intrusive and stigmatising as a test of circumstantial needs, especially if it entails intimate scrutiny of one's daily living arrangements and personal means. Social policy commentators have also argued that means testing is administratively complex on the one hand, and socially divisive on the other: there is an inherent danger that means-tested provision reserved for the poorest in society will tend to become an inferior or second-rate service (Titmuss, 1974; Deacon and Bradshaw, 1983). Nonetheless, supporters of means testing claim it is efficient. In countries such as Australia which rely principally on means-tested forms of social security provision – set at relatively generous levels – it is claimed that means testing need not be stigmatising (Castles and Mitchell, 1993). And at the global level, the so-called 'Washington Consensus' (Williamson, 1990) adhered to by the principal international financial institutions, contends that means-tested safety nets are the only kind of provision that is affordable in the poorest countries of the world.

'Human capital' is a lately fashionable concept encountered in Chapter Five when discussing the ways in which these same international financial institutions also appear to be appropriating and, arguably, misinterpreting Sen's notion of human capabilities. This conflation of concepts is possible in part, perhaps, because human capital is a concept lately explored by sociologists (see for example Bourdieu, 1997) as well as economists. The term itself was originally coined by Adam Smith (1776) to refer to the stock of skills and knowledge possessed by the wage labourer. Welfare economists such as Pigou (1928; see also Chapter Three, this book) used the term in a narrow utilitarian sense to refer to investment in personal productive capacity, but Becker (1993) firmly established the concept within standard economics to encompass the idea that public investment in individual education, training and healthcare amounted to an investment in productive human capital. The distinctive form of social liberalism that informed the beginnings of the British welfare state at the start of the 20th century (Fraser, 1984) drew on an implicit concept of human capital. The preoccupation of the era was the pursuit of national efficiency: to ensure the fitness of the nation's human stock to compete. There was more to this than crass utilitarianism, since promoting the health and literacy of the population as a whole meant focusing on particular needs. It required the development of dispensaries, clinics and health-visiting services; properly regulated and inspected schools; hygienic and better supervised housing; and forms of scrutiny and surveillance that reached into the particular spaces in which people lived out their lives (Ellis, 2000, pp 6-7). There was a realisation that the productive capacity of the national stock was vested in individual human beings. This particular era was later superseded by the Keynesian/Beveridgean strand of social liberalism. But the multifaceted policy regime associated with the so-called 'Third Way' (Giddens, 1998) that came to the fore at the close of the 20th century encompassed not only a utilitarian work-first approach, but also in several countries an explicitly human capital-oriented approach to welfare-to-work premised on post-Keynesian 'supply-side' economic principles. This amounted to a reversion to national efficiency principles, in the sense that the emphasis was on maximising the skills and productivity of the domestic labour force in order to better compete within a global economy. The human capital approach to welfare-to-work entailed attention to skills, motivational training, rehabilitation and support, mediated, for example, through the ministrations of personal advisers. The attention given to education policy was similarly instrumentally oriented to human capital production.

The revival of a particular human capital-oriented approach to individual need has been associated with new kinds of conditionality in social welfare provision (see Chapter Six). This is not the brutal conditionality of the workhouse test, but a more constructive conditionality that seeks to tailor the terms on which provision is made to a particular individual or family so as to enhance conditions for the creation of human capital. An example is the introduction of conditional cash transfer programmes in Latin America, where social assistance to poor families is made conditional on the children of the families attending health clinics and going to school (Britto, 2006). This is an example of how ambiguous social policy interventions can be. Is this a response that couples the families' circumstantial need for social assistance with the universal needs of the children for health and education provision? Or is it best understood as an intervention that targets the particular needs of children in poor households to develop their human capital?

The third way in which social policy addresses particular need is through measures to promote equality of opportunity so as to ensure that people can participate on equal terms as workers, consumers and users of public services (including education), whatever their particular needs. In our discussion of recognition in Chapter Five I referred to the implications of human diversity for the ability of social policies to meet human need. The distinctively liberal solution to the particularity of need is to try and guarantee equality of access to jobs, goods and services. This may be attempted by legislating to outlaw discrimination on the grounds of sex, 'race' and disability, and indeed sexuality and religion. The EU requires its member states to implement such legislation (Geyer, 2000; Marlier et al, 2007). The disadvantage of such legislation is that remedies against discrimination must usually be pursued by means of individual forms of legal redress, a process that can be technically difficult, while delivering, at best, personal relief rather than systemic change. The recent creation in the UK of an Equality and Human Rights Commission (also discussed in Chapter Five) explicitly links equality of opportunity issues to the human rights agenda. The implication is that particular needs associated, for example, with gender, ethnicity or disability are addressed within a framework of abstract principles and formal guarantees, which may or may not accord with the concrete experiences and substantive demands of women, minorities or disabled people. This is a discussion to which I shall return in Chapter Eight.

Common needs

Third, then, we turn to the bottom right hand quadrant in *Figure 7.1*, in which human need is thickly conceived but is interpreted. This encompasses what I have previously referred to as paternalistic approaches. They are paternalistic in the sense that human beings are regarded as being by nature vulnerable creatures in need of security and protection. They are thick interpretations in the sense that needs are situated axiomatically in their social context: security and protection are quintessentially social needs. There is a eudaimonic dimension to the way in which security is conceived, since it is not only physical security (protection against physical harm) but also ontological security (protection through belonging) that is valued. Needs are interpreted in the act of meeting them – by family or community elders, by sovereign protectors, by representative brokers and/or by benign policy makers. Needs, by definition, are held in common with others.

Locating common needs in relation to other models

People who satisfy common needs share common vulnerabilities as members of a particular society. In the above-mentioned study of popular discourse another of the 'moral repertoires' on which people were observed to draw was the *conformist* repertoire. The conformist moral repertoire assumes it is inevitable that some people in society will end up deprived. The maxim is 'The poor shall always be with us', and we must have compassion for the poor. It is by accepting our place within and our obligations to the social order that we ensure that everybody who belongs to that order is best protected from the risks of deprivation. Conformism is socially conservative.

Once again we can contrast the taxonomy presented in *Figure 7.1* with related two-dimensional conceptual schema:

- The corresponding quadrant in Mary Douglas's cultural theory schema is the *weak grid/strong group* quadrant that is inhabited in some versions of her scheme by the 'person under duress'. The notion of 'duress' implies that the person is under pressure to conform, which is consistent up to a point with the taxonomy in *Figure 7.1*, although where needs are perceived to be held in common, conformity can be achieved as much through acquiescence as duress.
- The corresponding quadrant in Galtung's liberally inspired typology of need is the *non-material need/actor-dependent* quadrant that is characterised by 'freedom' needs. Once again the resonance with the taxonomy in *Figure 7.1* is obscure until one considers Galtung's antonym. The antonym for freedom is 'repression', from which it may be seen that like Douglas, Galtung is concerned that conformity may be achieved by duress or an erosion of liberty. Provision to meet common needs may stifle freedom of choice.
- The corresponding quadrant on the EFSQ taxonomy is the *macro-societal/groups and communities* quadrant in which references are made to 'cohesion' on the one hand, and 'social recognition' on the other. In the context of EFSQ's aim to promote social quality, the notion of social cohesion reflects positively on the potential benefits of people sharing in the satisfaction of their common needs. The engagement with social recognition – a concept discussed in Chapter Five – implies that the needs of social groups and communities should be recognised and that in the pursuit of cohesion, sight should not be lost of human diversity.

From these contrasting theoretical perspectives it may be deduced that the space in which vulnerable or hard-pressed individuals must conform so as to have their common needs met is potentially repressive and neglectful of the diversity of need. What role has social policy played?

Safeguarding the common in practice

We consider now the kinds of social policy that represent a response attuned to *common* need. The word 'common' refers, sometimes simultaneously, to that which is ordinary and that which is shared. Common need, like common sense, is woven from the threads of precedent and custom: it is culturally constructed (Thompson, 1993). The essence of commonality is shared heritage on the one hand, and shared fortunes on the other. In social policy terms this is represented in at least three ways: through the traditions of *noblesse oblige* as the guarantee of social order; through the Catholic principle of subsidiarity; and through the development of risk-sharing forms of social insurance.

The obligations of the medieval Sovereign, the feudal Lord and the established Church to the common people, because they were supposedly divinely ordained, were to be gladly accepted. They purported to be borne not of cold charity, but sincere concern for the lower social orders. The reality could be different. Nonetheless, such notions of responsibility provided the impetus for informal welfare provision and for an inconsistent patchwork of provision through parish institutions. The influence and assumptions of the tradition survived the eclipse of aristocratic power and retained resonances within the expectations of a more or less deferent working class and the pretensions of an affluent but sometimes fearful middle class. The hope was that the common people would continue to look to their betters not directly for the satisfaction of their needs, but for the maintenance of the good order that guaranteed that such needs could properly be met. For example, when in England provision was first made in 1870 for universal elementary education, one of its primary purposes was held to be 'the safe working of our constitutional system' (Forster, 1870, pp 104-5).

Particularly important in Western Europe were principles and traditions – both catholic in a literal sense and Catholic in a religious sense – that placed great store on family and kinship networks as the foundations of an inclusive social order. The principle of subsidiarity – which would re-surface in European political discourse in the late 20th century (Geyer, 2000) – asserted that for the maintenance of natural order and social solidarity, responsibility for meeting needs should rest so far as practicable at the lowest possible level within the social hierarchy. Only if family could not provide should responsibility be accepted by other institutions. Family, therefore, was vested with considerable cultural and symbolic significance and this continues to be reflected in pro-family policies of conservative welfare state regimes (Esping-Andersen, 1990).

The most significant way in which common need has been met through modern social policy intervention occurred with the development of social insurance. This began at the end of the 19th century in Germany, whose Chancellor, Otto von Bismarck, sought tactically to outmanoeuvre the organised labour movement by providing systems, in the first instance, for health and accident insurance (Gilbert, 1966). Social insurance would become the big idea of the 20th century. It was imitated, adopted or adapted in countries around the world and extended to cover the risk not just of sickness, but unemployment. By extending coverage to the 'risk' of old age (that is, retirement), social insurance provided the basis for financing state pension schemes. The intentions of the original social insurance schemes were to guard against political unrest and to preserve social order. They succeeded precisely because they were capable of building and sustaining solidarity, of providing for needs held in common across the social classes. The popularity of the social insurance principle is enduring and rests to this day on people's endorsement of the idea that having paid contributions into a common fund they are morally entitled to have their needs met (Dean and Rodgers, 2004).

Universal needs

Finally, we come to the top right-hand quadrant in *Figure 7.1*, in which human need is thickly conceived but is regarded as inherent. This encompasses what I have previously referred to as humanistic or humanitarian approaches. They are humanistic in the ethical sense.[5] The human subject is construed not as passively vulnerable, but as a social actor, defined by her humanity. Such approaches are thickly conceived, because our species being is constituted through social engagement and because humanity, in the eudaimonic sense, requires fulfilment. Humanistic approaches entail inherent conceptions of need because the individual is construed as a relational self who must be able meaningfully to participate in human society. Such needs are universal.

Locating universal needs in relation to other models

People who satisfy universal needs would, in Heller's (1974) sense, be truly or 'radically' human. Alternatively, they may be thought of as citizens, whether citizens of a particular welfare state (Marshall, 1950) or even global citizens (Held, 1995). In the above-mentioned study of popular discourse the last of the 'moral repertoires' on which people were observed to draw was the *reformist* repertoire. The reformist moral repertoire considers it an injustice that some people in society should remain deprived. The maxim is 'Social justice for all'. The demand is for greater substantive equality in society and for fairness in the distribution of resources. Reformism, however, may be liberal collectivist on the one hand, or social democratic on the other.

Once more, we can contrast the taxonomy presented in ***Figure 7.1*** with a related two-dimensional conceptual schema.

- The corresponding quadrant in Mary Douglas's cultural theory schema is the *strong grid/strong group* quadrant that is inhabited in some versions of her scheme by the person who 'needs structure'. The need for structure in Douglas's theory is culturally imposed, although arguably what she regards as cultural imposition others might see as the realisation of a person's social humanity.
- The corresponding quadrant in Galtung's typology of need is the *non-material need/structure-dependent* quadrant that is characterised by 'identity' needs. Galtung, it would appear, is concerned lest universalism and an excess of structure should stifle the realisation of individual identity and people's need for eudaimonic well-being. His antonym for identity is 'alienation'.
- From the opposing ideological perspective of the EFSQ, the corresponding quadrant in its taxonomy is the *macro-societal/institutions and organisations* quadrant in which references are made to 'security' on the one hand, and 'social justice' on the other. Here there is a direct resonance with the taxonomy in ***Figure 7.1*** and the idea that social and economic security is a universal need and, by implication, structural reform that promotes provision for universal need is not inimical to eudaimonic well-being.

From these contrasting theoretical perspectives it may be deduced that the space in which our lives are lived may be justly structured to reformist ends in order to satisfy universal needs, although possibly, some would claim, at the expense of individual autonomy. So what has the role of social policy been?

Realising the universal in practice

As already indicated, social policy responses to *universal* need are premised on principles of social citizenship, a concept that is in itself capable of a spectrum of interpretations. In practice, universal needs may be variously construed. There is near consensus between social liberals and social democrats, however, that health is a universal need of all citizens that may be met by centrally funded healthcare provision. Beyond this, however, the citizen can appear in different guises: the worker citizen, the dependent citizen and the future citizen (Lister, 2003; Dwyer, 2004b).

Provision for worker citizens has in practice been made primarily, not by way of citizens' or basic income schemes (Fitzpatrick, 1999), but by way of modified forms of social insurance provision (Dean, 2002; Walker, 2005). The enduring assumption is that most needs should be met through wages from paid employment and that the function of social policy is to provide replacement incomes when employment is interrupted. Beveridgean national insurance schemes have aimed to make modest but comprehensive provision, while preserving the fiction of an actuarial link between the contributions that workers pay during their working lives and the benefits and pensions they may receive in the event of unemployment, sickness, maternity or in retirement. In reality, 'pay as you go' social insurance schemes can be extensively redistributive and social insurance schemes in some countries, especially the Nordic welfare regimes, are deliberately contrived to be both inclusive and generous to the point where benefits are virtually universal.

Dependent citizens, other than temporarily dependent workers, fare differently. Disabled people excluded from social insurance arrangements may receive contingent cash benefits to meet their income needs, social services to meet their care needs and/or other personal support to enable them to live independently. Citizens who provide unpaid care for disabled or frail elderly relatives may receive a contingent cash benefit. (There is a possibility that non-working parents [mainly mothers] who care for children, so long as they do not engage with the labour market and must depend on another wage earner, may temporarily cease in one sense to be 'social' citizens.)

The needs of children as 'future citizens'[6] may be met partly by way of contingent cash transfers (child benefits or family allowances) paid in recognition that society shares a universal responsibility for the care of future generations (Land, 1975), through other forms of support for families and directly through childcare provision. Just as fundamentally, however, from a humanistic perspective is children and young people's need for education. Education is regarded not merely as an integrative function catering to common need, or as an instrument of human capital development catering to particular needs, but as a universal human need required for the development of the human personality (Nowak, 2001).

The critics of universalistic social policy provision – from both left and right of the ideological spectrum (see Illich et al, 1977; Drover and Kerans, 1993, introduction) – contend that it vests too much administrative power in the apparatuses of the state and affords too much discretionary power to welfare professions. Judgements about what is or what might be universal about human need are made at too great a distance from the citizen. This is a concern I shall address in Chapters Eight and Nine.

Conclusion

The taxonomy proposed in this chapter is a highly reductive model. The categories of need defined by the taxonomy cut through the distinctions advanced in established theories. It can be seen, for example, that Doyal and Gough's (1991) theory of human need addresses both particular and universal needs. It is sometimes contended that Doyal and Gough's ostensibly universalistic theory entails a 'thin' conception of substantive need (Drover and Kerans, 1993), although, especially through its conceptualisation of critical autonomy, it undeniably offers the prospect of 'thick' interpretation. Bradshaw's (1972) taxonomy of human need skirts around and across both circumstantial and common needs categories, while illustrating the spectrum of needs interpretations to which policy makers may in practice react.

It is also the case that, although it can be articulated with the above model, Esping-Andersen's (1990) typology of welfare regimes does not map neatly against it. As an approximation it might be said that Liberal welfare regimes respond to particular needs, Conservative regimes to common needs and Social Democratic regimes to universal needs. In reality, however, it can be seen that the classic welfare states of the post-Second World War 'golden age' (Esping-Andersen, 1996) were responding to a mixture of common and universal needs, while the New Right assault on the welfare state in the 1980s and early 1990s (Jordan, 1998) was seeking to reframe it to respond to a mixture of circumstantial and particular needs. The Third Way (see above) and subsequent regime variants would seem to be responding to a complex and fluid mixture of need categories.

Notes

[1] The orientation of the diagram contained in *Figure 7.1* is consistent with similar diagrams used in my earlier work where I attempted to classify different approaches to popular moral discourse, to citizenship, to rights and to responsibilities. It is

worth clarifying that the orientation of the conceptual axes has always followed the convention established in the late Mary Douglas's writings on cultural theory, with the dimension equating (however loosely) with 'grid' or structure represented vertically and the dimension equating with 'group' or incorporation represented horizontally.

[2] This particular element of the analysis is quite esoteric and may possibly be of secondary interest to some readers. It is not essential to the main narrative content of the chapter.

[3] Distinguishing between morality and ethics inevitably courts confusion, if not controversy. I am concerned here with the distinction between *mores* (codes and customs) and *ethos* (doctrines and principles). By analogy, just as musicology entails critical reflection on music, so ethics entails critical reflection on morality.

[4] This study was discussed in some detail in Chapter Four.

[5] I have been using the term 'humanistic' and sometimes 'humanitarian' somewhat loosely. Humanism and humanitarianism are not strictly speaking interchangeable terms and each label can apply to more than one philosophy. Classical Greek humanism was concerned to distinguish humanity from nature; Renaissance humanism to liberate humanity from divine ordinances; Marxist humanism to assert the social nature of our species being. 'Humanitarian', on the other hand, is an everyday adjective that has been used to describe almost any intervention purporting to defend or advance human well-being, even military intervention. And curiously, perhaps, the arch-utilitarian, Bentham, looked on the prevention of cruelty to animals as 'humanitarian'. However, it should be clear from the context that I am referring to humanitarianism in a humanistic sense, drawing principally on the Marxist tradition. That tradition, as we have seen in Chapter Two, had its roots in early Marxist writings in which certain liberal assumptions about human nature are attacked, but others implicitly shared.

[6] In light of the provisions of the UN's 1989 Universal Convention on the Rights of the Child it may be argued that children should be regarded as citizens in their own right, not merely as future citizens.

Summary

In this chapter I have reduced the multiplicity of categorisations of human need to just four broad categories:

*   *Circumstantial needs:* these are needs that arise from everyday circumstances in a 'dog eat dog' world, in which everybody is expected to survive as best they can, while abiding by the rules. Provision for meeting circumstantial need is utilitarian and coercive in that assistance is conditional on willingness to labour or on a test of moral desert.

- *Particular needs:* these are needs that are particular to the competitive economic actor. Provision for meeting particular need is precisely targeted; it seeks to promote personal human capital and to ensure equality of opportunity.
- *Common needs:* these are needs that are shared in common. Provision for meeting common need relies on the perpetuation of traditional responsibilities through which the social order is constituted, including familial responsibilities, while promoting the sharing of common risk through social insurance.
- *Universal needs:* these are needs that are held to be universal to all. Provision for meeting universal need is based on concepts of social citizenship and the principle that for every member of society the state should provide or secure access to specific benefits, including healthcare, social security and education.

Questions for discussion:

- What is circumstantial about circumstantial needs?
- What is particular about particular needs?
- What is common about common needs?
- What is universal about universal needs?

eight

Translating needs into rights

- This chapter examines the ways in which human needs are translated into social rights.
- It draws distinctions, on the one hand, between 'top-down' doctrinal rights and 'bottom-up' claims-based rights and, on the other, between formal and substantive rights.
- A taxonomy or model that is related to that presented in Chapter Seven is introduced and explained and four broad categories of rights are identified: conditional, selective, protective and citizenship-based.
- The chapter argues that existing forms of social welfare provision are based on a mixture of different kinds of rights that in practice have failed adequately to address human need.

Human needs acquire particular meaning when they are expressed in terms of human rights. Some have dismissed the idea that needs may be translated into rights as 'a dangerous modern heresy' (Powell, 1972, p 12). If so, it is a heresy that may be traced back to Thomas Paine's (1791) treatise on *The rights of man*, in which he proposed the abolition of the Poor Laws and sketched out a scheme that would give the poor a *right* to relief. The idea that our essential needs may give rise to fundamental rights came of age with the advent of 20th-century social liberalism, perhaps most decisively, with Franklin D. Roosevelt's (1944) assertion that 'freedom from want' amounts to a human right. Human rights have been characterised not as a modern heresy, but as 'values for a Godless age' (Klug, 2000).

In previous chapters I dwelt on a distinction that may be drawn between inherent and interpreted needs. Correspondingly, there are two ways in which needs may be translated into rights. Inherent needs may be translated into 'doctrinal' rights and interpreted needs into 'claims-based' rights

(Dean, 2002). By doctrinal rights I refer to rights that are handed down, as it were, from above: rights conferred on us by nature or by God, birth rights preserved by our forbears, moral rights revealed by sages, priests or philosophers. By claims-based rights I refer to rights that are asserted from the bottom up: man-made rights defined by agreement or through struggle, rights framed through demands, in manifestos or by petition. As with inherent and interpreted conceptions of need, doctrinal and claims-based rights are difficult to disentangle because in the course of time each will inform the other. Charters, declarations and conventions of rights may enshrine doctrines established through past struggles.

When, as human beings, we *name* our needs there is a sense in which we implicitly claim a right to the means to satisfy those needs. However, there is a difference between needs that have been named for us by others and needs that we name for ourselves. The relationship between the two becomes clearer when we consider rights-based approaches to human need. This I shall discuss in the first part of the chapter. In the second part of the chapter I shall return to the subject of social citizenship (which was touched on in Chapter Six) and its relevance to human need.

Rights-based approaches

This short exploration of rights-based approaches will consider where ideas about rights come from before articulating the simplified taxonomy of needs just presented in Chapter Seven with a discussion of different kinds of rights-based approaches to human need.

The origins of rights

The modern conception of rights dates from the period of the so-called Western 'Enlightenment' of the 17th and 18th centuries. Enlightenment thought drew in part on old ideas from classical philosophers, but what was new about it was the break it made from a feudal era in which rights, insofar as they existed at all, were little more than arbitrary privileges. Kings and Queens ruled by divine right and could bestow privileges upon their Nobles.[1] The common people in practice had no rights other than a right to be guided or ruled by their superiors. The English Bill of Rights (1689), the American Declaration of Independence and Constitution (1776 and 1787, respectively) and the French Declaration of Rights (1789), although different in their substance and effect, shared a radically new conception of the human individual as a bearer of rights.

Rights were not uniformly conceived. In Chapter Six we explored a distinction between thin and thick conceptions of well-being. Thin conceptions are essentially liberal, thick conceptions essentially republican. The distinction reflects different constructions of the human individual and, by implication, of the rights she might bear: the abstract proprietor on the one hand; the vulnerable subject on the other. Hegel's contribution to Enlightenment thinking appears to have encompassed both, in the sense that it recognised *individual possession* – the freedom of property ownership – as the embodiment of an individual right, while also advocating poor relief, public healthcare and education as a means to ensure public or *social order* (see Fine, 1984, pp 57-9). The tension between these very different kinds of rights is reflected in distinctions between formal and substantive rights and in a variety of related or overlapping theoretical distinctions, such as those outlined in *Table 8.1*.

Table 8.1: Thin/formal *vs.* thick/substantive conceptions of rights

negative rights *[rights to the forbearance of others]*	vs.	positive rights *[rights that allow one to be oneself]*	(see Berlin, I. [1967] 'Two concepts of liberty', in A. Quinton (ed) *Political Philosophy*, Oxford University Press)
freedom rights *[liberties and immunities]*	vs.	entitlement rights *[claims and powers]*	(see Hohfeld, W. [1946] *Fundamental Legal Conceptions as Applied in Judicial Reasoning*, Yale University Press)
choice rights *[the right to exercise free will]*	vs.	benefit rights *[the right to pursue one's own interests]*	(see Campbell, T. [1988] *Justice*, Macmillan, ch 2)
background rights *[abstract – based on underlying principles]*	vs.	institutional rights *[concrete – based on policy or goals]*	(see Dworkin, R. [1977] *Taking Rights Seriously*, Duckworth)

It is a distinction that is swept aside by those who see something heretical in a rights-based approach to human need. Most famously, the idea that there could be some moral basis to rights was dismissed as 'nonsense on stilts' by the utilitarian philosopher Jeremy Bentham (1789), whose approach to human need we discussed in Chapter Six. For Bentham the only rights that mattered were 'black-letter' rights, rights that had been legally established and written down. This utilitarian and characteristically legalistic conception prioritises governance over rights (Osborne, 1996).

The ascendancy of this more narrow focus played some part, perhaps, in occluding debate about the connections between rights and needs until the emergence in the mid-20th century of the modern human rights agenda. The 1948 Universal Declaration of Human Rights (UDHR) consolidated what have been characterised as 'first-wave' human rights (see for example Klug, 2000); those liberally conceived civil and political rights that had been named and claimed since the Enlightenment. But it also named and claimed a 'second wave' of human rights, rights to economic, social and cultural security. At the level of grand rhetoric at least, human rights were explicitly connected to human needs. Bryan Turner has argued that 'it is from a collectively held recognition of individual frailty that rights as a system of mutual protection gain their emotive force' (1993, p 507). The human rights framework offered not only individual property rights, but also rights to security within a social order. It recognised the individual not only as a potentially autonomous being, but as a necessarily vulnerable being. Ostensibly, the new idea of human rights bowed both to a liberal and a republican conception of rights, but less consciously, it also gave expression to a deeper philosophical anthropology. According to Turner, human rights provide a substitute for the human species' lack of natural instincts (2006, p 29). While other sentient creatures' responses to their needs are more or less instinctive, this is not so for human beings. This is not simply because of the human capacity for rational calculation. The suffering – physical and emotional – that must to some degree attend the vicissitudes of a human life course is not only inevitable, it is also foreseeable. Human individuals are able to recognise their own frailty and the frailty of others and to construct social institutions for their mutual protection. But such institutions are in themselves fragile and require a socially constructed underpinning of rights.

This deeper or 'thicker' meaning is especially pertinent to any reading of second-generation human rights. In practice, however, second-generation rights remain more elusive than first-generation rights. The form in which they were written into the UDHR owed much to the Cold War tensions of that era (see for example, Hunt 1996). They represented an uncomfortable compromise between, on the one hand, a new-found, if guarded, willingness on the part of Western liberals to accommodate a mixed economy and permit a limited role for the state in the provision of social welfare and, on the other, attempts by the Soviet communist bloc to inflect the agenda away from liberally inspired civil and political freedoms in favour of its own interpretation of human rights, based on wholly state-organised economic and social guarantees (see for example Wronka, 1992). Despite rhetorical assertions as to the indivisibility and interdependence of all human rights, these tensions as to their substance – and, more particularly, as to the manner of their implementation and enforcement – led to the development of separate international covenants, one for civil and political rights, the other for economic, social and cultural rights. The latter have been consistently marginalised in favour of the former (Dean, 2002). Later, with the collapse of Soviet communism, human rights rhetoric became, for a time at least, less of a propaganda medium (UNDP, 2003). This may to an extent have opened the door to the possibility of global approaches to social policy issues (Deacon et al, 1997) and to rights-based approaches to problems such as global poverty (Pogge, 2007).

In the meantime, in response to the demands of the global South, the UN, through the Declaration of the Right to Development of 1986, had purported to institute a 'third generation' of human rights. The Declaration, although not binding, was intended in the words of the Senegalese delegate, to express for the poorest people of the world 'the right to live better'. It sought to establish the principle that all human beings should be enabled to participate in a process of social, economic and political development (Rosas, 2001). This latest generation of rights gives expression to shared human needs, incorporating demands for peace, for a healthy environment and for self-determination.

Rights-based rhetoric conceals a multitude of different meanings. However, this multitude of meanings rests on what Ignatieff has called 'the shared vocabulary from which our arguments can begin, and the bare minimum from which different areas of flourishing can take root' (2001, p 95). Let us see where that vocabulary leads.

A taxonomy of rights-based approaches

Having presented in Chapter Seven a taxonomy of needs-based approaches, let us now see whether, from that taxonomy, we can construct a parallel taxonomy of rights-based approaches to human need. Such a taxonomy is represented by the diagram in *Figure 8.1*.

In the diagram, the vertical axis from *Figure 7.1* in Chapter Seven is now replaced by an axis representing a dimension with doctrinally conceived rights at one end of the continuum and claims-based rights at the other. The horizontal axis from *Figure 7.1* is replaced by an axis representing a dimension with the thinly conceived autonomous subject as the bearer of rights at one end of the continuum and the thickly conceived vulnerable subject as the bearer of rights at the other. The model offers us four contested and (potentially) mutually contradictory ways of talking about rights:

Figure 8.1: A taxonomy of rights-based approaches to human need

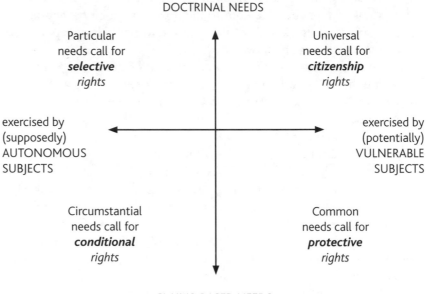

DOCTRINAL NEEDS

Particular
needs call for
selective
rights

Universal
needs call for
citizenship
rights

exercised by
(supposedly)
AUTONOMOUS
SUBJECTS

exercised by
(potentially)
VULNERABLE
SUBJECTS

Circumstantial
needs call for
conditional
rights

Common
needs call for
protective
rights

CLAIMS-BASED NEEDS

- *Circumstantial need and conditional rights:* circumstantial need reflects requirements for survival in a hazardous and competitive social environment. To the extent that anyone can claim against another a right to have such needs met is at best an ambiguous right, because it is necessarily conditional. Autonomous individuals may bargain with each other for the means to satisfy need and such bargaining may give rise to everyday claims or expectations, to which the term 'rights' may incidentally attach. Such rights are no more than the conditions on which bilateral exchanges are conducted. The concept of rights may, however, be transposed to a wider multilateral context. If a person is unable to satisfy her needs independently, she might possibly claim a right against society at large to the satisfaction of such need, upon condition that she deserves it. The administration of such rights requires the exercise of authority and judgement. Entitlement is conditional on obedience.
- *Particular need and selective rights:* particular need reflects requirements for autonomous enterprise in a harmoniously functioning market economy. The right to have such needs met is doctrinally conceived in the sense that the efficacy of markets is believed to depend on the application of formal principles, including the principle that there should be equal opportunity for everybody to participate and to do so on equal terms. Such a right, however, arises selectively where a particular need can be

proved to exist and where particular benefit will result from meeting that need. A right to targeted assistance can be said to arise if a person can show that – through unemployment or infirmity – she lacks the means of subsistence and therefore the ability to participate productively. If markets should prove incapable of developing the skills and maintaining the health of the labour force, then a right to education and healthcare will arise. The administration of such rights requires efficient public policy intervention with a view to promoting an effective market economy. Entitlement is premised on a civic duty ideal: the assumption that autonomous individuals should strive for productive participation and self-sufficiency.

- *Common need and protective rights:* common need reflects requirements for conformity and stability in a hierarchically ordered society. The right to have such needs met is claimed on the basis that one belongs to and accepts one's place in that society. Such rights arise because the common denominator shared by all members of society is a degree of present or potential vulnerability. Conceding rights to people may bind them together and so serve to protect them from subversive influences, to protect traditional institutions and practices on which social order depends and to protect against such risks as the people share in common. Entitlement is a matter of mutual moral obligation.
- *Universal need and citizenship rights:* universal need reflects requirements for human fulfilment. The right to have such needs met is a conception borne of reformist doctrine (whether social liberal or more radically, social democratic). Such rights arise through the creation of an effectively structured form of citizenship. They are axiomatically comprehensive in nature and unconditional in principle, although they may attach to citizens in response to different contingencies during different parts of the human life course. Entitlement is premised on an ideal of collective responsibility.

Once again, this is a model whose purpose is primarily heuristic. It helps us to understand the often confused and contradictory ways in which rights are spoken about in relation to human need. In practice, social policy makers and many commentators speak about social or welfare rights quite loosely and may, unwittingly or intentionally, muddle different meanings together. With this in mind, I want to return to the concept of social or welfare citizenship, since it is through the practical negotiation of welfare citizenship that rights to needs satisfaction can in practice emerge.

Welfare citizenship

Although I started this chapter with a discussion of *human* rights, it should be borne in mind that conceptions of human rights are of relatively recent provenance. The invention of *citizenship* rights predated the invention of human rights by over two millennia and it is citizenship rights that have provided the basic model on which human rights are founded (Clarke, 1996). Citizenship is both an ancient ideal and a current practice (Lister, 2003; Dwyer, 2004b). It is through citizenship of a nation state that human rights are most often realised in practice. We have already seen in Chapter Seven that although citizenship in capitalist welfare states accommodates a 'social' dimension, this is applied in different ways. Although people may be citizens in a legal sense, their needs may be construed within different capitalist welfare state regimes not as universal needs, but as circumstantial, particular or common needs. Drawing on Esping-Andersen's (1990) classification of welfare regimes:

- Whatever their classification, all kinds of welfare state regime (and many emergent economies with limited welfare provision) afford conditional rights, rights that respond to circumstantial need. This is especially the case where, for example, elements of work-first workfare have been introduced.
- Liberal welfare regimes are defined by their preference for selective rights, rights that respond to particular need.
- Conservative regimes are defined by their preference for protective rights, rights that respond to common need.
- Social Democratic regimes are defined by their preference for citizenship rights, rights that respond to universal need, although the needs of citizens at different stages of the life course are differently construed so that, for example, workers, dependants and children have different rights.

The economic, social and cultural rights defined by the UDHR and subsequent international instruments encompass rights to freely chosen work, an adequate standard of living, social security, housing, healthcare, education, participation in cultural life and to share in the benefits of scientific progress (Eide, 2001). The categories 'economic', 'social' and 'cultural' in practice overlap and it is common to roll these distinctions together under the umbrella of the term 'social rights' (see for example Marshall, 1950) or 'welfare rights'. The latter term acknowledges that, although clearly such rights have not necessarily achieved universal status, they have been addressed – however imperfectly – through the development of various capitalist welfare state regimes. Some might argue that the true ideal of social citizenship has yet to be fully achieved, even in the most highly developed welfare regimes, and for the purposes of our discussion of human need it makes sense to speak of welfare citizenship, rather than social citizenship.

The Marshallian compromise

The 'social' citizenship concept propounded by T.H. Marshall (1950) (and see the discussion in Chapter Six) is but a component of the welfare citizenship settlement. It was part of a compromise. Nonetheless the concept he elaborated is important, not least because it has been so influential. Marshall argued that three kinds of rights – civil/legal rights, political/democratic rights and social/welfare rights – could be compared to the legs of a three-legged stool. Just as a three legged-stool will be unstable if one of its legs is missing, weak or broken, so a society will be unstable if any of these three elements of citizenship should remain undeveloped or inadequate or if it should be undermined. Marshall advocated what he called the 'hyphenated society': *democratic-welfare-capitalism*. The hyphenated society depended on an essential equilibrium between political, social and civil rights. Marshall supposed that the state and the market existed as essentially opposing forces, but that democratic–welfare–capitalism achieved an optimum balance between accountability, fairness and freedom (Hindess, 1987). Political rights were necessary for democratic legitimacy, social rights to ensure some measure of social justice, civil rights to provide the conditions necessary for a market economy. For Marshall, the development of citizenship, which had begun with the Athenian city state in the 4th or 5th century BC, had come of age with the development of the 20th-century welfare state. Citizenship was no longer about self-government by a small and exclusive city elite, but about the dynamic regulation of a large and fully enfranchised industrialised nation that had to address the needs of its inhabitants.

Marshall was right that modern industrialised nations had, self-evidently, been obliged to address not only the needs of their individual citizens for some degree of formal autonomy (as economic actors and democratic subjects), but also their substantive welfare needs. His concept of social rights has been criticised, however, from several quarters. It is possible to group these criticisms according to the four different approaches to human need already outlined.

First, moral-authoritarian approaches (associated with circumstantial conceptions of need and conditional conceptions of rights) subscribe to those kinds of argument that tend to dismiss the idea of social rights as heresy. This is an approach for which individual autonomy is synonymous with self-sufficient survival: people should meet their own needs. The approach was reflected in the illiberal utilitarianism associated with Bentham. It has more lately been evident in New Right critiques of the social rights concept (Barry, 1987) and the ideas of commentators such as Charles Murray (1984) who argue, if not for an end to the welfare state, that the coercive power of the state should be harnessed not so much to provide for human needs as to make its citizens provide for themselves.

Second, economistic approaches (associated with particular conceptions of need and selective conceptions of rights) are inclined to the promotion of social standards, rather than social rights (Mishra, 1999). This is an approach for which individual autonomy and personal fulfilment is thought to flow from effective engagement as an economic actor. Social rights, it may be argued, cannot be universal rights in the way that civil and political rights should be, because provision for healthcare, education and social security is beyond the means of many developing countries (Cranston, 1976). It is only through economic development that social development and welfare citizenship become possible (Wilensky, 1975). What is more, while it is right to seek to promote higher standards of healthcare, education and social security, resources to this end must be sparingly applied and directed to where needs are greatest.

Third, paternalistic approaches (associated with common conceptions of need and protective conceptions of rights) are concerned less with individual rights to autonomy and more with the identification and negotiation of shared interests. Social rights in modern welfare states represent the outcome of brokered compromises between different interest groups. In classic corporatist welfare states this is likely to entail explicit tripartite compromises between business interests, trade unions and government. To a greater or lesser extent, however, capitalist welfare states can all be regarded as the outcome of what Poulantzas (1980, p 123) has called a 'condensation of class forces'. Marshall's conception of citizenship is criticised by Bottomore (1992) for its abstract nature. According to Marshall, citizenship is a logical settlement involving a state of equilibrium between abstract forces. In practice, Bottomore argues, even in liberal welfare regimes the demands of trade unions and the organised labour movement played a significant part in the development of welfare citizenship. Decisions about how the common needs of common people should be met may have involved significant compromises and were taken at a distance from those the labour movement purported to represent, but welfare citizenship had been the product of real-life negotiation, rather than the application of abstract principles.

Finally, it follows self-evidently that humanitarian approaches (associated with universal conceptions of need and citizenship rights) are the very expression of a social rights approach. The Marshallian compromise is broadly consistent with the welfare citizenship settlement to be found in social democratic welfare states, such as those to be found in the Nordic countries, which are nonetheless largely successful capitalist economies. The social democratic settlement has its critics: for example, from both socialist and feminist perspectives, both of which might endorse more radical notions of social rights. Socialist and neo-Marxist critics of the Marshallian compromise argue, on the one hand, that the welfare state has become both handmaiden and henchman for the market economy, managing and controlling labour supply in the interests of capital (for example Offe, 1984), and, on the other hand, that the application of liberal conceptions of individual rights is disempowering because it conceals the true character of capitalism's exploitative social relations of power (see for example Holloway and Picciotto, 1978). Feminist and social movement critics of the Marshallian compromise argue, on the one hand, that the welfare state has perpetuated patriarchal, racialised and disabling relations of power in industrialised societies (see for example Williams, 1989), and, on the other hand, that the application of androgynous or 'totalising' concepts of citizenship ignores or negates the relevance of social diversity and differing experiences and understandings of human need (see for example Pateman, 1989).

The limitations of welfare citizenship

On several counts, welfare citizenship has been a failure. First, as is evident from Chapter Four, the survival of poverty and inequality in spite of the development of the welfare state may be regarded as 'one of the wonders of the modern world' (Seabrook, 1985, p 12). Welfare citizenship may serve to ameliorate poverty and to abate need, but nowhere has it succeeded completely in eradicating it. In fact, some would argue that welfare citizenship has been implicated in perpetuating certain forms of poverty (Novak, 1988; Squires, 1990).

Second, in the developed countries of the global North, the nature of welfare citizenship has of late been increasingly reconstituted. Cox (1998) suggests that the conceptions of social rights have become more discursive and less associated with objective conditions of need. Certainly, it may be seen that New Right and Third Way attempts to reform state welfare have tended to reconstitute the citizen as a customer. Conventional explanations of the rise of welfare citizenship suggest that capitalist welfare states elected to varying degrees to 'de-commodify' the worker (Esping-Andersen, 1990). That is to say, by providing for the basic needs of workers the state not only ensured the efficient reproduction of labour power, it also enabled workers – up to a point – to live independently of the labour market. Because certain services such as social insurance, healthcare and education became available not as commercial commodities but as of right, labour power itself became less of a conventionally marketable commodity. Following the global crisis of the welfare state towards the end of the 20th century (see Chapters Two and Seven; and Esping-Andersen, 1996), there has been a certain trend to 'recommodification' (Offe, 1984). There have been several facets to this trend. At the level of labour market policy there was a trend away from demand-side policy informed by Keynesian economics to supply-side policy informed by monetarist economics and endogenous growth theory (see for example Dolowitz, 2004): put simply, the developed economies placed renewed emphasis on maximising domestic labour market participation and productivity. But at the same time such economies sought new ways to moderate or constrain their social spending, to reduce the *costs* of welfare citizenship. Not only was labour power to be recommodified, but so were public services addressed to meeting human needs.

Such recommodification occurred in various ways. In the UK, for example, during the period of Margaret Thatcher's premiership there were explicit attempts to privatise key elements of social welfare provision by, for example, the selling of public housing and the aggressive promotion of private pensions in place of the state pension scheme (Papadakis and Taylor-Gooby, 1987). The general trend has been towards a greater degree of pluralism in the provision of welfare services and the idea that the provision of human services ought not to be the exclusive preserve of the public sector (Johnson, 1987). The World Trade Organization (WTO) seeks to regulate against public sector monopolies in any form of human service provision, including healthcare and education (Deacon, 2007). At the same time, however, there have been attempts to change the basis on which those services that survived in the public sector should be managed. This – the 'new public managerialism' (Hood, 1991) – has expressed itself in various ways. First of all there has been a drive to 'marketise' public provision for personal needs. The intention has been to make public services more 'business-like', by importing the methods of business management and some of the characteristics of free markets into the administration of healthcare provision, education and social security. This entailed the development of mechanisms by which public sector agencies would compete with one another and the replacement of a public service ethos, with a customer service ethos. More recently, the new managerialism and new approaches to governance (Rhodes, 1997) has emphasised the need to 'modernise' (see for example Cabinet Office, 1999) and to 'personalise' public service provision (see for example PMSU, 2007). This has entailed the promotion of a more technical and pragmatic approach to welfare provision and subtler forms of performance management (Clarke, 2003; Henman and Fenger, 2006).

The essence of new governance approaches, whose tentacles have reached as far as the EU and the World Bank (Bekkers et al, 2007; Deacon, 2007), is that when needs are met by the state, the recipient's citizenship is defined by her civil status, not her social being. The relationship between recipient and provider is contrived to be like a market transaction, governed by civil not social rights, by contractarian rather than solidaristic principles. The recipient is construed not as a potentially vulnerable subject but as an autonomous economic actor, as a consumer. Goods such as healthcare, education and pensions are provided not to meet universal need, but are tailored to meet particular needs or preferences. Although such goods are available to everybody, an element of selectivity must apply to the transaction, even if this is limited to a requirement that the recipient must exercise choice, by choosing which hospital to attend, to which school to send one's child or to which pension fund to contribute. Defenders of such reform strongly argue this will be more effective than old-style welfare citizenship (Le Grand, 2003), yet it amounts to an erosion of the social citizenship ideal.

The third sense in which welfare citizenship has failed is that, although in various guises it is being adopted by several post-Soviet 'transition' countries, it has proved itself to be more or less irrelevant to many countries in the global South (see for example Deacon, 2007). Welfare citizenship is premised on two assumptions: first, that most citizens will meet their needs through earnings from paid employment in the labour market or within households sustained by such earnings; second, that a regulatory framework and some measure of provision for the needs of those excluded from labour market participation can be met under the aegis of a legitimate and functioning state apparatus. There are parts of the world where these assumptions do not completely hold or, indeed, may not hold at all. Gough et al (2004) have described different kinds of developing country regime. There are emergent welfare state regimes, for example, in several Latin American countries, but the provision or coverage of welfare provision is uneven and there are extensive rural enclaves and urban favelas which remain in the grip of an informal economy in which neither market nor state are fully functional. Throughout much of East Asia there are what might be described as 'productivist' regimes, once characterised as 'tiger economies', where economic production is prioritised over social policy and the role of the state remains limited. Across South Asia there are what might be called 'informal security' regimes, where the legacy of colonial rule is cumbersome yet often ineffective state bureaucracies, and where everyday human needs must be met through reliance on informal provision by family, kin and community. And across much of sub-Saharan Africa there are what are best described as 'insecurity' regimes, where neither market nor state are functional and everyday human needs may be met under the protection of chieftains, warlords, mafia leaders, corrupt officialdom or beneficent foreign aid workers. Finally, in China, the world's most populous nation, recent economic reforms have delivered spectacular economic growth but have, it is claimed, 'destroyed its socialist welfare system centred on the principles of equality and human needs' (Chan et al, 2008, p 195). Welfare reform in China lags behind economic reform and, in the absence of a liberal interpretation of democracy, what is emerging is not intended to approximate to any form of welfare citizenship.

The fourth sense in which welfare citizenship has failed stems from the difficulty of enforcing social rights. If human need is to be met through the creation of social rights, those rights must be enforceable. People who are denied their rights require some form of redress. This has been problematic. In practice, mechanisms of redress have generally involved the introduction of legal procedures and what has been called the 'juridification' of welfare (Teubner, 1987). Having recourse to judicial or quasi-judicial forms of redress has implications because legal systems have been created as a forum in which to address civil not social rights. Gunther Teubner has suggested that when at a national level legal systems and welfare systems are brought into a relationship with one another, one of three things tends to happen:

• The systems may prove incongruent. Fear of this has often motivated policy makers to insulate the administration of social welfare from judicial intervention and lawyers to resist involvement in matters of social policy for fear that their 'judicial purity' may be compromised (Dean, 2002, pp 158-9).
• Welfare arrangements can become over-legalised. Reference has been made in both Chapters Six and Seven to Habermas's distinction between system and life world and the extent to which the former may 'colonise' the latter (1987). The legal system may be an unsuitable instrument for dealing with decisions about how individual human needs may best be met (Tweedie and Hunt, 1994). This contention lies at the heart of a long-standing controversy as to whether meeting the 'legal needs' of welfare state citizens is an effective way of helping them satisfy such other needs as are supposedly guaranteed by social rights (see **Box 8.1**).

Box 8.1: The unmet legal need debate

T.H. Marshall's celebrated essay on citizenship, 'Citizenship and social class', coincided with legislation in the UK to extend provision of state funded legal aid and advice. Marshall himself regarded this as yet another extension of social rights. Nearly three decades later a Royal Commission on Legal Services was appointed to investigate further improvements to legal aid. It recommended largely incremental improvements to a system that in certain cases enabled poor clients to consult private lawyers at public expense. The Commission concluded that, although there were 'too many' people with unmet legal need:

> A society in which all human and social problems are regarded as apt for a legal remedy or susceptible to legal procedures would not be one in which it would be agreeable to live.... The improvements we propose are intended to remedy [the inadequacies in legal services] without creating an over litigious society. (Royal Commission on Legal Services [1976], para 2.28).

The report was greeted with dismay by the independent advice and law centres movement that was then burgeoning in the UK and had hoped for more public funding for proactive community-based legal service providers. The providers believed that problems of poverty and disadvantage could be addressed not by making people go to lawyers, but by bringing lawyers to the people. They sought to make community-based lawyers accountable to the communities they served and to bring legal expertise to bear not only on individual cases of social injustice, but upon the structural causes.

However, there were those who had counselled that:

> ... to say that someone has a legal problem is not a description of a state of fact; it is to suggest that he should take a certain course of action ... whether this is so or not will often be debatable and it may be that the appropriate course of action will be such that we should prefer to speak of that person having a political problem. (Lewis, P. [1973])

The Critical Legal Studies Movement has argued that bringing lawyers and the law closer to the people will not always empower them to meet their needs: it may secure some resources for some people, but not lasting gains for everybody; and despite the best intentions of enlightened practitioners, by constructing needs claims in terms of legal not social rights it can, potentially, individuate or dehumanise the citizen.

(For further discussion, see Dean, H. [2002], ch 9; and Unger, R. [1986]))

• The legal system can become over-socialised. The conventional courts may be drawn into policy matters with which they are ill-prepared to deal and which overburden them (Harden and Lewis, 1986). Certainly, there is evidence that a conservative judiciary can subvert the intentions of policy makers (Griffiths, 1991).

If legal redress for welfare citizens is weak, what are the alternatives? The international human rights framework is of little or no help to the individual citizen of a nation state, although I shall be discussing the scope for collective complaints in Chapter Nine. At an administrative level, most developed welfare states have a variety of quasi-judicial or purely administrative mechanisms for appeal or redress by citizens who are dissatisfied by decisions regarding their claims to social provision (see for example Skoler and Zeitzer, 1982). However, in harmony with the trend to new public managerialist 'modernisation' of public services, there has in recent times been a shift away from redress based on formal rights of appeal towards the application of customer charters and the use of customer complaints procedures (Dean, 2002). Increasingly, the recipient of state-administered healthcare, education or social security receives services not as a citizen claiming her rights, but as a customer exercising her choices. To the extent that she has rights of redress, it is not as a juridical subject, but as a discerning consumer.

Conclusion

This critique does not mean that we should dismiss the concept of social rights or the importance of actually existing forms of welfare citizenship. Amartya Sen (in UNDP, 2000, ch 1) has drawn on Kant's distinction between perfect and imperfect duties to argue that just because the rights demanded by or on behalf of the poor are neglected or repudiated by those with the power to observe them, this does not mean that such rights do not exist. Rights are social constructs and the language of rights provides a valuable discursive resource through which to name and claim human needs. The language of rights has a certain 'alchemical' force in the struggles of oppressed people. Referring specifically to the experiences of African-Americans in the US, Patricia Williams challenged the attempts of the Critical Legal Studies Movement (see **Box 8.1** above) to revert from a formal rights-based approach to a non-alienating needs-based approach by asserting:

> I by no means want to idealize the importance of rights …
> [which] are so often selectively invoked to draw boundaries, to

isolate, and to limit … [but] for the historically disempowered, the conferring of rights is symbolic of all the denied aspects of humanity: rights imply a respect which places one within the referential range of self and others, which elevates one's status from human body to social being.… "Rights" feels so new in the mouths of most black people. It is so deliciously empowering to say.… The concept of rights, both positive and negative, is the marker of our citizenship, our participatoriness, our relation to others. (Williams, 1987, pp 405, 416, 431)

We shall see, therefore, in the final chapter that a discourse of rights inevitably has a role to play in the politics of human need.

Note

[1] England's *Magna Carta* of 1215 is sometimes acclaimed for having laid the foundations of our human rights. In practice it amounted to little more than a reluctant concession by the Crown of certain restricted liberties made, in effect, exclusively to the Nobility.

Summary

- This chapter has been concerned with the ways in which needs are translated into rights and in particular into social rights, whether these are expressed as 'second-generation' human rights or as social rights of citizenship within a welfare state.
- Distinctions have been drawn, based in part on a discussion of the historical evolution of rights:
  - between doctrinally translated rights (premised on inherent needs) that are prescribed and handed down to the people from above and claims-based translations (premised on interpreted needs) that are formulated and demanded by the people from below;
  - between (thinly conceived) formal rights whose bearers are abstractly construed as autonomous subjects and (thickly conceived) substantive rights whose bearers are construed as potentially vulnerable and interdependent beings.
- A taxonomy or model has been proposed that draws on these two distinctions and which supplements the taxonomy of needs-based approaches presented in the last chapter with four corresponding categories of rights:
  - conditional rights that respond to circumstantial need;
  - selective rights that respond to particular need;
  - protective rights that respond to common need;
  - citizenship rights that respond to universal need.

- It has been emphasised that there is a difference between social rights, which may be realised in a variety of ways, and rights of social citizenship, arguing that:
    - the social welfare provision by which citizens of a welfare state can meet their needs may incidentally fulfil the social rights of some or even many citizens, but it will not necessarily guarantee an effective right of social citizenship unless it is a universal entitlement for all;
    - social citizenship remains an unrealised ideal and actually existing forms of welfare citizenship provide a mixture of conditional, selective and protective as well as citizenship rights;
    - the various forms of welfare citizenship associated with the 'golden age' of the capitalist welfare state appear to have been quite ineffectual: they have failed to abate poverty; in the global North they have been diluted, especially by managerial reform; in the global South their principles have proved to be partly or wholly irrelevant; and such mechanisms as have been provided for enforcing rights have been weak or inappropriate.

Questions for discussion:

- Is the claim that we may translate our needs into rights a heretical doctrine or an empowering ideal?
- In what ways do *social* rights give expression to human needs?
- In pursuit of the satisfaction of human needs why, if at all, should we aspire to citizenship of a welfare state?

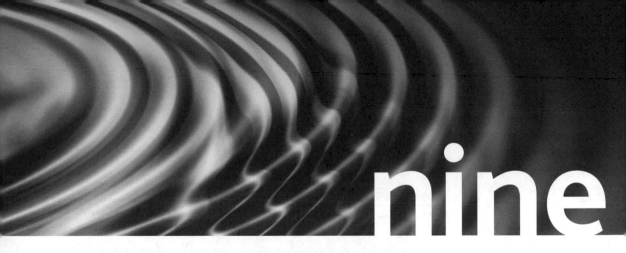

nine

The politics of human need

- This chapter argues that it is through politics that needs claims are translated into social rights.
- It critically discusses the old politics of welfare and specifically:
  - the politics that informed the creation and later the crisis of the capitalist welfare states of the global North;
  - the politics of social development in the global South, where there can be scepticism towards rights-based approaches.
- The scope for a new politics of need is examined: specifically, a politics of conviviality, which would empower ordinary people to name and claim their own needs, a Marxian approach to the strategic prioritisation of needs and what has been defined as a 'politics of needs interpretation'.
- While the idea of social rights is defended, this chapter emphasises that its justification depends on the promotion of the critical autonomy of the individual and a eudaimonic social ethic, concepts which are further explored.

In Chapter Eight we considered how human needs may be translated into rights. It is a process that is by nature political. Social rights are dependent for their realisation not only on the civil or legal rights by which people may enforce their claims against each other or against the state, but on political rights and the processes by which social policies are made. It is through politics that needs claims and social policies are formulated. The UDHR and the international human rights framework were the result of political negotiations between the signatory states. The specific social rights we may enjoy as citizens are the result of legislative and policy measures arrived at through political processes, in which the exercise of democratic rights may or may not play some part. In the everyday politics of personal relationships we continually negotiate and renegotiate the manner in which our needs are satisfied and the substance of our claims on and expectations of others (Ungerson, 1987; Finch and Mason, 1993). Declarations of rights may seem abstract, remote and alien from the perspective of ordinary lives and personal needs (Soysal, 1994), yet this does not mean that the personal cannot be political. Our personal troubles may be turned into public issues (Wright-Mills, 1959) and even the most intimate aspects of our personal lives are subject to relations of power (Hanisch, 1969). At every level, from the global to the personal, needs are political.

In this chapter I first discuss the old politics of 'welfare': the political dimensions to the rise and fall of the welfare state and the extent to which the politics of welfare has been apparently discredited. Second, I discuss alternative ways in which we might envision a politics of need. Finally, I return to and advance a defence of social rights as a foundation for a politics of need.

Old politics of 'welfare'

What we might refer to as the old politics of welfare is quintessentially associated with the idea of the 'welfare state'. The first use of the term 'welfare state' is attributed to Archbishop William Temple (1941; see also Timmins, 2001, p 36) who, in the midst of the Second World War, held out the hope that, when the war was over, Britain's warfare state, or 'power state', and its monolithic and burgeoning administrative apparatus, could be converted, like a sword into a ploughshare, into a peaceable and benevolent welfare state. The term caught on, not just in Britain, but throughout the developed world. Rather than reverting to a night watchman role and leaving provision for human need to the vicissitudes of the free market, the state could forge a new peacetime contract with its citizens. As mentioned in Chapter Eight, the coming of the welfare state and the development of the social rights of citizenship involved an element of de-commodification, in terms both of labour power and the human services required to reproduce and sustain labour power. Graham Room has suggested that this represented a shift from a system of distribution based on a cash nexus to one based on a 'needs nexus' (1979, p 59). But in another sense, the process reflected a sometimes progressive, albeit sometimes reluctant, compromise between what I crudely characterised in Chapter One as an economistic or market-oriented approach and a humanistic or humanitarian approach to need.

The compromise was not consistently drawn and could be unstable. Titmuss (1962) expressed concern that using the expression 'welfare state' to refer to any postwar Western democratic society elided the reality that welfare states were not static or uniform institutions, that in a rapidly changing world some were by no means unambiguously benign. On the contrary, the welfare state could readily be implicated in perpetuating social inequalities. While increasing levels of social and public expenditure in affluent societies, such as Britain, had indeed provided 'a better ordered, more efficient, more civilised social environment', it was clear that 'the rich benefited more than the poor ... [because] ... they knew how to make better use of this environment for more dignified living' (1962, p 52). If the brave new world captured in Temple's vision of a 'welfare state' did not come to pass quite as he might have envisioned it, a state-mediated needs nexus did now coexist with a market-mediated cash nexus. Although expenditure levels varied between different welfare state regimes, provision for human need was systematically organised through a democratic state apparatus. There was a politics of welfare.

In the meantime the expression 'welfare' – and especially 'social welfare' – took on a narrower and more pejorative meaning as a particular kind of state intervention addressed especially to 'the poor'. In the US the term 'welfare' is specifically applied not to social expenditures on health, education and pensions but to stigmatised forms of means-tested social assistance for the poorest of people. Increasingly, the ambiguity acquired by the word 'welfare' is reflected in the tone of current debates about 'welfare reform' across the Western world (see for example Lister, 2001). Nicholas Deakin, in his book *The politics of welfare* (1994), recalls from his own childhood an association between the term 'welfare' and the distinctive taste of the processed 'welfare orange juice' supplied by the local authority children's clinic. The welfare state considerably enhanced the satisfaction of human needs across society, but for some members of society it came with a slightly unpleasant flavour.

I have referred several times to the global crisis that befell the capitalist welfare state during the last quarter of the 20th century. At the root of that crisis, according to Mary Langan (1998), lay the politicisation of need, although paradoxically it might also be regarded as an attempt to depoliticise need, as a political attempt to unravel the needs nexus. The political demand was for the recommodification of welfare (Offe, 1984; see also Chapter Eight, this book). If human need could be depoliticised, social rights could be recommodified. As the New Right ideological orthodoxies of Reagan and Thatcher gave way to the more pragmatic Third Way orthodoxies of Clinton and Blair (Giddens, 1998; Jordan, 1998), the role of the welfare state was re-envisioned. Its job was no longer to meet individual needs but to enable its citizens to manage risk better, not so much to underwrite social rights as to promote individual responsibility. The essential infrastructure of the welfare state may have survived the 'ideological blizzard' fomented by the New Right (Le Grand, 1990b, p 350), but now it would undergo a technocratic shift. The old politics of need associated with the post-Second World War welfare state were conjured out of sight and replaced by 'modernised' forms of governance (Clarke and Newman, 1997). Control over and accountability for public service provision became a matter not of politics, but of management. In the capitalist welfare states of the global North, it would seem, discourses of need are no longer controversial. They have been eclipsed, for example, by the discourses of social exclusion, capability and recognition (see Chapter Five), discourses that are important and relevant but which take the politics of need in a new direction.

Meanwhile, in the global South the politics of need tends to be associated not with the social rights of welfare state citizenship, but with struggles to achieve the social rights promised by the UDHR and the pursuit of social development promised by the so-called 'third generation' of human rights (see Chapter Eight).

In the event, the UDHR has offered little substantive purchase for a politics of need. The UN Committee on Economic, Social and Cultural Rights (UNCESCR), created belatedly in 1985 to monitor the implementation of the 1966 International Covenant on Economic, Social and Cultural Rights (ICESCR), receives quinquennial reports from signatory state parties, but its jurisdiction is restricted to the making of 'general comments' on the implementation or violation of rights by those states. Since 1992 the Committee has invited critical submissions from non-governmental organisations (NGOs), but while international NGOs have been active in monitoring and campaigning for civil and political rights, they have shown much less interest in promoting or enforcing social rights (see for example Hunt, 1996). This is possibly because greater potential lay with the third generation of human rights portended by the 1986 Declaration of the Right to Development. The Declaration implied not only individual rights, but collective, group and solidarity rights. However, this has not so much added to the canon of rights already set out in the ICESCR as brought an element of ambiguity to the question of whether substantive needs claims are to be framed by citizens against their individual nation states or by poor nations against the wider international community. Paradoxically, perhaps, this has served to further marginalise the idea that social rights may be regarded as a global species of human rights that could or should in themselves be inalienable and unconditional. Certainly, aspirations based, for example, on group rights to self-determination and/or cultural freedom (Kymlicka, 1995; Perez-Bustillo, 2001) seek to enlarge our understanding of civil and political rights, but not social rights. In the struggle for the right to development, social rights have tended to take a back seat. The new social movements of the global South and their academic allies – the post-development theorists – tend to be hostile to the role of the state as a guarantor of welfare, or else they seek to transcend what they dismiss as the mere 'politics of demand' in favour of more worthy forms of political participation (Escobar, 1995; Waterman, 2001). It has been suggested that there is a fear on the part of 'new' social movements that the class-based demands of the 'old' Western-style labour movements may lead too easily to the kind of state corporatism that can be inimical to liberal democracy (Foweraker and Landman, 1997).

The struggle for social development tends therefore to take second place to struggles for political emancipation. Demands for the satisfaction of base needs are subordinated to the principled pursuit of a higher need for political autonomy and self-governance. The old politics of welfare associated with the capitalist North would seem to have become inherently suspect. It is regarded as a hollow and ineffectual 'politics of demand'. At one level, this bespeaks the extent to which faith has been lost in the capitalist welfare state model as a means of addressing human need. At another, it may imply an ascendancy of doctrinal liberalism at the expense of everyday claims making.

Beyond the politics of demand

Is it possible therefore to envisage an alternative politics? There are several candidates: Ivan Illich's politics of 'conviviality'; Marxist revolutionary politics or, at least, a Marxian 'politics of need' as envisioned by Kate Soper; or Nancy Fraser's 'politics of need interpretation'. I shall consider each in turn.

Illich's approach grew out of his own account of 'the history of needs' (1977). This entails a combination of the interpretive understandings of human need outlined in Chapter Three. On the one hand, Illich railed against the way in which advanced industrial societies – both capitalist and communist – either manufactured or imputed the needs of their citizens; on the other, against the way in which modern professionals dictated and disabled their clients' understanding of needs:

> … life without addictive access to commodities is rendered either impossible or criminal. Making do without consumption becomes impossible, not just for the average consumer but even for the poor. All forms of welfare … are of no help. The liberty to design and craft one's own distinctive dwelling is abolished in favor of the bureaucratic provision of standardized housing…. The organization of employment, skills, building resources, rules, and credit favor shelter as a commodity rather than as an activity. Whether the product is provided by

> an entrepreneur or an apparatchik, the effective result is the same: citizen impotence, our specifically modern experience of poverty. (Illich, 1977, pp vii–ix)

The need for housing, employment, healthcare and education is fashioned by market forces, state planning and/or the ministrations of professionals. The way forward, according to Illich, was to revert to a form of 'convivial austerity', the object of which would be 'to protect personal use value against disabling enrichment' (1977, p 16). It is a 'back to the future' prescription that is consonant, for example, with claims by ecologists that 'demand must be reduced, not expanded' (Porritt, 1984, p 136), or with Jordan's (2008) aim of restoring the notion of 'social value' to the public policy-making process (see Chapter Six). More fundamentally, however, a politics based on what Illich called conviviality would require new tools by which to reclaim the practical knowledge that would empower ordinary people to name and claim their own needs (Illich, 1973; see also Freire, 1972). Illich's is an essentially anarchistic and romantic quest. Elements of his analysis, however, especially his assertion that 'needs have become almost exclusively coterminous with commodities' (1977, p 13), are strongly redolent of Marxist thinking, albeit that Marx sought not to retreat from the effects of capitalist modernity but to transcend it.

In Chapter Two brief mention was made of Marx's concept of 'radical' needs. Agnes Heller sought to capture this elusive notion. Radical need could be defined as the expression of humanity's ultimate potential, something denied to us by capitalism that can only be realised through revolutionary action. Human beings need to work, but in the sense that they should be free to perform labour for its own sake; they need free time, in the sense that they should be free to be truly human; and they need universality, in the sense that they should be universally free to develop as individuals (Heller, 1974, pp 88-95). Central to the Marxist project is the concept of praxis: the synthesis between theory and action. The theory of which Marx spoke 'is actualised in a people only insofar as it actualises their needs.... A deep-going revolution can only be a revolution in basic needs' (cited in Heller, 1974, p 89). The satisfaction of radical needs, therefore, requires the revolutionary overthrow of capitalism.

One-and-a-quarter centuries since Marx's demise we might suppose that the revolutionary overthrow of capitalism is now a forlorn hope. Nonetheless, Kate Soper (1981) has attempted to address what a 'politics of need' might consist of. In Chapter Two, it may be recalled, I also explained the distinction that Marx made between use and exchange value. In a capitalist society we observe the relationships between the goods we consume and between the different sorts of work we perform not so much in terms of the extent to which they satisfy our needs as in terms of notions of their relative value as commodities. Marx's celebrated aphorism – 'from each according to his ability, to each according to his need' (cited by Soper, 1981, p 188) – was an attempt to imagine a society *without* commodities, in which need would replace value as the measure of things, in which work would be an expression of our species being and not an exchange of labour power. Marx had contended that 'only then can the narrow horizon of bourgeois rights be crossed in its entirety' (see Soper, 1981, p 188). His point was that the basis of rights under capitalism lay in the ownership and exchange of commodities. If human society were organised with a view to satisfying universal need, we would have no need of rights, at least not the kind of citizenship-based rights associated with capitalist liberal democracies.

To digress for a moment (since this was never a part of Marx's argument), might we yet conceive of some utopian form of cosmopolitan citizenship (Held, 1995) or 'deep' citizenship (Clarke, 1996) in which rights and needs become increasingly synonymous? And, in any event, rights could presumably still provide a necessary strategic resource in the event of an evolutionary as opposed to a revolutionary transition to socialism. Such a transition, according to Soper, required a politics that sought to plan for the meeting of needs. Soper argued that a society that read its needs from what it consumed was evading the question of needs (1981, pp 215–16). The implication here is that the capitalist welfare state did not and does not go far enough in addressing human need. A politics of needs entails decisions about what is needed and this requires *information* on which to base such decisions and mechanisms for social *participation* in the making of those decisions (1981, pp 210–11).

A glimpse of what this might entail is provided in Nancy Fraser's discussion of the 'politics of needs interpretation'. Fraser started from the premise that 'in late capitalist welfare state societies, talk about people's needs is an important species of political discourse' (1989, p 161). She proceeded to explore the ways in which needs were discursively interpreted and communicated. In doing so, she adopted what she later came to defend as a pragmatic approach to the study of discourse and communicative action (see Fraser, 1997, ch 6). The resulting account provides a distinctive perspective on social policy.

Fraser (1989, ch 8) identified three culturally constructed spheres of life or enclaves: the political, the economic and the domestic. She argued that for needs talk to enter the political sphere, it must be 'publicised', projected from the private sphere of commodities and market relations on the one hand and family and personal relations on the other into the public forum of political debate. Everyday livelihoods and personal needs were political, but private: a politics of needs interpretation might serve to democratise them. Social policy theorists, such as Esping-Andersen (1999), have discussed the extent to which capitalist welfare states may both 'decommodify' and 'defamilialise' (or may subsequently 'recommodify' and 'refamilialise') their citizens and/or the means by which the needs of citizens are met. Fraser discussed converse processes by which certain kinds of needs and needs talk could remain systemically depoliticised and confined to the economic or domestic spheres. But she also pointed to the circumstances in which the 'runaway needs' of, for example, exploited migrant workers or physically abused women could on occasions leak out of their enclaves and become politicised through what she called 'oppositional' forms of discourse. She was referring here to opposition at the level of everyday talking, contestation and argument.

Oppositional discourses may be met with 'reprivatisation' discourses that seek to '(re)depoliticise' such needs. In addition to oppositional and reprivatisation discourses, Fraser identified a third kind of needs discourse, 'expert' discourses. These were the discourses of the professional problem solvers who, as 'the politics of needs interpretation devolves into the administration of needs satisfaction' (1989, p 177), sought to colonise the definition of needs. Fraser's argument here is strikingly similar to that of Illich (see above). The implication is that a more effective and enduring politics of needs interpretation might require, as Illich and Soper each suggested, some means for the democratisation of information and of expert knowledge.

In describing the dialogic nature of claim and counterclaim, definition and redefinition, that are entailed in the politics of need interpretation, Fraser captured precisely the nature of the relationship that is referred to throughout this book between inherent and interpreted conceptions of human need. It is what may be called a 'dialectical' relationship in which one kind of definition both informs and feeds off the other. Additionally, in her discussion of the chains of association between consequentially connected needs, she expressly alluded to the distinction and the relationship between 'thin' and 'thick' needs (1989, p 163), also discussed in this book. Her model of a politics of needs interpretation envisaged how struggles over needs could potentially promote new synergies between inherent and interpreted conceptualisations of need, while also leading to progressively 'thicker' understandings of need.

However, Fraser acknowledged two unresolved issues. First, how were we to decide between competing needs claims? This, she said, must involve 'balancing democracy and equality' (1989, p 182). In later essays (1997, chs 1 and 3), she cast more light on what this might mean. In her critique of the liberal democratic public sphere (already discussed in Chapter Five above) she called for 'parity of participation', for steps to ensure that silent and oppressed groups or 'publics' should be enabled to access the political sphere on equal terms with vocal and powerful publics. Fundamentally connected with this call was a wider demand that a politics of recognition should go hand in hand with a politics of redistribution (Fraser and Honneth, 2003). A politics of need interpretation must recognise and include everybody's claims in order to negotiate a just distribution of resources. The intention here would seem to go some way to fulfilling Soper's participation requirement.

The second unresolved issue is the relationship between needs claims and rights. We have seen in this chapter and the last that this is an ambiguous and contested relationship. Fraser, for her part, decided to align herself 'with those who favour translating justified needs into social rights' (1989, p 183).

In defence of social rights?

Despite the failings of the old politics of welfare, the concept of social rights with which it has been associated remains an essential strategic element in any politics of need. Rights provide an important discursive resource within processes of political struggle or transition (Dean, 2008a). But I would argue that the translation of what Fraser refers to (but does not define) as 'justified' needs into social rights requires two things. Justification implies first, the critical autonomy of the human subject, and second, a polity founded on a eudaimonic ethic. These are concepts briefly encountered earlier in this book, but which I shall now explore in greater depth.

Critical autonomy

Doyal and Gough (1991) coined the term 'critical autonomy'. While personal autonomy, that is, 'basic' autonomy of agency, may be minimally necessary for a human being to exist with dignity, optimal needs satisfaction requires 'critical autonomy', a higher level of autonomy associated with political freedom and with the opportunity to 'question and to participate in *agreeing or changing* the rules' (Doyal and Gough, 1991, p 67; emphasis in original). Critical autonomy is not the autonomy of the isolated and independent individual, but of the connected and engaged political subject. In this sense critical autonomy is a condition precedent for a politics of needs interpretation. Doyal and Gough's concern was that, to be effective, the participation required to achieve critical autonomy required not only culturally specific competencies, but also an awareness of alternative cultural realities (1991, pp 187-9). It is not enough that people should be free to participate in a society if the cultural milieu of that society is repressive: they should be free to challenge or to reject that which is unacceptable in such a society. In this context Doyal and Gough placed special emphasis on educational needs, including the importance of higher education. This chimes to an extent with the demands of Illich (see above, and also Illich, 1971) and Freire (1972), albeit that Illich and Freire are rather more radical in their approach to the role of education.

Freire remains especially significant. Just as Fraser would have us 'publicise' those unseen and unheard needs that are experienced in private, Freire spoke of the 'culture of silence' that subdued oppressed peoples and called for a process by which people became conscious of their oppression and committed themselves to challenging it. He described this process, rather clumsily, as 'conscientisation'. For Freire existing forms of institutional education were deeply implicated in perpetuating the culture of silence. And alternative, liberating pedagogic techniques were necessary as a means to conscientisation. The basis of this pedagogy is dialogue. In place of top-down monologues and slogans, there should be dialogical cultural action: teachers and students, leaders and people should be engaged together as subjects in the creation of knowledge. These ideas are not necessarily confined to the realms of educational practice, but extend to everyday politics. They are ideas that speak simultaneously to Fraser's concept of a politics of needs interpretation and to Doyal and Gough's concept of critical autonomy. They also engage with my contention that inherent and interpreted conceptions of need exist in dialogical or dialectical relation to each other. Social rights are created at the point at which doctrines and claims engage with one another.

Insofar as the old politics of welfare had clearly entailed elements of negotiation around the recognition of needs and the specification of rights, they had not been fully dialogic in the sense envisaged by Freire. Popular discourses have been silenced or muted by hegemonic assumptions, resulting in restricted needs claims; or else they have been compromised by ideological orthodoxies, and have been reflected in compromised policy prescriptions. Drawing on the various interlinking categories developed in previous chapters, we might say:

- Survivalist forms of popular discourse have informed but have in turn been silenced by moral-authoritarian assumptions that tend to blame the individual should she fail to meet her own needs. This has tended to result in restricted notions of circumstantial need and the acceptance of conditional social rights.
- Conformist forms of popular discourse have informed but have in turn been silenced by paternalistic assumptions that situate the individual's

needs in relation to her place within the social order. This has tended to result in restricted notions of common need and social rights that, although they may be protective, are not necessarily liberating.

• Entrepreneurial forms of popular discourse have supported but have in turn been conditioned by a spectrum of economistic doctrine that equates the individual's needs with her freely expressed preferences. This has tended to result in compromised notions of particular needs and the acceptance of selective social rights.

• Reformist forms of popular discourse have supported but have in turn been conditioned by a spectrum of humanistic doctrine that equates the individual's needs with variously conceived categorical imperatives. This has tended to result in more or less compromised notions of universal need and social rights that, although they may be citizenship-based, can be substantively deficient.

An alternative politics of need would require a cultural shift towards the democratisation of knowledge and expertise in relation to the provision of services for meeting human needs, more meaningful opportunities for people to participate in decision-making processes and more dialogical forms of negotiation concerning the substance of people's claims to needs satisfaction. This formulation has much in common with Habermas's (1987) intriguing but infuriatingly abstract construction of the 'ideal speech situation' in which the identification and satisfaction of our needs would be achieved through un-coerced forms of negotiation (see Chapter Three). Critical autonomy may be achieved through the substantive framing and enforcement of rights to needs satisfaction, provided this is a process that can be rendered inclusive. This is the point at which grand but abstract ideas must be translated into more banal but plausible suggestions.

We have seen above that it has been difficult for the UNCESCR to provide an effective global forum for dialogue over the implementation of social rights. Similarly, at a European level, the Council of Europe's European Committee on Social Rights, created in parallel with the UNCESCR under the Council of Europe's Social Charter of 1961, has provided a somewhat limited forum. The European Social Charter was revised in 1996 so as to allow the Committee to receive representations or complaints from trade unions and NGOs, but the procedure has still to be fully ratified by all state parties and appears underused. Social rights have been written in, often symbolically, to national constitutions in a number of countries, including India, Brazil and South Africa, but with mixed and generally limited results in terms of their capacity to promote dialogue as to the substance of the needs whose satisfaction is to be guaranteed (Hunt, 1996).

There have been proposals by NGOs for the establishment of national Social Charters in both the UK (Coote, 1992) and Canada (Bakan and Schneiderman, 1992). These have generated academic debate, but nothing more. The Canadian proposal, framed as an alternative to a government proposal for a more limited social clause within the Canadian constitution, was presented by the National Anti-Poverty Organization (now called Canada Without Poverty). It has been defended by Jennifer Nedelsky and Craig Scott (1992; see also Hunt, 1996, pp 185-7) since it was seen to promote social rights as 'sites of dialogue', not as 'trumps', as 'sites of social struggle' and not as 'debate-stopping conclusions'. The alternative Social Charter proposed the creation of a supervisory social rights council as a forum with educative and monitoring functions in which it was envisaged that people would 'converse about different claims regarding different values and relationships' (Nedelsky and Scott, 1992, p 62). Nedelsky and Scott attempt to ground the potential role of a social rights council in everyday life by conceiving of 'rights as relationships', reflecting the ways in which rights structure relationships of interdependency (1992, p 69). With this in mind it is difficult to imagine that a *national* social rights council could ever provide an intimate enough forum for meaningful and inclusive dialogue. However, what scope might there be for networks of *local* social rights councils?

In Chapter Three I discussed the potential and the drawbacks of participatory approaches to need interpretation (see also Barnes et al, 2007). Local social rights councils might provide a different kind of mechanism for effective participation through a standing forum in which anybody might participate. There are many precedents for strictly localised kinds of standing forum. In England, for example, the chequered history of parish councils can be traced back 1,000 years or more. They were once distinctly undemocratic bodies with direct responsibility for the local relief of poverty, a responsibility that tended to be arbitrarily observed, if at all. They are now democratically elected, but virtually powerless. In more recent memory, there were experiments in the 1970s with non-statutory urban neighbourhood councils (Cockburn, 1977), with local community relations councils (created under the 1968 Race Relations Act but discontinued after 1976) and community health councils (statutorily created in 1974, but eventually abolished, except in Wales, in 2003). We should not romanticise the achievements of these local forums, which could co-opt as much as empower local inhabitants and which were not always socially inclusive, but in some neighbourhoods they succeeded in attracting substantial levels of participation and provided a site for quite vibrant political debate relating specifically and immediately to the needs of local people. A more recent and very different example of local participation in a politics of needs interpretation has been the participatory budget-making process in Porto Alegre, Brazil (Wainwright, 2003). It is perhaps, therefore, not too fanciful to envisage the creation of local social rights councils as forums in which vernacular discourses of need could be promoted and claims and grievances framed, councils that would wield real influence over local human service providers and have an effective voice in national policy-making processes.

These would have to go further than the kinds of public participation initiative and service user forums that have recently been tried out, for example, in Britain. A study of such initiatives has concluded that the outcomes:

> ... were not enough to sustain participation over time. Material and/or institutional change was also necessary. The evidence ... suggests that such change is not much in evidence as an outcome of new deliberative practices. For example ... the impact that each of the 'community governance' initiatives [we studied] was having on mainstream service providers appeared limited.... this was in part because little power was invested in any of the initiatives: their status was almost exclusively advisory. (Barnes et al, 2007, pp 201-2)

Similarly, local social rights councils would have to be more than consultative forums, managed by researchers or technocrats, such as the participatory poverty assessments championed in the developing world by the World Bank (Narayan et al, 2000). They would have to have a remit empowering them to articulate and to authentically interpret human need, and to negotiate for the satisfaction of such need as of right. They would have to be democratically constituted, locally managed and permanent. They would have to be more than trade unions for 'the poor', since they would be inclusive promoters of the social rights of all. National mechanisms through which the voices of local forums are concerted would have to ensure that it was not only the noisier voices that were heard. It is also just as possible that social rights councils might be established to articulate the voices of communities founded on criteria other than locality, such as those based on particular kinds of shared experience.

However, a book such as this is not the place to model detailed proposals, but merely to illustrate that there are ways in which an inclusive dialogic process for translating needs into rights could be built from the local level upwards. Critical autonomy for all of humanity – including hitherto isolated individuals, excluded minorities, isolated communities and silent majorities – might yet become a practical rather than an imaginary possibility.

A eudaimonic ethic

The second requirement for the translation of human needs into more effective social rights would be the ascendancy of a eudaimonic social ethic. When introducing the distinction between thin and thick interpretations of human need in Chapter Six, I discussed the closely related distinction between hedonic and eudaimonic notions of well-being. I suggested that social policy based, for example, on principles of social insurance or universal social provision reflected elements of a eudaimonic approach in the sense that they were concerned not only to prevent suffering, but also to promote human flourishing. Insurance-based social provision can be insufficiently inclusive and universal provision can be inadequate in relation to particular need, but both, nonetheless, set out to do more than satisfy people's survival requirements; they set out to enable people to share the risks they face and/or to be protected as citizens.

And earlier in Chapter Five, when discussing the need for recognition and for care, I mentioned both Honneth's conception of the ethical life (that requires mutual recognition through love, solidarity and rights) and the feminist conception of the ethic of care. I have concurred with those (for example Clement, 1998) who suggest that although an ethic of care may enjoin us to embrace the mutual responsibilities we have as interdependent but vulnerable beings, it is important that this should extend to recognising the needs and rights of distant strangers as much as those of intimates and neighbours. Let us call this more extensive ethic, which requires an acceptance of rights as relationships (Nedelsky and Scott, 1992, p 69), a eudaimonic ethic.

Insofar as I have previously referred to moral-authoritarian approaches to human need, it is important that I explain what I mean by 'an ethic'. In everyday English the terms 'morality' and 'ethics' may be used as if they were synonymous. Although the two are intimately connected, there is a philosophical distinction. Morals are concerned with cultural *mores*, with norms, customs and what may be commonly deemed to be *good*. Ethics are concerned with cognitive *ethos*, with values, principles and what can be systemically deduced to be *right*. Morality may implicitly be informed by some kind of ethic. An ethic, on the other hand, is an explicit reflection on morality. A hedonic ethic is concerned with the duties incidentally owed to others by individuals in pursuit of the satisfaction of their own needs, duties that will ensure that others are not denied fair opportunity. A eudaimonic ethic is concerned with the mutual or collective responsibility that is shared between people who depend on each other for the satisfaction of their needs, but more than this, it is concerned that others too should realise their human potential.

A eudaimonic ethic, by its nature, transcends the boundaries of national citizenship. The eudaimonic ethic is a principle of social development. Insofar as it may invoke the language of social rights in order to give expression to human needs, it is not necessarily to the social rights of citizenship that it must turn so much as to the social rights component of the human rights agenda. Alternatively, it might require the evolution of some form of transnational, post-national or global citizenship (Falk, 1994; Dwyer, 2004b, ch 10). Whatever form it were to take, global citizenship, as suggested above, would be more cosmopolitan and/or deeper in nature and attenuate the distinction between the naming of needs and the claiming of rights.

There is a campaign for the establishment of a UN Parliamentary Assembly (see http://en.unpacampaign.org), which may or may not represent a step towards a new architecture for global governance, based on global citizenship. As matters stand, however, there is a fundamental tension between current agencies of the UN. We have already seen in Chapter Six that agencies such as the World Bank and the WTO favour a social development strategy premised on free trade in human services, with selective welfare safety nets, whereas the ILO favours social insurance or universal social security provision. There is no agreement as to how even the most basic needs of the poorest members of humanity may be met.

At the turn of the current millennium, of the world's 6.1 billion people, 2.8 billion (46%) were living in 'severe poverty' on less than $US2 per day at purchasing power parity (PPP), and 1.2 billion (20%) were living in 'extreme poverty' on less than $1 per day (UNDP, 2000; Townsend and Gordon, 2002). The poorest 2.8 billion had 1.2% of global income, while the 0.9 billion people living in high-income OECD countries had 80%. And yet a 1% shift of aggregate global income from the OECD countries to the poorest 2.8% of humanity would alleviate their poverty (Pogge, 2002, p 2). The extent of international commitment through the Millennium Development Goals to alleviate poverty is to merely halve, between 1990 and 2015, the proportion of humanity living in extreme poverty. Robert Goodin has argued that the ethical basis of our responsibility towards other human beings, whether they are our own children or needy neighbours, lies in their vulnerability and that, 'individually or collectively, we have the same sort of strong responsibilities towards all those who are vulnerable to our actions and choices' (Goodin, 1985, p xi). Given that poor countries are significantly disadvantaged relative to rich countries by virtue of their colonial past and the current terms of international trade, he concludes:

> ... that we do have a responsibility to aid distant peoples in
> distress but that it is a collective rather than an individual

responsibility. While people in the Third World may not be vulnerable to us in the First World as individuals, they are enormously vulnerable to us as a collectivity. Saying that the responsibility is a collective one does not exempt individuals from responsibility: it merely changes the character of their responsibilities. (1985, p 163)

If this were accepted, it would clearly imply that a far greater commitment is required to the social rights of humanity as a whole.

In the poorest parts of the world there are grounds for profound pessimism. Wood and Newton (2005) argue that there are in the world many 'unsettled societies', societies that lack not only a formalised labour market, but any legitimate state apparatus. In these circumstances a politics of need could not take hold without fundamental reform of the political order. Such societies are governed principally if not militarily or coercively, through patrimonialism or clientalism, such that much of the population can achieve basic existential security only by way of a 'Faustian bargain' that perpetuates their material poverty. On the other hand, Peter Townsend (2007), the stalwart veteran of academic social policy, insisted it was clearly possible for the international community to enforce the observance of the rights to social security and to an adequate standard of living contained in UN human rights instruments and in the standards set by the ILO. He demanded an international legal framework to regulate the conduct of transnational corporations and the contribution they could make to social development, and the institution of a Currency Transfer Tax (or Tobin Tax) (Nissanke, 2003; see also *Table 9.1*) as a means of securing the necessary resources.

In the meantime, key thinkers are divided between those who consider that the needs of the poorest members of humanity are best addressed by regulating the conduct of the rich and those who seek mechanisms for giving effect to the rights of the poor against the rest of humanity. Pogge (2007, ch 1) regards severe poverty as a human rights violation, an injustice. He seeks ways of reigning in the practices by which the most affluent have shaped the world order to the disadvantage of the poorest. He seeks an international fiscal mechanism by which to achieve global justice: the Global Resource Dividend (Pogge, 2002, ch 8; see also Bertram, 2008; and *Table 9.1*). Campbell (2007), on the other hand, believes that extreme poverty is a violation of human rights, not merely because it is unjust, but because it is an affront to the humanity of poor people themselves. All human rights, he argues, derive from the existence of human needs (2007, p 59), and so he seeks to give effect to social rights, to rights to subsistence and the resources required for a truly human life. Poverty is as specific a violation of human rights as torture or slavery and, for this reason, humanity must come before justice. Elements of Campbell's argument are perhaps confusing,[1] but the thrust of it is very similar to the idea that it is a humanitarian and essentially eudaimonic ethic that should prevail over a justice-based and essentially hedonic ethic. Humanitarianism is not the same as charity; it cannot be optional in the sense that it encompasses the essence of our species being, which can only be fulfilled in relationship with other human beings. Consistent with this argument, Campbell's favoured international fiscal mechanism is a Global Humanitarian Levy (2007, pp 67-8; see also *Table 9.1*).

Table 9.1: *International fiscal mechanisms for meeting human need*

Tobin Tax, or Currency Transaction Tax (CTT)	Global Resources Dividend (GRD)	Global Humanitarian Levy (GHL)
First proposed by the Nobel Laureate, James Tobin, who suggested a 1% tax on all speculative currency transfers as a way to tame global markets and fund social development.	Proposed by Thomas Pogge (2002, ch 8) as tax to redistribute from those in the world who made the greatest demands upon the world's natural resources to those who made the least.	Proposed by Tom Campbell (2007, 67-8) as a mechanism for enforcing global humanitarian obligations through the progressive taxation of wealthier individuals.
*****	*****	*****
Subsequent variants on the proposal have suggested more modest levies – from 0.005% to 0.25% on all currency transfers around the world, something that is technically feasible since virtually all such transactions are electronically conducted or recorded. Since currency to the value of $US2 trillion or more is exchanged each day, this could generate substantial funds to be administered for development aid by UN agencies.	All countries that use or sell limited natural resources extracted from their own territories should pay a dividend for the benefit of those elsewhere in the world who have a stake in those resources. The GRD payable on crude oil extraction, for example, might be $2 per barrel. Pogge's aim was to generate of the order of 1% of aggregate global income: enough to lift the incomes of the poorest 2.8 billion people above the $2 per day poverty line.	All national governments would levy an additional tax of, say, 2% on all personal incomes of more than US$50,000 (or the equivalent) and 2% on all personal wealth above US$500,000. The funds raised at national level would be accumulated and administered globally. The mechanism would replace existing bilateral and multilateral Overseas Development Aid (ODA) arrangements.

Emerging from organisations such as the anti-globalisation movement and the World Social Forum there is now also what some have characterised as a resurgent global Left (de Sousa Santos, 2006). Clear policy prescriptions are seldom advanced within this movement and, certainly, there is resistance to social development models that originate in the global North (Hardt and Negri, 2000; Deacon, 2007). Writers like de Sousa Santos (2006) would argue that the mono-cultural epistemology of the global North constrains and obscures alternative forms of knowledge and understanding about needs and rights and he calls for an epistemology of the South. It is a call premised on an ethical dimension that de Sousa Santos calls an 'axiology of care'. This might be construed as a eudaimonic ethic that resonates on the one hand with the feminist ethic of care (Sevenhuijsen, 1998) and on the other with Marxist conceptions of radical need (Heller, 1974). In a characteristically obtuse way, de Sousa Santos suggests that clues to the future lie in the present and this might be taken to imply more pragmatic and strategic approaches to human need and social development. Callinicos (2003), in his *An anti-capitalist manifesto*, for example, suggests ways in which familiar demands for reform, that already command support across a variety of constituencies, might be advanced in concert so as to mount a fundamental challenge to global capitalism. He argues for the pursuit on a global basis of universal basic income schemes, progressive and redistributive forms of taxation, widespread reductions in working hours and the defence of public services.

Whether it is informed by debates between and within the family of UN agencies, within academia or from the global Left, a eudaimonic ethic in social policy and social development would be premised on a very particular conception of human need. That premise, I suggest, is that our humanity depends not on survival and satisfaction; but on social engagement and self-fulfilment. This implies approaches that are:

- *Universal:* they should aim to reach 'people as people'. The phrase is redolent of aphorisms from ubuntu philosophy (Ramose, 2003), an ancient pan-African humanistic tradition and an example of an 'epistemology of the South'. The wellspring of our needs is our personhood, which is defined not through productive or trading relations, but through the way that human beings care for and about each other. The purpose of social policy and social development is to underwrite the mutual obligations and attachments that people have for one another.
- *Unconditional:* provision for meeting human need should put life needs first and should not be conditional on compliance with particular norms of behaviour. The primary aim should not be, for example, to promote the formation of human capital required for national productivity and

competitiveness, but to guarantee the capabilities required for human development and 'ethical life' (cf Honneth, 1995).

• *Globally contextualised but locally grounded:* this applies in two senses. On the one hand, to achieve social development it may be necessary in some instances to overcome the alienating or disabling effects of local relations of power. On the other hand, local demands and epistemologies may provide alternative understandings of human well-being that supersede hegemonic assumptions. Workable solutions occur when human needs are translated into meaningful rights, at the point where top-down and bottom-up demands are resolved through inclusive negotiation.

Conclusion

At the very end of Chapter One I announced my argument that translating the essential nature of human interdependency into an effective range of human rights requires a politics of human need. That argument has been addressed in this final chapter. The politics of need is all around us. It goes on in our everyday relationships as much as in parliamentary debating chambers. Wherever human beings negotiate to have their needs recognised and satisfied, they are engaged in a politics of need. That is why need is such a central concept in social policy. It is precisely because need is a concept that bears a great many meanings that the politics of need is constituted through contests over meaning: top-down *versus* bottom-up meanings; thin *versus* thick meanings.

In the conduct of such contests critical autonomy is essential to ensure that claims-based interpretations of need can meaningfully and effectively inform the doctrinal framing of inherent needs. A eudaimonic ethic is essential to promote 'thicker' more universal accounts that situate human need in the context of human interdependency over the life course and between the generations, while always taking account of 'thinner' forms of individual need when these must take short-term priority.

Articulating this with the categories of need discussed in Chapter Seven, we might suppose that an alternative politics of need would transcend the struggle for survival. It would be concerned with more than the satisfaction of circumstantial need. It would be a politics centred on an open and negotiable understanding of universal need, an understanding that looks to accommodate particular need on the one hand, and to incorporate common need on the other. This is not a utopian quest but merely a way of taking human need seriously.

Note

[1] Campbell appears uncertain as to whether the duty of one human being to relieve the suffering of another should be attributed to some form of 'positive utilitarianism' or to 'neo–Kantianism', and likens the difference between these two interpretations as a 'family quarrel'. In one sense, this illustrates admirably my contention that humanitarian approaches can be hybrid in nature, drawing on competing moral discourses. In another sense, it elides those humanitarian approaches which are informed by neo–Marxist theories of human need.

Summary

- This chapter has argued that the creation in various forms across the industrialised world of the capitalist welfare state had crystallised a particular politics of need. It is suggested that:
  - this was a politics of welfare within a mixed economy in which a state-mediated needs nexus coexisted with a market-mediated cash nexus;
  - by the end of the 20th century, the limitations of that accommodation had become apparent. Processes of state mediation were challenged, for very different reasons, by pro-market neoliberals on the one hand, and by the emergence of a new culturally or identity-oriented politics on the other;
  - in the 'developing' world, the prospects of social development premised on a politics of welfare comparable to that which applied in the global North were dismissed as a misguided 'politics of demand', as a distraction from the particular and often desperate needs of the global South.
- Radical alternatives to the politics of welfare have been explored:
  - Illich's 'politics of conviviality' represents a kind of back to the future vision of how people might regain knowledge of their own needs;
  - the Marxist notion of 'radical need' implies a revolutionary politics whose ultimate objective is to realise humanity's ultimate potential. However, a more gradualist politics of need would necessarily entail explicit and participative processes by which to plan the meeting of needs;
  - Fraser's 'politics of needs interpretation' attempts to capture the possibility that we might transcend the old politics of welfare by instituting a politics concerned not only with social justice and distribution of resources to meet need, but also with parity of participation and the recognition of the needs of oppressed or marginalised people.
- It has been argued that a politics of needs interpretation, while depending on a rights-based approach, would require an explicit commitment to:
  - critical autonomy, that is, the substantive capacity of all members of any society to participate in a politics of need as it affects every aspect of their lives, a capacity based on critical understanding and parity of recognition;

- a eudaimonic ethic, that is, a guiding premise that holds that a 'good life' necessarily entails fulfilment through social contribution and involvement as well as individual comfort and stimulation.

Questions for discussion:

- What has politics got to do with human need?
- Has the politics of welfare and of the 'old' welfare state necessarily had its day?
- How do you think we should set about politicising or 'publicising' human need? Is a rights-based strategy the best way?

Afterword

I ended the last chapter, as promised, with a normative conclusion. Whether readers agree is less important than that they take away from this book a better understanding of why all students of social policy should take human need seriously.

There is a very obvious sense in which social policy engages with issues of human need: with people's needs for various forms of human services and to be safeguarded from various kinds of harm. In the ordinary course of our lives we need health provision, education, housing and social security and at times of special vulnerability we may need personal care and protection. Social policy may, but does not necessarily, entail translating human need into social rights. That, at least, is the premise on which this book has been written. It is strange, perhaps, that there is relatively little academic literature within the social policy subject area that focuses specifically on human need. It is a topic that, potentially, offers us a window into the fundamental principles that underpin social policy.

In recent times, social policy students' introduction to the idea of human need has been focused, principally, on two sources: Doyal and Gough's theory of human need (1984, 1991) and Bradshaw's taxonomy of social needs (1972). Doyal and Gough's contribution is a theory that posits the existence of universal needs that vest in and are experienced by every human being: the needs for health on the one hand, and for an element of autonomy on the other. The job of social policy is to optimise access to the intermediate satisfiers by which these fundamental needs may be met. Bradshaw's taxonomy is a pragmatic interpretation of the different ways in which policy makers can interpret needs: through normative judgement, personal experience, express demand or comparative analysis. Beyond this point, further reflection on human need tends by and large to be overshadowed by concerns about social justice and the question of which needs or whose needs must take priority. This is wholly understandable, but it pulls the student immediately into the sphere of ideological contests between liberals, social democrats, communitarians, feminists and others.

This is essential to an understanding of the principles of social policy, but too easily it draws the student away from everyday meanings and intimate experiences of need, from an understanding that our needs are rooted in our interdependency as human beings, from the very basics of human need.

When writing this book, I endeavoured to start from an understanding of everyday meanings or 'discourses' of need. This built in part on thinking informed by my previous research in which I explored the ways in which people profess to understand and talk about the underlying moral issues associated with state welfare provision (Dean, 1999). Helpful comments obtained by the publishers from an anonymous reader on an early version of the typescript for this book included a complaint about my use in certain passages of 'high fallutin language (discourse especially)', when paradoxically, my discussion of 'discourse' was intended precisely to demonstrate how important everyday language and expression is to our understandings of human need. My argument started (then and now) from a very simple account of the different responses to human need that may be found in everyday popular discourse. That leads on, inevitably, to a more complex and nuanced debate, which I have made, I hope, as clear as reasonably possible. In this brief afterword, however, I attempt to reprise my argument as succinctly and straightforwardly as I can.

My starting point has been to challenge the reader to think about the different and contradictory ways in which people talk about everyday human needs. I have suggested there are perhaps four ways in which any or all of us might sometimes do so:

- *In moralistic (or moral-authoritarian) ways:* what people need or ought to be able to do is to survive without impinging on the lives of others.
- *In economistic ways:* what people need is demonstrated by the preferences they express through their behaviour under free market conditions.
- *In paternalistic ways:* what people need or ought to have and do is reflected through common customs in the community or society to which they belong.
- *In humanistic (or humanitarian) ways:* what people need is defined by some ideal vision of what constitutes human fulfilment.

The next stage in my argument entailed an attempt to unpick the distinction between absolute and relative need. I did this by drawing out two intersecting and dynamic distinctions: one between abstractly formulated inherent definitions and concretely formulated interpreted definitions; the other between 'thin' and 'thick' definitions of need. Doyal and Gough's theory, incidentally, represents an example of an inherent definition. Bradshaw's taxonomy is an instance of interpretive definition.

The 'thin'/'thick' distinction (which is not necessarily used in the same way as other commentators) is linked with the philosophical distinction between hedonic and eudaimonic well-being, or, more crudely, between happiness and the fulfilment of a good life.

Along the way, I digressed from the central core of my argument: first, to relate concepts of need to debates central to social policy concerning poverty and inequality; second, to consider relatively recent concepts – social exclusion, capabilities and recognition – that bear on and may have served to displace discussion of human need. The purpose, and, I hope, the effect, of these digressions is to locate the relevance of human need as a concept and to deepen our understanding of it.

I then brought together the elements of my argument in order to present an alternative taxonomy or model. This model applies the analytical distinctions between inherent and interpreted conceptualisations of need on the one hand, and thin and thick conceptualisations on the other, in order to relate the four everyday 'discourses' of need to four broad approaches to human need that may be seen to be historically and contemporarily evident in the development of social policy:

- *Circumstantial need:* a conception with roots in moral–authoritarian approaches, which has been reflected in the development of conditional forms of welfare provision.
- *Particular need:* a conception with roots in economistic approaches, which has been reflected in the development of targeted forms of welfare provision.
- *Common need:* a conception with roots in paternalistic approaches, which has been reflected in the development of policies that organise the sharing of risks.
- *Universal need:* a conception with roots in humanitarian approaches, which has been reflected in the development of policies based on social citizenship rights.

These conceptions are very broadly defined and in practice they overlap. Substantive social policy may combine different conceptions of need. It may do so in ways that are complex, or even contradictory. The model is a way to help us understand how human need, as a contested concept, informs social policy.

At this point in my argument I turned to focus specifically on the ways in which human needs may be translated into social rights and on the political conditions in which that process might be advanced. My aim was to contribute to current debate about the future of social policy. Rights to social welfare can be framed in different ways – as conditional, selective, protective or citizenship-based – depending on the approach to human need that informs them. The challenge for a politics of need, I argued, is to achieve more effective and meaningful social rights. Social rights entail political negotiation: a contest between top-down and bottom-up meanings, between thin and thick definitions. My ideal would be an open understanding of human needs that are universal, not merely circumstantial, yet which can accommodate a variety of what I have defined as particular and common needs. This brings us back to ideological debate about the nature and substance of social justice (see for example Craig et al, 2008), but it does so through a careful consideration of human need.

In my attempt simultaneously to simplify and elaborate the potentially bewildering array of concepts that lie at the heart of the notion of human need, it has been necessary to strike a balance. I set out quite deliberately to achieve an element of analytical parsimony that may be welcome to some but will fail, no doubt, to satisfy everybody. There is so much more that could be written about human need, especially as we contemplate the uncertainty of the future that humanity – by its own failings – now faces. My hope, nonetheless, is that this book will serve as a resource for the teaching of social policy and for those who wish to re-examine or re-engage with the idea of human need.

Resources

Key additional reading and sources of interest

On human need and social policy

- Doyal, L. and Gough, I. (1991) *A theory of human need*, Basingstoke: Macmillan.
- Goodin, R. (1988) *Reasons for welfare: The political theory of the welfare state*, Princeton, NJ: Princeton University Press.
- Hewitt, M. (1992) *Welfare ideology and need: Developing perspectives on the welfare state*, Hemel Hempstead: Harvester Wheatsheaf.

On related concepts and issues

- Lister, R. (2004) *Poverty*, Cambridge: Polity Press.
- Held, D. and Kaya, A. (eds) (2007) *Global inequality*, Cambridge: Polity Press.
- Hills, J., Le Grand, J. and Piachaud, D. (eds) (2002) *Understanding social exclusion*, Oxford: Oxford University Press.
- Sen, A. (1999) *Development as freedom*, Oxford: Oxford University Press.
- Fraser, N. and Honneth, A. (2003) *Redistribution or recognition?*, London: Verso.
- Jordan, B. (2008) *Welfare and well-being: Social value in public policy*, Bristol: The Policy Press.

On needs and rights

- Dean, H. (2002) *Welfare rights and social policy*, Harlow: Prentice Hall.

On needs and politics: alternative approaches

- Illich, I. (1977) *Towards a history of needs*, New York, NY: Bantam/Random House.
- Soper, K. (1981) *On human needs*, Brighton: Harvester Wheatsheaf.
- Fraser, N. (1989) *Unruly practices: Power, discourse and gender in contemporary social theory*, Minneapolis, MN: University of Minnesota Press.

Selected websites of potential interest

On poverty and disadvantage

- in Britain, The Poverty Site: www.poverty.org.uk/
- in Europe, Employment, Social Affairs and Equal Opportunities: http://ec.europa.eu/employment_social/social_inclusion/jrep_en.htm#joint_report
- in the US, the National Poverty Center: http://npc.umich.edu/poverty/
- globally, the United Nations Development Programme: www.undp.org

On social attitudes to need

- in Britain, the National Centre for Social Research: www.natcen.ac.uk/natcen/pages/op_socialattitudes.htm
- globally, the World Values Survey: www.worldvaluessurvey.org

On alternative/critical approaches

- capability approach, the Human Development and Capability Association: www.capabilityapproach.com
- Max-Neef model of human-scale development: www.rainforestinfo.org.au/background/maxneef.htm
- anti-autistic economics: www.autisme-economie.org
- happiness index, Happiness Foundation: www.happiness.org/Resources/Happiness_Studies/Happiest_Countries.aspx

References

Adler, M. and Posner, E. (2006) *New foundations of cost-benefit analysis*, Cambridge, MA: Harvard University Press.

Alcock, P. (2006) *Understanding poverty*, Basingstoke: Palgrave.

Alkire, S. (2002) *Valuing freedoms: Sen's capability approach and poverty reduction*, New York, NY: World Bank/Oxford University Press.

Althusser, L. (1994) *Althusser: A critical reader* (edited by G. Elliott), Oxford: Blackwell.

Andrews, F. and Withey, S. (1976) *Social indicators of well-being*, New York, NY: Plenum Press.

Annetts, J., Law, A., McNeish, W. and Mooney, G. (2009) *Understanding social movements and social welfare*, Bristol: The Policy Press.

Arnstein, S. (1969) 'A ladder of citizen participation', *Journal of the American Institute of Planners*, vol 35, pp 216-24.

Assiter, A. (2000) 'Bodies and dualism', in K. Ellis and H. Dean (eds) *Social policy and the body*, Basingstoke: Macmillan.

Auletta, K. (1982) *The underclass*, New York, NY: Random House.

Baers, J., Beck, W., van der Maesen, L., Walker, A. and Herriman, P. (2005) *Renewing aspects of the social quality theory for developing its indicators*, Amsterdam: European Foundation on Social Quality.

Bakan, J. and Schneiderman, D. (1992) *Social justice and the constitution: Perspectives on a social union for Canada*, Ottawa, Canada: Carleton University Press.

Baker, J., Lynch, K., Cantillon, S. and Walsh, J. (2004) *Equality: From theory to action*, Basingstoke: Palgrave Macmillan.

Barnes, M., Newman, J. and Sullivan, H. (2007) *Power, participation and political renewal: Case studies in political participation*, Bristol: The Policy Press.

Barry, B. (2002) 'Social exclusion, social isolation and the distribution of income', in J. Hills, J. Le Grand and D. Piachaud (eds) *Understanding social exclusion*, Oxford: Oxford University Press.

Barry, N. (1987) *The New Right*, London: Croom Helm.

Baudrillard, J. (1970) *The consumer society: Myths and structures*, London: Sage Publications.

Baudrillard, J. (1988) *Selected writings* (edited by M. Poster), Cambridge: Polity Press.

Bauman, Z. (1993) *Postmodern ethics*, Oxford: Blackwell.

Bauman, Z. (1998) *Work, consumerism and the new poor*, Buckingham: Open University Press.

Beck, U. and Beck-Gernsheim, E. (2001) *Individualization*, London: Sage Publications.

Beck, W., van der Maesen, L. and Walker, A. (1997) *The social quality of Europe*, Bristol: The Policy Press.

Becker, G. (1993) *Human capital*, Chicago, IL: University of Chicago Press.

Becker, G. (1998) *Accounting for tastes*, Cambridge, MA: Harvard University Press.

Bekkers, V., Dijkstra, G., Edwards, A. and Fenger, M. (2007) *Governance and the democratic deficit*, Aldershot: Ashgate.

Bentham, J. (1789) 'An introduction to the principles and morals of legislation', in M. Warnock (ed) *Utilitarianism*, Glasgow: Collins.

Benton, T. (1988) 'Humanism = specieism: Marx on humans and animals', *Radical Philosophy*, vol 50, pp 4–18.

Beresford, P. and Croft, S. (2001) 'Service users' knowledges and the social construction of social work', *Journal of Social Work*, vol 1, pp 293–316.

Berlin, I. (1967) 'Two concepts of liberty', in A. Quinton (ed) *Political philosophy*, Oxford: Oxford University Press.

Bertram, C. (2008) 'Globalisation, social justice and the politics of aid', in G. Craig, T. Burchardt and D. Gordon (eds) *Social justice and public policy*, Bristol: The Policy Press.

Beveridge, W. (1942) *Social insurance and allied services*, London: HMSO.

Bochel, C. and Bochel, H. (2004) *The UK social policy process*, Basingstoke: Palgrave.

Bochel, H., Bochel, C., Page, R. and Sykes, R. (2005) *Social policy: Issues and development*, Harlow: Pearson/Prentice Hall.

Booth, C. (1889) *The life and labour of the people in London*, London: Macmillan.

Bottomore, T. (1992) 'Citizenship and social class, forty years on', in T. Marshall and T. Bottomore (eds) *Citizenship and social class*, London: Pluto.

Bourdieu, P. (1997) 'The forms of capital', in A. Halsey, H. Lauder, P. Brown and A. Wells (eds) *Education, culture, economy, society*, Oxford: Oxford University Press.

Bourdieu, P. (1999) *The weight of the world: Social suffering in contemporary society*, Cambridge: Polity.

Bradshaw, J. (1972) 'The concept of social need', *New Society*, 30 March.

Bradshaw, J. and Finch, N. (2003) 'Overlaps in dimensions of poverty', *Journal of Social Policy*, vol 32, no 4, pp 513-25.

Britto, T. (2006) 'Conditional cash transfers in Latin America', in UNDP (United Nations Development Programme) (ed) *Social protection: The role of cash transfers – Poverty in focus*, Brasilia: International Poverty Centre.

Brown, M. (1977) *Introduction to social administration in Britain*, London: Hutchinson.

Bull, M. (2007) 'Vectors of the biopolitical', *New Left Review*, vol 45, pp 7-25.

Burchardt, T. (2006a) *Foundations for measuring equality: A discussion paper for the Equalities Review*, CASEpaper 111, London: CASE/STICERD, London School of Economics and Political Science.

Burchardt, T. (2006b) 'Happiness and social policy: barking up the right tree in the wrong neck of the woods', in L. Bauld, K. Clarke and T. Maltby (eds) *Social Policy Review 18*, Bristol: The Policy Press/Social Policy Association.

Burchardt, T. and Vizard, P. (2007) *Definition of equality and framework for measurement: Final recommendations of the Equalities Review Steering Group on Measurement*, CASEpaper 120, London: CASE/STICERD, London School of Economics and Political Science.

Burchardt, T., Clark, D. and Vizard, P. (2008) *Overall project briefing for EHRC and GEO specialist consultation on selection of indicators for Equality Measurement Framework*, Briefing Paper No 1, London: OPHI/CASE.

Burchardt, T., Le Grand, J. and Piachaud, D. (2002) 'Introduction', in J. Hills, J. Le Grand and D. Piachaud (eds) *Understanding social exclusion*, Oxford: Oxford University Press.

Cabinet Office (1999) *Modernising government*, London: The Stationery Office.

Callinicos, A. (2003) *An anti-capitalist manifesto*, Cambridge: Polity Press.

Callinicos, A. (2007) *Social theory: A historical introduction*, Cambridge: Polity Press.

Campbell, T. (1988) *Justice*, Basingstoke: Macmillan.

Campbell, T. (2007) 'Poverty as a violation of human rights: inhumanity or injustice?', in T. Pogge (ed) *Freedom from poverty as a human right: Who owes what to the very poor*, Oxford: UNESCO/Oxford University Press.

Castles, F. and Mitchell, D. (1993) 'Worlds of welfare and families of nations', in F. Castles (ed) *Families of nations: Patterns of public policy in Western democracies*, Aldershot: Dartmouth.

Chambers, R. (1997) *Whose reality counts?*, London: Intermediate Technology Publications.

Chambers, R. and Conway, G. (1992) *Sustainable rural livelihoods: Practical concepts for the 21st century*, IDS Discussion Paper 296, Brighton: Institute of Development Studies.

Chan, C.-K., Ngok, K.-L. and Phillips, D. (2008) *Social policy in China*, Bristol: The Policy Press.

Clarke, J. (2003) 'Managing and delivering welfare', in P. Alcock, A. Erskine and M. May (eds) *The student's companion to social policy*, Oxford: Blackwell.

Clarke, J. (2004) 'Dissolving the public realm? The logics and limits of neo-liberalism', *Journal of Social Policy*, vol 33, pp 27-48.

Clarke, J. and Newman, J. (1997) *The managerial state*, London: Sage Publications.

Clarke, P. (1996) *Deep citizenship*, London: Pluto.

Clement, G. (1998) *Care, autonomy and justice: Feminism and the ethic of care*, Boulder, CO: Westview Press.

Cockburn, C. (1977) *The local state: Management of cities and people*, London: Pluto Press.

Coote, A. (1992) *The welfare of citizens: Developing new social rights*, London: Rivers Oram/IPPR.

Court, W. (1965) *British economic history 1870–1914*, Cambridge: Cambridge University Press [in particular pp 288-94].

Cox, R. (1998) 'The consequences of welfare reform: how conceptions of social rights are changing', *Journal of Social Policy*, vol 27, pp 1-16.

Craig, G., Burchardt, T. and Gordon, D. (2008) *Social justice and public policy: Seeking fairness in diverse societies*, Bristol: The Policy Press.

Cranston, M. (1976) 'Human rights, real and supposed', in N. Timms and D. Watson (eds) *Talking about welfare*, London: Routledge & Kegan Paul.

CRE (Commission for Racial Equality) (2006) *Fact file 1: Employment and ethnicity*, London: CRE.

Croft, S. and Beresford, P. (1992) 'The politics of participation', *Critical Social Policy*, vol 12, pp 20-44.

Cutler, T., Williams, K. and Williams, J. (1986) *Keynes, Beveridge and beyond*, London: Routledge & Kegan Paul.

Davis, K. and Moore, W. (1945) 'Some principles of stratification', *American Sociological Review*, vol 10, pp 242-9.

de Schweinitz, K. (1961) *England's road to social security*, Perpetua, PA: University of Pennsylvania.

de Sousa Santos, B. (2006) *The rise of the global Left: The World Social Forum and beyond*, London: Zed Books.

Deacon, A. and Bradshaw, J. (1983) *Reserved for the poor: The means-test in British social policy*, Oxford: Blackwell.

Deacon, B. (2007) *Global social policy and governance*, London: Sage Publications.

Deacon, B., Hulse, M. and Stubbs, P. (1997) *Global social policy*, London: Sage Publications.

Deakin, N. (1994) *The politics of welfare: Continuities and change*, Hemel Hempstead: Harvester Wheatsheaf.

Dean, H. (1991) *Social security and social control*, London: Routledge.

Dean, H. (1999) *Poverty, riches and social citizenship*, Basingstoke: Macmillan.

Dean, H. (2002) *Welfare rights and social policy*, Harlow: Prentice Hall.

Dean, H. (2003) *Discursive repertoires and the negotiation of wellbeing: Reflections on the WeD frameworks*, WeD Working Paper 04, Bath: Wellbeing in Developing Countries ESRC Research Group.

Dean, H. (2004) *The ethics of welfare: Human rights, dependency and responsibility*, Bristol: The Policy Press.

Dean, H. (2006) *Social policy*, Cambridge: Polity Press.

Dean, H. (2008a) 'Social policy and human rights: re-thinking the engagement', *Social Policy and Society*, vol 7, pp 1-12.

Dean, H. (2008b) 'Towards a eudaimonic ethic of social security', in J. Bradshaw (ed) *Social security, happiness and wellbeing*, Antwerp: FISS/Intersentia.

Dean, H. (2009) 'Critiquing capabilities: the distraction of a beguiling concept', *Critical Social Policy*, vol 29, no 2, pp 261-78.

Dean, H. and Rodgers, R. (2004) 'Popular discourses of dependency, responsibility and rights', in H. Dean (ed) *The ethics of welfare*, Bristol: The Policy Press.

Dean, H. and Taylor-Gooby, P. (1992) *Dependency culture: The explosion of a myth*, Hemel Hempstead: Harvester Wheatsheaf.

Dean, M. (1991) *The constitution of poverty: Toward a genealogy of liberal governance*, London: Routledge.

Deneulin, S. and Stewart, F. (2000) 'A capability approach for people living together', VHI Conference, 'Justice and Poverty: Examining Sen's Capability Approach', St Edmunds College, Cambridge.

Di Tella, R. and MacCullough, R. (2007) 'Gross national happiness as an answer to the Easterlin paradox', 14th FISS Research Seminar on Issues in Social Security: 'Social Security, Happiness and Well-being', Sigtuna, Sweden.

Dixon, J. (1999) *Social security in global perspective*, Westport, CN: Praeger.

Dolowitz, D. (2004) 'Prosperity and fairness? Can New Labour bring fairness to the 21st century by following the dictates of endogenous growth?', *The British Journal of Politics and International Relations*, vol 6, pp 213-30.

Dorling, D., Rigby, J., Wheeler, B., Ballas, D., Thomas, B., Fahmy, E., Gordon, D. and Lupton, R. (2007) *Poverty, wealth and place in Britain, 1968 to 2005*, York: Joseph Rowntree Foundation.

Douglas, M. (1977) *Natural symbols*, Harmondsworth: Penguin.

Douglas, M. and Ney, S. (1998) *Missing persons: A critique of the social sciences*, Berkeley, CA: University of California Press.

Doyal, L. and Gough, I. (1984) 'A theory of human needs', *Critical Social Policy*, vol 4, pp 6-38.

Doyal, L. and Gough, I. (1991) *A theory of human need*, Basingstoke: Macmillan.

DRC (Disability Rights Commission) (2007) *Disability briefing*, London: DRC.

Drover, G. and Kerans, P. (1993) *New approaches to welfare theory*, Aldershot: Edward Elgar.

DSS (Department of Social Security) (1998) *New ambitions for our country: A new contract for welfare*, London: The Stationery Office.

Durkheim, E. (1893) *The social division of labour*, New York, NY: Free Press.

Dworkin, R. (1977) *Taking rights seriously*, London: Duckworth.

DWP (Department for Work and Pensions) (2001) *Households Below Average Income 1994/5-2000/01*, London: The Stationery Office.

DWP (2007) *Households Below Average Income 1994/5-2006/7*, London: The Stationery Office

Dwyer, P. (2004a) 'Creeping conditionality in the UK', *Canadian Journal of Sociology*, vol 25, pp 261-83.

Dwyer, P. (2004b) *Understanding social citizenship*, Bristol: The Policy Press.

Easterlin, R. (2005) 'Building a better theory of well-being', in L. Bruni and P. Porta (eds) *Economics and happiness*, Oxford: Oxford University Press.

EHRC (Equalities and Human Rights Commission) (2009) *Business Plan 2009/10*, London: EHRC.

Eide, A. (2001) 'Economic, social and cultural rights as human rights', in A. Eide, C. Krause and A. Rosas (eds) *Economic, social and cultural rights: A textbook*, Dordrecht: Martinus Nijhoff.

Elias, N. (1978) *The civilising process: The history of manners*, Oxford: Blackwell.

Ellis, K. (2000) 'Welfare and bodily order: theorising transitions in corporeal discourse', in K. Ellis and H. Dean (eds) *Social policy and the body*, Basingstoke: Macmillan.

Ellis, K. (2004) 'Dependency, justice and the ethic of care', in H. Dean (ed) *The ethics of welfare: Human rights, dependency and responsibility*, Bristol: The Policy Press.

Ellis, K. and Dean, H. (2000) *Social policy and the body: Transitions in corporeal discourse*, Basingstoke: Macmillan.

EOC (Equal Opportunities Commission) (2006) *Women and men in Britain*, Manchester: EOC.

Equalities Review (2007) *Fairness and freedom: The final report of the Equalities Review*, London: Cabinet Office.

Erskine, A. (2002) 'Need', in P. Alcock, A. Erskine and M. May (eds) *The Blackwell dictionary of social policy*, Oxford: Blackwell.

Escobar, A. (1995) 'Imagining a post-development era', in J. Crush (ed) *The power of development*, London: Routledge.

Esping-Andersen, G. (1990) *The three worlds of welfare capitalism*, Cambridge: Polity Press.

Esping-Andersen, G. (1996) *Welfare states in transition*, London: Sage Publications.

Esping-Andersen, G. (1999) *The social foundations of post-industrial economies*, Oxford: Oxford University Press.

Fabian Society (2006) *Narrowing the gap: The Fabian Commission on life chances and child poverty*, London: Fabian Society.

Falk, R. (1994) 'The making of a global citizenship', in B. van Steenbergen (ed) *The condition of citizenship*, London: Sage Publications.

Fanon, F. (1967) *Black skin, white masks*, New York, NY: Grove Press.

Field, F. (1989) *Losing out: The emergence of Britain's underclass*, Oxford: Blackwell.

Finch, J. and Mason, J. (1993) *Negotiating family responsibilities*, London: Routledge.

Fine, B. (1984) *Democracy and the rule of law: Liberal ideals and Marxist critiques*, London: Pluto Press.

Fine, B. (2001) *Social capital versus social theory*, London: Routledge.

Fitzpatrick, P. (2005) *New theories of welfare*, Basingstoke: Palgrave.

Fitzpatrick, T. (1999) *Freedom and security: An introduction to the basic income debate*, Basingstoke: Macmillan.

Fitzpatrick, T. (2001) *Welfare theory: An introduction*, Basingstoke: Palgrave.

Fitzpatrick, T. (2008) *Applied ethics and social problems*, Bristol: The Policy Press.

Fletcher, R. (1965) *Human needs and social order*, London: Michael Joseph.

Forder, A. (1974) *Concepts in social administration: A framework for analysis*, London: Routledge & Kegan Paul.

Forster, W. (1870) 'Speech introducing Elementary Education Bill, House of Commons', in S. Maclure (ed) *Education documents*, London: Methuen.

Foster, P. (1983) *Access to welfare: An introduction to welfare rationing*, Basingstoke: Macmillan.

Foucault, M. (1977) *Discipline and punish*, Harmondsworth: Penguin.

Foucault, M. (1979) *The history of sexuality*, London: Allen Lane.

Foweraker, J. and Landman, T. (1997) *Citizenship rights and social movements: A comparative and statistical analysis*, Oxford: Oxford University Press.

Fraser, D. (1984) *The evolution of the British welfare state*, Basingstoke: Macmillan.

Fraser, N. (1989) *Unruly practices: Power, discourse and gender in contemporary social theory*, Minneapolis, MN: University of Minnesota Press.

Fraser, N. (1997) *Justice interruptus: Critical reflections on the 'postsocialist' condition*, London: Routledge.

Fraser, N. (2007) 'Reframing justice in a globalising world', in D. Held and A. Kaya (eds) *Global inequality*, Cambridge: Polity Press.

Fraser, N. and Honneth, A. (2003) *Redistribution or recognition?*, London: Verso.

Freire, P. (1972) *Pedagogy of the oppressed*, Harmondsworth: Penguin.

Freud, S. (2006) *The Penguin Freud reader* (edited by A. Phillips), London: Penguin Books.

Friedman, M. (1993) 'Beyond caring: the de-moralisation of gender', in M. Larabee (ed) *An ethic of care: Feminist and interdisciplinary perspectives*, New York, NY: Routledge.

Fromm, E. (1976) *To have or to be?*, London: Abacus.

Frost, L. and Hoggett, P. (2008) 'Human agency and social suffering', *Critical Social Policy*, vol 28, pp 438-60.

Fukuyama, F. (1992) *The end of history and the last man*, New York, NY: Basic Books.

Gaarder, J. (1996) *Sophie's world*, London: Phoenix.

Galbraith, K. (1958) *The affluent society*, London: Hamish Hamilton.

Galtung, J. (1980) 'The basic needs approach', in K. Lederer (ed) *Human needs: A contribution to the current debate*, Cambridge, MA: Oelgeschlager, Gunn & Hain.

Galtung, J. (1994) *Human rights in another key*, Cambridge: Polity Press.

Garland, D. (1981) 'The birth of the welfare sanction', *British Journal of Law and Society*, vol 8, no 1, pp 29-45.

Gasper, D. (2007) 'Conceptualising human needs and wellbeing', in I. Gough and J. McGregor (eds) *Wellbeing in developing countries*, Cambridge: Cambridge University Press.

Geertz, C. (1973) *The interpretation of cultures*, New York, NY: Basic Books.

George, V. and Howards, I. (1991) *Poverty amidst affluence*, Aldershot: Edward Elgar.

Geras, N. (1983) *Marx and human nature: Reflection of a legend*, London: Verso.

Germani, G. (1980) *Marginality*, New Brunswick, NJ: Transaction Books.

Geyer, R. (2000) *Exploring European social policy*, Cambridge: Polity Press.

Giddens, A. (1998) *The third way*, Cambridge: Polity Press.

Gilbert, B. (1966) *The evolution of National Insurance in Great Britain*, London: Michael Joseph.

Gilligan, C. (1982) *In a different voice: Psychological theory and women's development*, Cambridge, MA: Harvard University Press.

Giradin, J.-C. (2000) 'Towards a politics of signs: reading Baudrillard', in M. Gane (ed) *Jean Baudrillard, vol I*, London: Sage Publications.

Goodin, R. (1985) *Protecting the vulnerable*, Chicago, IL: University of Chicago Press.

Goodin, R. (1988) *Reasons for welfare: The political theory of the welfare state*, Princeton, NJ: Princeton University Press.

Goodin, R. (1990) 'Relative needs', in A. Ware and R. Goodin (eds) *Needs and welfare*, London: Sage Publications.

Goodin, R. and Dryzek, J. (2006) 'The macro-political uptake of mini-publics', *Politics and Society*, vol 34, pp 219-44.

Gordon, D. (2006) 'The concept and measurement of poverty', in C. Pantazis, D. Gordon and R. Levitas (eds) *Poverty and social exclusion in Britain*, Bristol: The Policy Press.

Gordon, D. and Pantazis, C. (1997) *Breadline Britain in the 1990s*, Aldershot: Ashgate.

Gough, I. (2003) *Lists and thresholds: Comparing the Doyal-Gough theory of human need with Nussbaum's capability approach*, WeD Working Paper No 1, Bath: ESRC Research Group on Wellbeing in Developing Countries.

Gough, I. and McGregor, J.A. (2007) *Wellbeing in developing countries: From theory to research*, Cambridge: Cambridge University Press.

Gough, I., Bradshaw, J., Ditch, J., Eardley, T. and Whiteford, P. (1997) 'Social assistance in OECD countries', *Journal of European Social Policy*, vol 7, no 1, pp 17-43.

Gough, I., Wood, G., Barrientos, A., Bevan, P., Davis, P. and Room, G. (2004) *Insecurity and welfare regimes in Asia, Africa and Latin America: Social policy in development contexts*, Cambridge: Cambridge University Press.

Griffiths, J. (1991) *The politics of the judiciary*, London: Fontana.

Gudex, C. (1986) *QALYS and their use by the health service*, Discussion Paper 20, York: Centre for Health Economics.

Habermas, J. (1962) *The structural transformation of the public sphere*, Cambridge, MA: MIT Press.

Habermas, J. (1987) *The theory of communicative action: Vol 2: Lifeworld and system*, Cambridge: Polity Press.

Hadley, R. and Hatch, S. (1981) *Social welfare and the failure of the state*, London: Allen and Unwin.

Hall, A. and Midgley, J. (2004) *Social policy for development*, London: Sage Publications.

Halmos, P. (1973) *The faith of the counsellors*, London: Constable.

Hanisch, C. (1969) 'The personal is political', in Redstockings Inc (ed) *Feminist revolution*, New Palz, NY: Redstockings Inc.

Harden, I. and Lewis, N. (1986) *The noble lie: The Bitish constitution and the rule of law*, London: Hutchinson.

Hardt, M. and Negri, A. (2000) *Empire*, Cambridge, MA: Harvard University Press.

Harris, J. (2007) 'Principles, poor laws and welfare states', in J. Hills, J. Le Grand and D. Piachaud (eds) *Making social policy work*, Bristol: The Policy Press.

Hayek, F. (1976) *Law, legislation and liberty: Vol 2 – The mirage of social justice*, London: Routledge & Kegan Paul.

Heclo, H. (1986) 'General welfare and two American political traditions', *Political Science Quarterly*, vol 101, pp 179-96.

Hefner, R. (2000) 'Baudrillard's noble anthropology', in M. Gane (ed) *Jean Baudrillard, vol I*, London: Sage Publications.

Hegel, G. (1821) *Elements of the philosophy of rights*, Cambridge: Cambridge University Press.

Held, D. (1987) *Models of democracy*, Cambridge: Polity Press.

Held, D. (1995) *Democracy and the global order: From the modern state to cosmopolitan governance*, Cambridge: Polity Press.

Held, D. and Kaya, A. (2007) *Global inequality*, Cambridge: Polity Press.

Heller, A. (1974) *The theory of need in Marx*, London: Alison & Busby.

Heller, A. (1980) 'Can "true" and "false" needs be posited?', in K. Lederer (ed) *Human needs: A contribution to the current debate*, Cambridge, MA: Oelgeschlager, Gunn & Hain.

Henman, P. and Fenger, M. (2006) *Administering welfare reform: International transformations in welfare governance*, Bristol: The Policy Press.

Hewitt, M. (1992) *Welfare ideology and need: Developing perspectives on the welfare state*, Hemel Hempstead: Harvester Wheatsheaf.

Hewitt, M. (2000) *Welfare and human nature: The human subject in twentieth century politics*, Basingstoke: Macmillan.

Hills, J., Le Grand, J. and Piachaud, D. (eds) (2002) *Understanding social exclusion*, Oxford: Oxford University Press.

Hindess, B. (1987) *Freedom, equality and the market*, London: Tavistock.

Hirsch, F. (1977) *The social limits to growth*, London: Routledge & Kegan Paul.

Hirst, P. (1994) *Associative democracy*, Cambridge: Polity Press.

Hobbes, T. (1651) *Leviathan*, Cambridge: Cambridge University Press.

Hobcraft, J. (2003) 'Social exclusion and the generations', in J. Hills, J. Le Grand and D. Piachaud (eds) *Understanding social exclusion*, Oxford: Oxford University Press.

Hobsbawm, E. (1968) *Industry and Empire*, Harmondsworth: Penguin.

Hohfeld, W. (1946) Fundamental legal conceptions as applied in judicial reasoning, New Haven, CT: Yale University Press.

Holloway, J. and Picciotto, S. (1978) *State and capital: A Marxist debate*, London: Arnold.

Honneth, A. (1995) *The struggle for recognition: The moral grammar of social conflicts*, Cambridge: Polity Press.

Hood, C. (1991) 'A public management for all seasons?', *Public Administration*, vol 69, pp 3–19.

Hunt, P. (1996) *Reclaiming social rights*, Aldershot: Dartmouth/Ashgate.

Ignatieff, M. (1984) *The needs of strangers*, London: Chatto and Windus.

Ignatieff, M. (2001) *Human rights as politics and idolatory*, Princeton, NJ: Princeton University Press.

Illich, I. (1971) *Deschooling society*, London: Calder & Boyers.

Illich, I. (1973) *Tools for conviviality*, London: Calder & Boyars.

Illich, I. (1977) *Towards a history of needs*, New York, NY: Bantam/Random House.

Illich, I., McKnight, J., Zola, I., Caplan, J. and Shaiken, H. (1977) *Disabling professions*, London: Marion Boyars.

ILO (International Labour Organization) (2006) *Social security for all: Investing in global social and economic development*, Geneva: ILO.

Inglehart, R. (1990) *Culture shift in advanced industrial society*, Princeton, NJ: Princeton University Press.

Inglehart, R., Foa, R., Peterson, C. and Welzel, C. (2008) 'Development, freedom and rising happiness', *Perspectives on Psychological Science*, vol 3, no 4, pp 264–85.

Jessop, B. (2002) *The future of the capitalist state*, Cambridge: Polity Press

Johnson, N. (1987) *The welfare state in transition: The theory and practice of welfare pluralism*, Brighton: Harvester Wheatsheaf.

Johnston, G. and Percy-Smith, J. (2003) 'In search of social capital', *Policy & Politics*, vol 31, pp 321–34.

Jordan, B. (1998) *The new politics of welfare*, London: Sage Publications.

Jordan, B. (2008) *Welfare and well-being: Social value in public policy*, Bristol: The Policy Press.

Keane, J. (1988) *Democracy and civil society*, London: Verso.

Kincaid, J. (1975) *Poverty and equality in Britain: A study of social security and taxation*, Harmondsworth: Penguin.

Kind, P., Rosser, R. and Williams, A. (1982) 'Valuation of quality of life', in M. Jones-Lee (ed) *The value of life and safety*, Amsterdam: Elsevier Science Publishing Co.

King, D. (1999) *In the name of liberalism: Illiberal social policy in the United States and Britain*, Oxford: Oxford University Press.

Kittay, E., Jennings, B. and Wasunna, A. (2005) 'Dependency, difference and the global ethic of long-term care', *The Journal of Political Philosophy*, vol 13, pp 443-69.

Klein, R., Day, P. and Redmayne, S. (1996) *Managing scarcity: Priority setting and rationing in the National Health Service*, Buckingham: Open University Press.

Klug, F. (2000) *Values for a godless age: The story of the United Kingdom's new bill of rights*, London: Penguin.

Kymlicka, W. (1995) *Multicultural citizenship: A liberal theory of minority rights*, Oxford: Clarendon Press.

Lacan, J. (1977) *Ecrits* (translated by A. Sheridan), London: Tavistock.

Land, H. (1975) 'The introduction of Family Allowances', in R. Hall, H. Land, R. Parker and A. Webb (eds) *Change choice and conflict in social policy*, London: Heinemann.

Langan, M. (1998) *Welfare: Needs, rights and risks*, London/Milton Keynes: Routledge/The Open University.

Law, I. (1996) *Racism, ethnicity and social policy*, Hemel Hempstead: Harvester Wheatsheaf.

Layard, R. (2003) 'Happiness: has social science a clue?', Lionel Robbins Memorial Lectures, London: London School of Economics and Political Science.

Layard, R. (2005) *Happiness: Lessons from a new science*, London: Penguin.

Le Grand, J. (1990a) *Quasi-markets and social policy*, Bristol: SAUS /University of Bristol.

Le Grand, J. (1990b) 'The state of welfare', in J. Hills (ed) *The state of welfare: The welfare state in Britain since 1974*, Oxford: Clarendon.

Le Grand, J. (2003) *Motivation, agency and public policy: Of knights, knaves, pawns and queens*, Oxford: Oxford University Press.

Le Grand, J., Propper, C. and Robinson, R. (1992) *The economics of social problems*, Basingstoke: Macmillan.

Lederer, K. (1980) *Human needs: A contribution to the current debate*, Cambridge, MA: Oelgeschlayer, Gunn & Hain.

Leiss, W. (1978) *The limits of satisfaction*, London: Calder.

Lenoir, R. (1974) *Les exclus*, Paris: Seuil.

Levitas, R. (1996) 'The concept of social exclusion and the new Durkheimian hegemony', *Critical Social Policy*, vol 16, no 1, pp 5-20.

Levitas, R. (1998) *The inclusive society? Social exclusion and New Labour*, Basingstoke: Macmillan.

Lewis, G., Gewirtz, S. and Clarke, J. (2000) *Rethinking social policy*, London: Sage Publications.

Lewis, P. (1973) 'Unmet legal need', in P. Morris et al (eds) *Social needs and legal action*, Oxford: Martin Robertson.

Liddiard, M. (2007) 'Social need and patterns of inequality', in J. Baldock, N. Manning and S. Vickerstaff (eds) *Social policy*, Oxford: Oxford University Press.

Lis, C. and Soly, H. (1979) *Poverty and capitalism in pre-industrial Europe*, Brighton: Harvester Wheatsheaf.

Lister, R. (2001) 'New Labour: a study in ambiguity from a position of ambivalence', *Critical Social Policy*, vol 21, pp 425-47.

Lister, R. (2003) *Citizenship: Feminist perspectives* (2nd edn), Basingstoke: Macmillan.

Lister, R. (2004) *Poverty*, Cambridge: Polity Press.

Lødemel, I. and Trickey, H. (2001) *'An offer you can't refuse': Workfare in international perspective*, Bristol: The Policy Press.

McGregor, J.A. (2007) 'Researching wellbeing: from concepts to methodology', in I. Gough and J. McGregor (eds) *Wellbeing in developing countries: From theory to research*, Cambridge: Cambridge University Press.

McKay, S. (2004) 'Poverty or preference: what do "consensual deprivation indicators" really measure?', *Fiscal Studies*, vol 25, pp 201-23.

Macintyre, A. (2007) *After virtue*, Notre Dame, IN: Notre Dame Press.

Mack, J. and Lansley, S. (1985) *Poor Britain*, London: Allen and Unwin.

Macnicol, J. (1987) 'In pursuit of the underclass', *Journal of Social Policy*, vol 16, pp 293-318.

Marcuse, H. (1964) *One dimensional man: Studies in the ideology of advanced industrial society*, Boston, MA: Beacon Press.

Markus, G. (1978) *Marxism and anthropology*, Assen, The Netherlands: Van Gorcum.

Marlier, E., Atkinson, A., Cantillon, B. and Nolan, B. (2007) *The EU and social inclusion: Facing the challenges*, Bristol: The Policy Press.

Marshall, T.H. (1950) 'Citizenship and social class', in T. Marshall and T. Bottomore (eds) *Citizenship and social class*, London: Pluto Press.

Marx, K. (1844 [1975 edn]) 'Economic and philosophical manuscripts', in L. Colletti (ed) *Early writings*, Harmondsworth: Penguin.

Marx, K. (1845) 'Theses from Fuerbach (extract from)', in T. Bottomore and M. Rubel (eds) *Karl Marx: Selected writings in sociology and social philosophy*, Harmondsworth: Penguin.

Marx, K. (1887) *Capital, vols I, II, III*, London: Lawrence & Wishart.

Marx, K. and Engels, F. (1848) *The Communist manifesto*, New York, NY: Pathfinder Press.

Maslow, A. (1943) 'A theory of human motivation', *Psychological Review*, vol 50, pp 370-396.

Maslow, A. (1970) *Motivation and personality*, New York, NY: Harper & Row.

Mead, G.H. (1934) *Mind, self and society from the standpoint of a social behaviorist*, Chicago, IL: University of Chicago Press.

Milanovic, B. (2007) 'Globalization and inequality', in D. Held and A. Kaya (eds) *Global inequality*, Cambridge: Polity Press.

Mishra, R. (1984) *The welfare state in crisis*, Hemel Hempstead: Harvester Wheatsheaf.

Mishra, R. (1999) *Globalisation and the welfare state*, Hemel Hempstead: Harvester Wheatsheaf.

Monaghan, P. (2003) 'Taking on "rational man": dissident economists fight for a niche in the discipline', *Chronicle of Higher Education*, 24 January.

Mooney, G. (2004) *Work: Personal lives and social policy*, Bristol: The Policy Press.

Morris, L. (1994) *Dangerous classes*, London: Routledge.

Murray, C. (1984) *Losing ground: American social policy 1950–1980*, New York, NY: Basic Books.

Murray, C. (1990) *The emerging British underclass*, London: Institute of Economic Affairs.

Murray, C. (1994) *Underclass: The crisis deepens*, London: Institute of Economic Affairs.

Myrdal, G. (1963) *Challenge to affluence*, New York, NY: Random House.

Narayan, D., Chambers, R., Shah, M. and Petesch, P. (2000) *Voices of the poor: Crying out for change*, Washington, DC: World Bank.

Nedelsky, J. and Scott, C. (1992) 'Constitutional dialogue', in J. Bakan and D. Schneiderman (eds) *Social justice and the constitution: Perspectives on a social union for Canada*, Ottawa, Canada: Carleton University Press.

Nissanke, M. (2003) *The revenue potential of the currency transfer tax for development finance: A critical appraisal*, WIDER Discussion Paper No 2003/81, Helsinki: United Nations.

Novak, T. (1988) *Poverty and the state*, Milton Keynes: Open University Press.

Nowak, M. (2001) 'The right to education', in A. Eide, C. Krause and A. Rosas (eds) *Economic, social and cultural rights*, Dordrecht: Martinus Mijhoff.

Nozick, R. (1974) *Anarchy, state and utopia*, Oxford: Blackwell.

Nussbaum, M. (2000a) 'The future of feminist liberalism', *Proceedings and Addresses of the American Philosophical Association*, vol 74, pp 47-9.

Nussbaum, M. (2000b) *Women and human development: The capabilities approach*, Cambridge: Cambridge University Press.

Nussbaum, M. (2006) *Frontiers of justice: Disability, nationality, species membership*, Cambridge, MA: Harvard University Press.

Offe, C. (1984) *Contradictions of the welfare state*, Cambridge, MA: MIT Press.

Offer, A. (2006) *The challenge of affluence*, Oxford: Oxford University Press.

Oliver, M. and Barnes, M. (1998) *Disabled people and social policy: From exclusion to inclusion*, Harlow: Longman.

Osborne, T. (1996) 'Security and vitality: drains, liberalism and power in the nineteenth century', in A. Barry, T. Osborne and N. Rose (eds) *Foucault and political reason*, London: UCL Press.

Pahl, J. (1989) *Money and marriage*, Basingstoke: Macmillan.

Pahl, R. (1995) *After success: Fin-de-siecle anxiety and identity*, Cambridge: Polity Press.

Paine, T. (1791) *The rights of man*, Harmondsworth: Penguin.

Pantazis, C., Gordon, D. and Levitas, R. (2006) *Poverty and social exclusion in Britain: The Millennium Survey*, Bristol: The Policy Press.

Papadakis, E. and Taylor-Gooby, P. (1987) *The private provision of public welfare: State, market and community*, Brighton: Harvester Wheatsheaf.

Pareto, V. (1909) *Manuel d'economie politique*, Paris: Giard.

Park, R. (1928) 'Human migration and the marginal man', *American Journal of Sociology*, vol 33, pp 881-93.

Parker, H. (1998) *Low cost but acceptable: A minimum income standard for the UK*, Bristol: The Policy Press.

Parker, R. (1981) 'Tending and social policy', in E. Goldberg and S. Hatch (eds) *A new look at the personal social services*, London: Policy Studies Institute.

Pateman, C. (1989) *The disorder of women*, Cambridge: Polity Press.

Peck, J. (2001) *Workfare states*, New York, NY: Guilford Press.

Perez-Bustillo, C. (2001) 'The right to have rights: poverty, ethnicity, multiculturalism and state power', in F. Wilson, N. Kanji and E. Braathen (eds) *Poverty reduction: What role for the state in today's globalised economy?*, London: CROP/Zed Books.

Persky, J. (1995) 'Retrospectives: the ethology of homo economicus', *Journal of Economic Perspectives*, vol 9, pp 221-31.

Phillips, D. (2006) *Quality of life: Concept, policy and practice*, London: Routledge.

Piachaud, D. (1981) 'Peter Townsend and the Holy Grail', *New Society*, 10 September.

Piachaud, D. (2002) *Capital and the determinants of poverty and social exclusion*, London: London School of Economics and Political Science.

Pigou, A. (1928) *A study in public finance*, London: Macmillan.

Pigou, A. (1965) *Essays in applied economics*, London: Frank Cass.

Plant, R., Lesser, H. and Taylor-Gooby, P. (1980) *Political philosophy and social welfare*, London: Routledge & Kegan Paul.

Plato (1974 edn) *The Republic*, Harmondsworth: Penguin.

PMSU (Prime Minister's Strategy Unit) (2007) *Building on progress: Public services*, London: Cabinet Office.

Pogge, T. (2002) *World poverty and human rights*, Cambridge: Polity Press.

Pogge, T. (2007) *Freedom from poverty as a human right: Who owes what to the very poor?*, Oxford: Oxford University Press.

Porritt, J. (1984) *Seeing green*, Oxford: Blackwell.

Porter, D. and Craig, D. (2004) 'The third way and the third world: poverty reduction and social inclusion in the rise of "inclusive" liberalism', *Review of International Political Economy*, vol 11, pp 387-423.

Poulantzas, N. (1980) *State, power, socialism*, London: Verso.

Powell, E. (1972) *Still to decide*, London: Elliot Right Way Books.

Powell, M. and Hewitt, M. (2002) *Welfare state and welfare change*, Buckingham: Open University Press.

Putnam, R. (2000) *Bowling alone*, New York, NY: Simon & Schuster.

Ramose, M. (2003) 'Globalisation and ubuntu', in P. Coetzee and A. Roux (eds) *The African philosophy reader*, London: Routledge.

Raphael, D., Renwick, R., Brown, I. and Rootman, I. (1998) 'Quality of life indicators and health: current status and emerging conceptions', *Social Indicators Research*, vol 39, pp 65-88.

Rawls, J. (1972) *A theory of justice*, Oxford: Oxford University Press.

Rhodes, R. (1997) *Understanding governance: Policy networks, governance, reflexivity and accountability*, Buckingham: Open University Press.

Rist, G. (1980) 'Basic questions about basic human needs', in K. Lederer (ed) *Human needs: A contribution to the current debate*, Cambridge, MA: Oelgeschlager, Gunn & Hain.

Roche, M. (1992) *Re-thinking citizenship*, Cambridge: Polity Press.

Rodgers, G., Gore, C. and Figueiredo, J. (1995) *Social exclusion: Rhetoric, reality, responses*, Geneva: International Labour Organization.

Room, G. (1979) *The sociology of welfare: Social policy, stratification and political order*, Oxford: Blackwell/Martin Robertson.

Roosevelt, F.D. (1944) 'State of the Union address to Congress 11 January', in S. Rosenman (ed) *The public papers and addresses of Franklin D. Roosevelt, vol XIII*, New York, NY: Harper.

Rosas, A. (2001) 'The right to development', in A. Eide, C. Krause and A. Rosas (eds) *Economic, social and cultural rights: A textbook*, Dordrecht: Martinus Nijhoff.

Rose, N. (1999) *Powers of freedom: Reframing political thought*, Cambridge: Cambridge University Press.

Rowntree, B.S. (1901/2000) *Poverty: A study of town life*, London: Macmillan, 2000 edn – J. Bradshaw (ed), Bristol: The Policy Press.

Rowntree, B.S. (1941) *Poverty and progress: A second social survey of York*, London: Longman.

Royal Commission on Legal Services (1976) *Final report*, London: HMSO.

Runciman, G. (1966) *Relative deprivation and social justice*, London: Routledge & Kegan Paul.

Runciman, G. (1990) 'How many classes are there in contemporary British society?', *Sociology*, vol 24, no 3, pp 377-96.

Ryan, R. and Deci, E. (2001) 'On happiness and human potentials: a review of research on hedonic and eudaimonic wellbeing', *Annual Review of Psychology*, vol 52, pp 141-66.

Ryan, R. and Sapp, A. (2008) 'Basic psychological needs: a self-determination theory perspective on the promotion of wellness across development and cultures', in I. Gough and J. McGregor (eds) *Wellbeing in developing countries: From theory to research*, Cambridge: Cambridge University Press.

Sahlins, M. (1974) *Stone Age economics*, London: Tavistock.

Salais, R. and Villeneuve, R. (2004) *Europe and the politics of capabilities*, Cambridge: Cambridge University Press.

Sandel, M. (1982) *Liberalism and the limits of justice*, Cambridge: Cambridge University Press.

Saunders, P. (1984) 'Beyond housing classes: the sociological significance of private property rights in means of consumption', *International Journal of Urban and Regional Research*, vol 8, pp 208-27.

Scaff, L. (1998) 'Max Weber', in R. Stones (ed) *Key sociological thinkers*, Basingstoke: Palgrave Macmillan.

Schmidt, S. and Bullinger, M. (2008) 'Cross-cultural quality of life assessment approaches and experiences from the health care field', in I. Gough and J. McGregor (eds) *Wellbeing in developing countries: From theory to research*, Cambridge: Cambridge University Press.

Scott, A. (1990) *Ideology and new social movements*, London: Unwin Hyman.

Seabrook, J. (1985) *Landscapes of poverty*, Oxford: Blackwell.

Searle, B. (2008) *Well-being: In search of a good life?*, Bristol: The Policy Press.

Sen, A. (1985) *Commodities and capabilities*, Amsterdam: Elsevier.

Sen, A. (1992) *Inequality re-examined*, Oxford: Oxford University Press.

Sen, A. (1999) *Development as freedom*, Oxford: Oxford University Press.

Sen, A. (2005) 'Human rights and capabilities', *Journal of Human Development*, vol 6, pp 151-66.

SEU (Social Exclusion Unit (1997) *Social Exclusion Unit: Purpose, work priorities and working methods*, Briefing document, London: Cabinet Office.

Sevenhuijsen, S. (1998) *Citizenship and the ethics of care*, London: Routledge.

Sevenhuijsen, S. (2000) 'Caring in the third way: the relation between obligation, responsibility and care in "Third Way" discourse', *Critical Social Policy*, vol 20, pp 5-37.

Skoler, D. and Zeitzer, I. (1982) 'Social security appeals systems: a nine-nation review', *International Social Security Review*, vol 35, pp 57-77.

Smith, A. (1759) *The theory of moral sentiments*, Indianapolis, IN: Liberty Fund.

Smith, A. (1776) *An inquiry into the nature and causes of the wealth of nations*, London: George Routledge.

Smith, D. (1998) *Tax crusaders and the politics of direct democracy*, New York, NY: Routledge.

Soper, K. (1981) *On human needs*, Brighton: Harvester Wheatsheaf.

Soper, K. (1993) 'The thick and thin of human needing', in G. Drover and P. Kerans (eds) *New approaches to welfare theory*, Aldershot: Edward Elgar.

Soysal, Y. (1994) *Limits of citizenship: Migrants and postnational membership in Europe*, Chicago, IL: Chicago University Press.

Springborg, P. (1981) *The problem of human needs and the critique of civilisation*, London: George Allen & Unwin.

Squires, P. (1990) *Anti-social policy: Welfare ideology and the disciplinary state*, Hemel Hempstead: Harvester Wheatsheaf.

Stafford-Clark, D. (1965) *What Freud really said*, Harmondsworth: Penguin.

Stedman-Jones, G. (1971) *Outcast London*, Oxford: Clarendon Press.

Stenner, P. and Taylor, D. (2008) 'Psychosocial welfare: reflections on an emerging field', *Critical Social Policy*, vol 28, pp 415-37.

Stenner, P., Barnes, M. and Taylor, D. (2008) 'Editorial introduction', *Critical Social Policy*, vol 28, pp 411-14.

Tao, J. (2004) 'The paradox of care: a Chinese Confucian perspective on long-term care', in P. Kennett (ed) *A handbook of comparative social policy*, Aldershot: Edward Elgar.

Tawney, R. (1913) 'Poverty as an industrial problem', in R. Tawney (ed) *Memoranda on the problems of poverty, vol 2*, London: William Morris Press.

Taylor, C. (1992) *Multiculturalism: Examining the politics of recognition*, Princeton, NJ: Princeton University Press.

Taylor, D. (1998) 'Social identity and social policy: engagements with post-modern theory', *Journal of Social Policy*, vol 27, pp 329-50.

Taylor-Gooby, P. and Dale, A. (1981) *Social theory and social welfare*, London: Edward Arnold.

Temple, W. (1941) *Citizen and churchman*, London: Eyre & Spottiswoode.

Teubner, G. (1987) *Dilemmas of law in the welfare state*, Berlin: Walter de Gruyter.

Thane, P. (1982) *Foundations of the welfare state*, Harlow: Longman.

Thompson, E.P. (1993) *Customs in common*, New York, NY: The New Press.

Thomson, G. (1987) *Needs*, London: Routledge & Kegan Paul.

Timmins, N. (2001) *The five giants: A biography of the welfare state*, London: HarperCollins.

Titmuss, R. (1974) *Social policy*, London: Allen and Unwin.

Titmuss, R. (2001 [1955]) 'Lecture at the University of Birmingham in honour of Eleanor Rathbone', in P. Alcock, H. Glennerster, A. Oakley and A. Sinfield (eds) *Welfare and wellbeing: Richard Titmuss' contribution to social policy*, Bristol: The Policy Press.

Titmuss, R. (2001 [1962]) 'Lecture at the University of California', in P. Alcock, H. Glennerster, A. Oakley and A. Sinfield (eds) *Welfare and wellbeing: Richard Titmuss's contribution to social policy*, Bristol: The Policy Press.

Townsend, P. (1979) *Poverty in the UK*, Harmondsworth: Penguin.

Townsend, P. (1993) *The international analysis of poverty*, Hemel Hempstead: Harvester Wheatsheaf.

Townsend, P. (2007) *The right to social security and national development: Lessons from OECD experience for low-income countries*, Discussion Paper 18, Geneva: International Labour Organization.

Townsend, P. and Gordon, D. (2002) *World poverty: New policies to defeat an old enemy*, Bristol: The Policy Press.

Tronto, J. (1994) *Moral boundaries: A political argument for an ethic of care*, New York, NY: Routledge.

Turner, B. (1993) 'Outline of a theory of human rights', *Sociology*, vol 27, pp 489-512.

Turner, B. (2006) *Vulnerability and human rights*, Pennsylvania, PA: Pennsylvania State University.

Tweedie, J. and Hunt, A. (1994) 'The future of the welfare state and social rights: reflections on Habermas', *Journal of Law and Society*, vol 21, no 2, pp 288-316.

UN (United Nations) (1995) *The Copenhagen Declaration and Programme of Action*, New York, NY: UN.

UNDP (United Nations Development Programme) (2000) *Human development report 2000*, New York, NY: Oxford University Press.

UNDP (2003) *Human development report 2003 – Millennium Development Goals: A compact among nations to end human poverty*, New York, NY: Oxford University Press.

UNDP (2008) *Human development report 2007/08*, New York, NY: Oxford University Press.

UN (United Nations) General Assembly (2000) *United Nations millennium declaration (Resolution 2 Session 55)*, New York, NY: UN.

Unger, R. (1986) *The critical legal studies movement*, Cambridge, MA: Harvard University Press.

Ungerson, C. (1987) *Policy is personal: Sex, gender and informal care*, London: Tavistock.

UNICEF (United Nations Children's Fund) (2007) *Child poverty in perspective: An overview of child well-being in rich countries*, Florence: UNICEF Innocenti Research Centre.

Vale, D., Watts, B. and Franklin, J. (2009) *The receding tide: Understanding unmet needs in a harsher economic climate – The interim findings of the Mapping Needs Project*, London: The Young Foundation.

Veblen, T. (1899) *The theory of the leisure class*, New York, NY: Random House.

Veenhoven, R. (1996) 'Happy life expectancy: a comprehensive measure of quality of life', *Social Indicators Research*, vol 39, pp 1-58.

Veit-Wilson, J. (1986) 'Paradigms of poverty: a rehabilitation of B.S. Rowntree', *Journal of Social Policy*, vol 15, no 1, pp 69-99.

Veit-Wilson, J. (1999) 'Poverty and the adequacy of social security', in J. Ditch (ed) *Introduction to social security: Policies, benefits and poverty*, London: Routledge.

Vizard, P. and Burchardt, T. (2007) *Developing a capability list: Final recommendations of the Equalities Review Steering Group on Measurement*, CASEpaper 121, London: CASE/STICERD, London School of Economics and Political Science.

Wainwright, H. (2003) *Reclaim the state: Experiments in popular democracy*, London: Verso.

Waldfogel, J. (2004) *Social mobility, life chances and the early years*, CASEpaper 88, London: CASE/STICERD, London School of Economics and Political Science.

Walker, A. (1990) 'Blaming the victims', in C. Murray (ed) *The emerging British underclass*, London: Institute of Economic Affairs.

Walker, R. (2005) *Social security and welfare: Concepts and comparisons*, Maidenhead: Open University Press.

Walzer, M. (1983) *Spheres of justice*, Oxford: Blackwell.

Walzer, M. (1994) *Thick and thin*, Notre Dame, IN: University of Notre Dame Press.

Waterman, P. (2001) *Globalization, social movements and the new internationalisms*, London: Continuum.

WHOQOL (World Health Organization Quality of Life) Group (1995) 'The World Health Organisation quality of life assessment: position paper from the WHO', *Social Science and Medicine*, vol 41, pp 1403-9.

Wilensky, H. (1975) *The welfare state and equality: Structural and ideological roots of public expenditure*, Berkeley, CA: University of California Press.

Wilkinson, R. (1996) *Unhealthy societies: The afflictions of inequality*, London: Routledge.

Wilkinson, R. (2005) *The impact of inequality: How to make sick societies healthier*, New York, NY: The New Press.

Williams, A. (1974) 'Need as a demand concept', in A. Culyer (ed) *Economic policies and social goals*, London: Martin Robertson.

Williams, F. (1989) *Social policy: A critical introduction*, Cambridge: Polity Press.

Williams, P. (1987) 'Alchemical notes: reconstructing ideals from deconstructed rights', *Harvard Civil Rights – Civil Liberties Review*, vol 22, p 401.

Williamson, J. (1990) 'What Washington means by policy reform', in J. Williamson (ed) *Latin American adjustment: How much has happened?*, Washington, DC: Institute for International Economics.

Wisner, B. (1988) *Basic human needs and development policies*, London: Earthscan.

Wollstonecraft, M. (1792) *A vindication of the rights of women*, Harmondsworth: Penguin.

Wood, G. and Newton, J. (2005) 'From welfare to well-being regimes: engaging new agendas', Arusha Conference, 'New Frontiers of Social Policy', World Bank.

World Bank (2001) *World development report 2000/2001*, Oxford: Oxford University Press.

Wright-Mills, C. (1959) *The sociological imagination*, New York, NY: Oxford University Press.

Wronka, J. (1992) *Human rights and social policy in the 21st century*, Lanham, MA: University Press of America.

Young, I. (2008) 'Structural injustice and the politics of difference', in G. Craig, T. Burchardt and D. Gordon (eds) *Social justice and public policy*, Bristol: The Policy Press.

Younghusband, E. (1964) *Social work and social change*, London: Allen & Unwin.

Index

Page references for notes are followed by n